The Man
I Might Become

The
Man
I Might
Become

GAY MEN WRITE
ABOUT THEIR FATHERS

EDITED BY
BRUCE SHENITZ

FOREWORD BY
ANDREW HOLLERAN

MARLOWE & COMPANY ■ NEW YORK

THE MAN I MIGHT BECOME: *Gay Men Write About Their Fathers*
Compilation and introduction © 2002 by Bruce Shenitz
Foreword © 2002 by Andrew Holleran
Please consult page 265 for additional copyright
information on individual selections.

Published by
Marlowe & Company
An Imprint of Avalon Publishing Group Incorporated
161 William Street, 16th Floor
New York, NY 10038

Library of Congress Cataloging-in-Publication Data

The man I might become : gay men write about their fathers /
edited by Bruce Shenitz.
p. cm.
ISBN 1-56924-564-9 (trade paper)
1. Gay men—United States—Family relationships. 2. Fathers and sons—
United States. 3. Gay men's writings, American. I. Shenitz, Bruce.
HQ76.3.U5 M335 2002
305.38'9664'0973—dc21   2002141440

9   8   7   6   5   4   3   2   1

Designed by Pauline Neuwirth, Neuwirth & Associates

Printed in Canada
Distributed by Publishers Group West

FOR MY FATHER AND MOTHER
AND FOR STAN

Contents

Acknowledgments

Even more than most books, an anthology of original work is highly collaborative, with many people providing insights, advice, and assistance along the way. This book had its genesis in a series of conversations with Clifford Chase, whose anthology, *Queer 13: Lesbian and Gay Writers Recall Seventh Grade,* suggested to me the rich possibilities of the form; it was Cliff whose example showed that putting together an anthology was actually a feasible undertaking. Alberto Manguel, writer, essayist, and anthologist, encouraged me to tackle this project long before I was convinced I should.

My agent Richard Parks took on the project despite something of an uphill battle in selling serious gay nonfiction these days, and offered advice and counsel throughout the process. Chris Bull, an outstanding journalist, author, and editor, introduced me to Matthew Lore, a publisher whose enthusiasm, passion, and dedication were a wonderful inspiration and a resource throughout. Sue McCloskey kept this complex project organized and running smoothly. Tita Gillespie provided judicious copyediting.

When Judy Wieder, Corporate Editorial Director of Liberation Publications Inc., hired me as executive editor of *Out* magazine two years ago, she gave me the opportunity to work in a stimulating environment where I've been constantly challenged to examine my assumptions about important gay issues. Brendan Lemon, editor-in-chief at *Out,* provided valuable insights during the course of my workdays in dealing with expository nonfiction and the people who write it. He also offered thoughtful advice at several crucial points during the editing of the anthology. I'm also grateful to the entire *Out* editorial staff, who make the magazine such an exciting place to work.

The writers who submitted pieces—especially those who made a commitment to do so long before there was a promise of publication—deserve my heartfelt thanks. I knew that the topic hit home because of the extreme reactions I received as I approached potential contributors. They ranged from "I've been waiting to write a piece like that all my life," to "I don't even want to *touch* the topic." The back-and-forth process of editing has resulted in rich ongoing conversations, mostly by email, occasionally in person, about writing, about life in general, and a mix of the two. A special thanks is due to writers whose work I was unable to include for reasons of space.

Patrick Merla generously suggested several writers whose work he had previously collected in *Boys Like Us: Gay Writers Tell Their Coming Out Stories.*

Many friends offered encouragement and support throughout the long gestation period. They include Matt, Kate, and Maggie Perlman, Shelley Karson and Harriet Mendlowitz, Ann Miller, Rob Kahn, Joan Westreich, Peter Fish, Bart Ziegler and Jim Zarroli, David Bornstein, and Eric Marcus.

My partner, Stan Scott, offered his eyes and ears as well as providing computer-tech support throughout the course of this project, and listened to more than his share of the arcana of book publishing.

Foreword

ANDREW HOLLERAN

Many men, straight and gay, wish they'd been closer to their fathers. To this day when I see in public a man and his son talking, or holding hands as they walk down a street, I linger on the sight. Once, in a restaurant, I watched a boy sit down in the next booth with his father and a group of friends. Tired from an afternoon of fishing, the boy proceeded to rest his head against his father's shoulder, and then the father rested his head on top of his son's, so that the two of them were folded together like chimpanzees that had just groomed each other. I could scarcely contain myself. The image of this father and son expressing their affection, their trust, their intimacy, in so unself-conscious a way, was astounding to me—it seemed so what I was never able to do with my own.

Of course there are many sons who are as affectionate with their fathers as this boy in the restaurant was, but for some reason—connected no doubt to the role the paterfamilias plays—the more common feeling I suspect is one of awe or distance. Our fathers may be perfectly available—but even when they are good and generous we feel some gulf between us. I don't know if it was guilt, or love, or boredom that induced my father from time to time to take me for a drive on a deserted country road so I could sit in his lap and steer the car—but while doing this I always felt I had to make small talk, as if with a perfect stranger, now that we were finally alone. I didn't know how to amuse this august man. Finally, on the way to a father-son banquet sponsored by the Boy Scouts one night when I was ten, I felt like such an impostor I jumped out of the car rolling down our driveway rather than attend—it seemed so fraudulent to pretend there was a bond between us. Or at least it was much more complicated than any father-son banquet could admit; it lay too deep for words. To his credit my father did not question me; we went back inside the house and returned to our reading.

In his book *Being Homosexual,* Richard Isay suggests that this alienation between gay men and their fathers begins in childhood when the father, sensing they are different, withdraws. This is not to say that fathers are still not enormous presences in the lives of their gay sons. Fathers have always been, in life and literature, a mystery we believe we must decipher before we can understand ourselves. The classic account of a gay man's trying to do this is the English writer J. R. Ackerley's masterpiece *My Father and Myself.* Written over a period of thirty years, and published posthumously, *My Father and Myself* uncovers secrets that most fathers admittedly do not live with; but the instinct—to go back, to find out what if anything one's homosexuality had to do with one's progenitor—is common, I suspect, whether in the occasional reverie or literary excavation. With gay sons the problem may seem doubly perplexing in part because it is (or was, till recently) assumed that sons acquired their masculinity by identifying with their fathers. A recent spate of books about young boys takes the premise that masculinity is in fact a rather fragile construct, easily skewed by cultural expectations and careless adults. But in real life boys are simply expected to end up "a chip off the old block." Gay sons may think they have done something wrong, therefore, when it turns out they are unlike their fathers in one fundamental way; they're not looking for a girl like dear old Mom, they're searching for—what?—the man they were supposed to be, the man they want to surrender to, or merge with, so that, as Isay suggests, they can heal the wound the estrangement from their fathers caused.

It may be reductive to observe that in some persistent way gay men seem to be searching for masculinity, or some version of their father in another man. Even if there is some truth to it, however, this search clearly has many permutations. The anecdotes one hears in any gay lifetime include every conceivable combination of fathers and sons—fathers who were despised, adored, crucial, irrelevant, remote, or intimate—just like the fathers of straight men and women. In a biography of Abraham Lincoln I am reading, I was surprised to learn that Lincoln's oldest son Robert, who sobbed unrestrainedly at his father's deathbed, had always felt deeply awkward in his presence.

Relations between fathers and sons are, at best, a loaded combination of love and rivalry tinctured with the unpleasant fact of mortality. Sons, after all, are here to replace their fathers—to one day play his part; and they seem to do this by either trying to imitate him or emphatically insisting on the opposite. Some sons make a point, like Lincoln, to be what their father was not; the president people called Father Abraham would not even attend his own father's funeral. Others long to be carbon copies ("The acorn doesn't fall far from the tree") or improvements on their model. (What else is a family supposed to do but make social progress?) Lincoln—who wanted to get off his father's farm in the worst way— never said one word in praise of his sire, and ascribed all that was best in him to his stepmother. Yet Lincoln himself was notorious for doting on his sons—letting them run wild through the White House. The variations are endless. Fathers may be anything—even, nowadays, with recent changes in conception, mere donors of sperm. Yet when I walked into the local hardware store this morning and saw two young boys standing with their father at the check-out counter, I instinctively bristled—thinking, This is what I missed. Fathers, to some extent, no matter what else they do, are supposed to initiate their sons into the male role, the realm of men, which is to say, the world.

The world turns out to contain a hazard for gay sons that their fathers did not have to face, however—being homosexual—though of course there are gay sons with gay fathers. Even if the son does resemble his father, there is one rather important aspect the gay son cannot replicate. This aspect has huge consequences for his life. The psychologist Walt Odets has said there's not a gay man alive who does not feel that he's let his family down. I never told my father I was gay because I couldn't imagine his hearing, much less processing, that fact. I could only picture his incomprehension, or disgust. There was therefore a chasm between us—so much so that I was amazed, and touched, when I overheard him one evening tell an old friend on the phone that although I had not married I seemed happy—and that was all that mattered.

That this came as a shock shows how little I knew my father, but I suspect this is not uncommon in children. Our fathers remain the family Zeus; a creature on Mount Olympus who's capable of throwing lightning bolts. Our fathers are our progenitors; we fear (or want) their judgment. We often don't even know what that is, because most of the time our fathers die without our ever explaining ourselves to them, or vice versa. This unfinished business, this gap, becomes eternal, perhaps a template for the estrangement we feel from all people. Then one day we find ourselves tapping our fingers in a certain way, smiling or talking to someone in just the way he did.

One doubts the things in this book could have been or even now be said face-to-face to the fathers who are being portrayed, and, I suppose, evaluated, here; yet in some sense that is just what the sons writing about their fathers are doing in this book—speaking to them. When William James's father died, he was in Europe and could not get home for the funeral; so his brother Henry, who, for a change, happened to be in Massachusetts, took the letter William had written to his father, but which had arrived too late, and read it aloud to their father's grave in the Cambridge cemetery. It is among the most touching of scenes in literary history—this attempt to speak across the grave. Yet, whether the obstacle is the grave, or something else, it is what some of the people in this book are doing— and for good reason. Though it's been a long time since Jacob and Esau sought their father's blessing in the Bible, it is still that blessing we seek.

Introduction

BRUCE SHENITZ

> Mothers are soft and yielding. Fathers are hard and rough,
> and to teach us the way of the world, which is rough, which
> is mean, which is selfish and prejudiced.
>   —*I Never Sang for My Father,* by Robert Anderson

I used to be convinced that there really should be only two titles for essays that sons write about their fathers: "I Never Played Catch with My Father, and Then He Died," and "I Played Catch with My Father, But He Died Anyway." Beneath the quip was an element of truth: the predominant mode of the remembrance of fatherhood seems to be one of missed opportunities and regrets. I would sneer at many of these essays, because I assumed that the straight men who were doing the writing had no cause to complain: They, after all, never had to deal with the fundamental cause for alienation that any gay man who came out had to reckon with. I've since realized that the father-son story is almost always a complicated one for any man, straight or gay. Still, I continued to note that few examples in the floodtide of writing about fathers that I read reflected the experience of gay men—either the ways in which it was similar to or radically different from our straight brethren.

So why a collection of essays exclusively by gay men writing about fathers? The unfolding discovery of differentness, culminating in the knowledge of being gay, has usually played a major role in how we relate to our fathers. Navigating connections across differences is a universal in human relations, one that we all face in almost every relationship we have, whether sexual, platonic, familial, or even in the workplace. The lessons that gay men have learned in this arena, however hard won, can be both moving and instructive.

In the case of men who don't actually come out to their fathers, the very absence of that moment can remain a force throughout their lives. For Brian Malloy, who lost his father when he was fifteen, the unspoken words in "Things I Never Told My Father" take on a powerful life as he imagines the conversation that will never take place. Joseph Hansen doesn't even try to imagine what that scene would be like. As the 79-year-old doyen of gay mystery writers puts it, for his generation, "Coming out was tantamount to self-destruction." For Felice Picano, who belongs to the in-between generation of men active in Gay Liberation beginning in the late 1960s, the subject was discussable, but just barely.

For most of the writers here, the act of coming out is a pivotal, defining moment in their relationship with this first man in their lives. The initial reactions generally range from uncomprehending to hostile, but these narratives offer parallel, alternate accounts of the consequences that ripple out from that moment. The anthology is bookended by contrasting accounts: the first selection, which chronicles Peter M. Krask's wrenching coming out, may fit a stereotype of troubled-gay-son–straight-father relations, but his essay expands our understanding of the emotional costs incurred by these rifts. In the final piece, Bernard Cooper, who has writen about his father with grace, humor, and compassion on several occasions over the years, offers a richly textured portrait of binding ties in all their complexity.

Most writers in this collection navigate similarly complex territory, finding ways to relate to fathers who, despite some sense that their sons might be different from other boys, probably never thought too much about homosexuality—and certainly not as a life option for their sons. These essays move sequentially from alienation toward reconciliation with several intermediate steps—puzzled incomprehension, grudging acceptance, strained attempts at understanding—and a detour into sexual mythologies. Whether they are read in sequence or at random, they provide a rough typology of father-son relationships that are richly different from each other. There are no simple explanations of why some of these relationships deepen while others never move beyond painful confrontations; what these writings offer is the suggestion of a range of possibilities.

I CONSIDER MYSELF lucky to have been spared the demands of a macho father. (My father and I did toss one of those metaphor-laden baseballs occasionally, but no one suggested that I ought to try out for Little League in addition to—or instead of—taking piano lessons.) But I often assumed this was exceptional. If, like me, you grew up in the years before gay characters exploded on the TV screen, and your early knowledge of homosexuality came from the furtive perusal of psychology books in the library—you might have read about the binding-mother–distant-father model of homosexual pathology and fit your own life into it even if the fit was uncomfortable. Years later, as I listened to other men—yes, in a men's consciousness-raising group in California, no less—I began to hear more and more stories that went against the grain: straight sons who found it nearly impossible to talk to fathers, and gay sons who had emerged from the coming-out process into a new honesty with their fathers.

Which is not to say that this collection is filled with tales of redemptive love that miraculously blossom in hostile surroundings. Far from it. Part of the reason, I think, can be found in the received wisdom that says that our mothers love us unconditionally while we have to earn our fathers' approval. The kernel of truth in the truism is that traditionally, at least, men ground their relationships in the world of the physical—work and sports being its two major arenas. Our earliest memories of our fathers often involve our perceptions of their work: Tom Donaghy connects his father's work in the roofing business with the changing skyline of downtown Philadelphia.

My own father is a CPA, and one of my most frequent associations with him occurs when I open my wallet. When I was first old enough to have one, my father often told me to put the larger bills in back and arrange them by decreasing denomination so that the singles would be in the front. You'll never confuse a ten with a one, he'd tell me, something I've occasionally done as I reach into my chronically disheveled wallet.

It's hardly the most important lesson I learned from him. That would have to be the time that he told me, after he received a clean bill of health following a tumor biopsy, that if the results had been unfavorable, he probably would have wanted to continue the life he was leading. As a teenager who was accustomed to thinking of the world in more dramatic terms, I found that it was a great lesson in seeking satisfaction in everyday things. Yet I'm probably more likely to think of my father when I deal with the daily physical reality of my wallet.

So what does all this have to do with being gay? Naturally, the numbers of sons who sit around and discuss the details of their sexual lives with their fathers is relatively small. A few years ago, the Australian movie *The Sum of Us* told the story of a father who took an overly healthy interest in his son's sex life; as implausible as it was, and as unbearable as many might find it in real life, the story was appealing in part because of a level of acceptance that few men experience. It's a rarity in the pieces in this collection, which sometimes makes the very effort moving. Kai Wright's father immediately responds to a coming-out letter by writing back to tell him about a relatively obscure James Baldwin work which is "the only book I have ever bothered to read which depicts gay love in the same way that heterosexual love is shown." Wright reminds us, too, that even when we manage to come through coming out, there is no escaping the burdens that life brings to parents and children alike: aging, disease, and loneliness.

These paternal meditations may have something else to teach us—the possibility of a normalization of the previously pathological. While psychology by and large no longer looks for "causes" of homosexuality in an unhealthy home, we are still in the process of replacing the old models with new images of what a developmentally normal gay life might look like. James M. Saslow's playful exploration of Greek mythology and childhood memory in "Daddy Was a Hot Number" suggests that gay men search for, as Andrew Holleran notes in his foreword, a gay male equivalent of someone "just like the girl, who married dear old Dad." Douglas Sadownick takes this a step further in his discussion of what a new psychology of gay male sexuality in relation to fathers would look like.

Finally, it is because most of us have been pushed into levels of self-revelation beyond what our straight counterparts ever contemplated that I believe our stories are worth telling. For the most part gay men have, at least until recently, been deprived of a fundamental point of commonality with their fathers—becoming fathers themselves. As the essay by Jesse Green suggests, becoming a parent opens up new possibilities for gay men to overcome some of the traditional differences that have divided fathers and gay sons. Those of us without that point of contact will continue to forge those relations from a perspective of "otherness" that is perhaps only a more radical version of the way that all personal connections are made. Certainly, many of the essays in this collection suggest that some sort of rapprochement is possible, even if the path to it is difficult. That we can forge connections at all strikes me as something miraculous, and the stories that chronicle that effort have something to teach all of us, parents and children, gay, straight, or other. The stories of fathers and sons who remain locked in opposition and anger have something to teach us as well—the price exacted when conformity is valued over the integrity of the self.

The Man
I Might Become

PETER M. KRASK

The Question I Asked Him

for Dr. John Kavanaugh

I must have thought that no one was home, or perhaps that no one would hear me. How old was I—seven? Nine? Maybe an unlikely and embarrassing ten? I don't recall thinking anything beyond this: My mother's dress—white silk, long, with a high gathered waist, and printed with large purple flowers—was laid out on her bed in anticipation of the party she and my father would be attending that night. It was there, spilling over the edge of the bed onto the floor, a cascade of blossoms poured out through a cloud. It was *there*.

Even though I never put the dress on, I knew enough to shut the slatted door. Fantasy sparked the impulse toward privacy, or, even then—it's possible—toward shame. In thrall more to some silly movie spoof from the *Carol Burnett Show* than the desire for drag, I held the dress up, the corners tucked tight under my arms, and swayed and dipped before the mirror. And in the finest magnolia-steeped southern accent I could manage, kept spurning some nameless cad's bold—and secretly welcomed—advances.

"Why y'aw so fray-ush!" I said, turning on my heel fast enough to make the silk dance. "Ah said fray-ush!"

I didn't hear the knob turn. Then, in mid-flounce: "What are you doing?"

My father must have listened through the door—"So vairy fray-ush!"—before he decided to enter. But he never completely crossed the threshold either. I stood silent before him, still holding the dress under my arms, the blossoms falling to rest—an afterthought—at my feet.

The trouble I was in was greater than I could know; and nameless, too.

"Put it down," he said. "Men don't do those kinds of things." He stepped back. He shut the door.

THE BEST EXPLANATION I've heard of the often-fraught nature of the relationship between fathers and their gay sons comes from gay psychiatrist Richard Isay. Dr. Isay theorizes—and I'm simplifying—that a father, early in his son's infancy, intuits that his son is somehow, well . . . *different*. He knows that the tiny crying life he holds so close to his chest, that boy with hands as big as spoons, the one on the edge of settling into sleep under the shadow of his stubbled chin, will never be—but how he hopes!—a man like him.

After making this unpleasant discovery, a father spends the rest of his life running from this knowledge, which also means away from his son. The strain of keeping this knowledge at bay—of being two steps ahead always—warps the bond between father and son into one forever twisting barbed-wire coil of rejection. The son, marked like Cain, but with a secret he has yet to understand, wanders the land unable to get near. Dad's forever out of reach—*there!*—just over the horizon.

Theories are tricky, I know. And Dr. Isay's, with its many Freudian trimmings, raises all kinds of big, messy questions. Even so, the fundamental dynamic he describes, that endless reaching for the hand that won't be grasped, has the bedrock feel of truth to me. For too many years, I entered into a fatal footrace with my own father, a man, I thought, who had the advantage of an enormous head start. And since I could never catch up to him, clearly the fix was in. My only thought (should I properly call it hope?): Call to him; get him to look back, turn his head just once, goddamnit, to see me gaining on him.

You've seen me before, maybe yesterday when you passed the playground. I was the boy running hard by himself. My steps began to falter and slow, even as they grew wilder. The urgency in my feet transformed into the heat of panic and tears in my voice as I cried, "C'mon! Wait up! C'mon, please! Wait! . . ."

(A useful life, a happy life, a life burnished with love will not be built on the habit of pursuit.)

I've missed something here. Truth, after all, wills out. As we endlessly ran toward safety, my father and I could not see we were also being pursued. Our secret selves would not be left behind. No matter where we ran.

I GOT THE call when I lived far from home, at a time when I was lost in the wilderness of a broken heart and unprepared for it to shatter further. I want to say it was nine years ago; I can never remember exactly. Mom would be all right. My oldest brother kept saying that. She wasn't hurt, even though she had driven her car off the road. Something about a massive panic attack. The doctors weren't sure—yet. When the ambulance brought her in, she looked like she might die. Mom will be all right. My brother wanted me to know that. She will. But she says she won't go back.

Won't go back where?

. . . with Dad. Not with him.

My brother added something else: It's the drinking.

There. It had been said. With that, the seam had been rent; the forty-two years of my parents' marriage—and, with it, my family—unraveled overnight into nothing.

I saw my mother the next day, but only after a nurse first unlocked the door to the psych ward.

AS I SIFT through my memories of When I Came Out—a task that brings no pleasure—it would be easy for me to paint my father as a vicious man. So easy. But dishonest, too. It wouldn't take into account the man who can improvise mad hilarious songs on the piano for children. The Ph.D. student at the University of Chicago who was nearly expelled because of his delicious itch for vaudeville and burlesque. The prodigious boy who performed a Saint-Saëns piano concerto at the Chicago World's Fair. The father who taught me how to cook as we sat together at the kitchen table while he artfully sliced vegetables for soups and chop suey. The handsome soldier who, after playing a round of dueling pianists, once accompanied a singing movie star at a USO show, a star who also took him out to dinner afterward—at least that's what the newspapers said. The scientist who made sure all five of his children got graduate degrees, and they did, too. The wounded soldier—age twenty, I think, and shot in the leg—who rescued another wounded young man pinned under a fallen tree during a German bombing raid in France. The brave proud man who was awarded a Purple Heart, a Silver Star, a Bronze Star, and a Good Conduct Medal. The curious man who, when his beard came in white, took a tube of mascara and brushed it black as Satan's just to see what people would say.

But these details can in no way account for the fury, the hurricane of hatefulness, my father let loose upon me when I came out to him. Here are facts I can work like an endless string of beads. Before I left home for good, to be with a man I thought I'd spend my life with, my father said, "I hope to God you can find a job with health insurance for when you get it." "Get what?" I asked, unwittingly setting up the punch line. "AIDS, of course," he said. "What else?" After noticing that most of my writing had gone unpublished and unproduced for years, my father called up to say, "Well, I guess there was no reason for you to have gone into such debt with that fancy graduate school since you wasted it all on that gay writing."

There's more. Yes, much more.

But I'll stick with the first. My father wrote me a letter—twelve pages in longhand from a yellow legal pad—after I told him I was gay. I still have it somewhere, in a box, I think; I can't read it, nor can I throw it out. It began, "I will never be able to forgive you for what you have done to your family." And he meant it. It ended with this: "Those boys in college were right. [He meant the ones who had harassed me, the boys who had vandalized my room with a picture of two men having anal sex, drawn life-size in indelible purple ink.] You are a fruit. A fairy. A faggot. A queer." Then this: "I've seen the life you chose." And this: "When I travel, there are places where I won't ever go. They disgust me so."

Then my father, who had once held me, his youngest son, in his arms, hoping to rock me to sleep, refused to speak to me for a very long time.

I CAME TO a crossroads with my father one night during a drunken phone call. Alcohol turned into venom the second it entered my father's blood. He called in a poisonous, incoherent rage. My parents would not divorce, and my mother had tried once more to live with him. When her health again became perilously at risk, my siblings and I intervened; no matter what, married or not, she could not live with him again—ever. For my father, it was the final damning proof of just how ungrateful his children were. He had been right all along.

I should have hung up when I heard his first slurred word. His wrath was stoked to such a pitch, I thought he'd have a heart attack. Everything he'd ever done for us. Everything he'd ever given up. For *what?* And you. You big disappointment. You're the one who betrayed me most. (Did he say this to each of his children? I've never thought to ask this before.) Everything you've done was done for spite. To rub my face in it. What I expected. Worst of all, I'm sick just thinking about it, the things you do with men. Those foul *things* . . . I expected better. You owe me. Where's my respect?

"Dad," I said, not knowing where the words were coming from, "I'm going to hang up. But understand one thing: You always talk about respect. You insist that everyone owes you respect. Well, I demand respect, too. Until you can speak to me with even the barest trace of respect, I want nothing to do with you. I mean it. *Nothing.*"

Silence. Then a wail of the purest, most concentrated, brilliant, incandescent anger. Before it could fully pierce my ear, I hung up.

Like father, like son. After that, I didn't speak to my father for a very long time.

In describing this, in thinking it through, I notice most my father's crushing resentment of his children. Should I instead call it envy? In the dark, aren't they the same thing?

I wonder about this; it tugs at me in a way I would not have expected.

LET ME BE clear. I won't be misunderstood. I'm not equating alcoholism with homosexuality. But much in their respective languages is similar: Condition. Predisposition. Choice. Practicing. Nature. Nurture. Treatment. Cure. *Denial.* These words are necessary and true, but it's in my nature to resist them, to contest their power to trump the singularity of experience. Yet it is experience—the steady, sometimes tedious, labor of untangling my father's life and mine—that dares me to connect the two. There is a law of patterns, a logic of secrets, that arises in any life spent fleeing the havoc unleashed by desire. When I first came out, I was shocked by the depth of my parents' surprise—weren't the signs always there? Not long ago, I spoke with my oldest brother who figured out that my father had started drinking much earlier than we'd ever thought. Why were we so surprised, so caught off guard? Weren't the signs always there?

As I slowly learn to live my life with greater freedom, I've begun to think of being gay as a way of learning to live without expectations, or, more accurately, of getting past them. After all, what boy, whose eyes have lingered a little too long on the brown hair peeking over the front collar of that man's white T-shirt—the shirt, like his skin, which moves with that man's every breath—doesn't learn a hard lesson? And early, too. All bets are off. Life's not gonna be what you think it is, no sir. If he survives that shock, if he's not too dazed, or doesn't run from it, the boy stands a chance as a man to hold life closer, to ride its mysteries with grace.

(When love costs that much, its value is hard to forget.)

For a man like me who's always considered himself a total failure as a homosexual, who doesn't know what or where the "gay community" is, the irony is sublime: My life turned out to be one giant gay cliché, a father's worst nightmare. I couldn't be a bigger fag. I earn my living as a florist. Much of my writing life involves the rarefied, exquisite world of opera. I've been known to use the phrase *organza overlay* in conversation. (A friend sweetly, but unthinkingly, remarks after dinner, "Why, you're the female Martha Stewart!") It's nothing I ever wanted.

Or expected.

All I can do is laugh.

Fate, holding a grudge for all the years—those wasted years—I spent running from Her and Her plans, wanted to make sure the question would never come up again. As a form of divine retribution, it's been enormously kind and freeing. Now, with the trappings of my life draped in rainbow-striped bunting, the pressure's off. I can get on with it. On the days I forget to do this, the odd times when someone asks me what I do and the sulfurous taste of shame rises unwelcome in the back of my throat, fate has given me a subtle and valuable reminder to once again seize the freedom I had long ago asked for.

If coming out is a question about freedom—and it is—it's a question about several kinds of freedom. Yes, it's about being free to be one's self, and being free enough to accept one's self. But there's another, even more demanding, kind of freedom at stake, too. It's the freedom that seeks out the furthest limits of love's bonds, the ties that usually hide from daylight. It's no small thing to ask another person—in the name of love, for the sake of love—this question: *Will you grant me the freedom to choose my life whatever the consequences?* Just to summon the courage for the asking can take a lifetime.

But it is harder, more difficult—isn't it?—to be the one who is asked. Harder to be the one to put aside all ideas, hopes, beliefs, and plans. Isn't it? More difficult to give up, well, everything. To stand alone, naked, bereft, with only empty hands. To say: *Yes. I'll give you my hand. It's all that I've got, and together we'll go*—where?

(I cannot say now which takes the greater faith.)

I didn't understand this until my father chose a bottle of scotch over his family.

Because that's what he did.

In that first terrible year after my mother's breakdown, my brothers and sisters held out much more hope than I ever did. They tried longer and harder, and with lasting pain, to do something—*anything*—to get my father to seek help. It defied belief; the choice was so clear, so simple. Surely he could see his family was at stake. Surely he'd want to save that. But he didn't. My father knew what an alcoholic was—a drunk passed out in a gutter covered in his own filth—and that wasn't him. It's easy to say my father was in denial, that, in alcohol's death grip, he couldn't see how completely he fit the classic standard profile, the stereotype, of an alcoholic. Saying it, however, wouldn't—and doesn't—solve the problem. Saying it denies him the dignity of choice, his freedom to say *No.*

My father made his decision. His decision was willful, perverse, cruel, and catastrophic. But it was *his.* And I think—it's hard to admit this—he knew what he was choosing; it wasn't only the alcohol talking. My father told me once that he'd done his duty. Called back to duty one final time, my father refused. He said *No.* He'd show us all. At last, he'd finally ask for the freedom to choose the course of his life, whatever the consequences.

Maybe I'm letting myself off the hook. Maybe I could have done more, or believed more, to get my father sober. My conscience is far from clear. But I knew then—without hesitation or hope—during those dreadful uncertain weeks when my mother was hospitalized that my father had made up his mind. "It's useless," I told my sister-in-law. "Dad's already decided." I think she thought I was bitter, and perhaps I was. But perhaps I also knew a little more about how a man's secret self, when it simply cannot stand it anymore, insists on itself and its prerogatives. The day comes when freedom can wait no more. It can be a terrible reckoning.

My father, for all of the wrong stupid reasons he could think of, asked me the same question I had once asked him. I ask you: How could I say no? He had the right to ask. He had the right to choose. To grant my father his freedom, to tell him *Yes,* meant offering only my open hand knowing, in the end, he would never take it.

Love's never what you think it is.

I write this as if I've made some kind of peace. That's not true, though. I claim no wisdom here. Some mornings I wake up and still can't believe what's happened. Despite its fair share of pleasures and happiness, much in my life went quietly and deeply awry after my parents separated. Recently, I dated an alcoholic. One night he was literally falling-down drunk. He fell on me and knocked me to the floor, where I had to struggle to push him off me. Two more months had to pass before I had the sense to leave. After an important professional success of mine, my mother called to tell me my father cried when he heard the news. She thought I'd want to know. I told this to a friend who said, "That must make you proud and happy." To which I replied, surprising myself, "Yeah. Well. Whatever. He can go fuck himself for all I care."

And there's always that awkward inevitable moment during a date. The conversation is going well, nerves have started to settle, and then the man says, "Tell me about your dad and mom." I never know what to say. Partly, it's shame. But it's not nearly as simple as that. It never is.

Here's the thing about grief: Even if you learn to live with it, once it gets inside you, it won't go away.

SEVERAL YEARS AGO I had the privilege of meeting Dennis Shepard, Matthew's father. He was waiting to tape an interview in a television studio where I had come to install some flowers. Most people had gathered around Matthew's mother, Judy, and Dennis sat by himself. I went up to him, introduced myself, and told him how much I admired his courage, the extraordinary bravery he showed in sparing the life of his son's murderer. Before I could continue, he stopped me. "You've come out, haven't you?" he asked. I told him I had. "Then you've told your father, haven't you?" I started to answer, but he pressed on. "How did it go? How did he take it? What's it like now between you?"

"It was a disaster," I replied. Dennis winced. "As for now . . ." *Estranged* wasn't the right word. I couldn't think. *Distant,* perhaps. *Complicated?* I wanted to be as accurate as I could. My brain seemed to stop working.

"It's okay," Dennis said. "I want you to know one thing. You were the brave one for telling him. You have far more courage than I."

I thought I might faint if I didn't leave the room that instant.

Dennis looked at me, right in my eyes. "Peter," he said, "I am so very proud of you."

He took me in his arms. "Peter," he asked, his eyes searching, "we fathers and gay sons. What do we do? What do we do?"

He held me tight. I didn't let him go.

WHEN I WAS twenty, I fell in a love with a boy, but I was too afraid to call it by its proper name. Its secrecy only inflamed it—the love, its confusion—further. The boy I loved—and I see him in my mind that way—once gave his life over to despair. The boy I loved swallowed a bottle of pills. I found him. He lived anyway. Two days later my father found me crying. " You must stop this," he said. He studied me, his eyes bright with rage. "The things I saw . . . when I was your age . . ." he said. " Listen to me. I'm your father. You don't know the first thing about suffering." He grabbed my shoulder, then walked away.

The cruelty of this memory makes me flinch. Yet, I see now, although I didn't understand it this way at the time, that my father had told me something of real significance about his life, no matter how mysterious the details. Maybe things would have been easier between us had I understood this earlier.

I first became a writer in the hope of uncovering the tragic secret that would explain my father's life. I was certain the secret existed. I wrote so much about him, always thinking that the next page would turn up an answer. It never did. Hypnotized by the prevailing wisdom of the day, the nonsense that masqueraded as compassion, which, in turn, got a generation to believe the big lie that "we are all victims of victims of victims," I wrote and wrote and wrote words that added up to not a lot. I can't read any of it now. It should be burnt.

One day I tired of this. I wanted to live my own life instead of my father's.

The tragic secret of my father's life, it turns out, is far simpler than I ever thought: My father was unhappy. He worked hard. He loved his wife and kids as he was able. He was a good provider. He was kind when he could be kind. These count a great deal. My brothers and sisters are all excellent parents; I know something got through. But I also know my father probably never wanted to be married and have five children. He lived a life he didn't want, and it made him profoundly unhappy.

Beyond that, I cannot say.

Unhappiness is enough, however, to drown a man. Life so seldom falls to pieces on one tragic secret, anyway. It's like this: A man dives into the ocean not knowing his foot is caught on a line. The line is light and very long. The man can still swim. He can swim out far, meeting the waves head-on, all the while unaware of the line unspooling behind him, the line slowly and imperceptibly pulling him under as the shore disappears from view. Suddenly he can go no further, even as he kicks harder, beating the water into foam. He's alone. All he can feel is the line, but he has no blade to cut it.

One kind of man keeps his wits. It's not too late to swim back to shore, the safety of land where he can free himself. Another kind of man—a man like my father—panics or rages. He fights and pulls against the line until the effort exhausts him. He begins to sink. He doesn't know he can turn back. He doesn't know that someone on land might be able to help free him. He sinks further, gasping for breath. He sinks ever downward. He sinks; sinks until all he can see is a ceiling of sea, and the ever-receding, ever-silent shadows of the waves, the waves, the waves.

My father is slowly dying now. He has emphysema. Two months ago, he coughed so hard he passed out and hit his head. He won't see a doctor. He refuses all help, all care. And we've tried. He called me not too long ago to tell me that all the advice he had ever given me was wrong. Then he hung up before I could say anything. On his birthday, two of his grandchildren came to visit. It was morning—always the best time to see him, he hasn't had a drink yet—and they came bearing cupcakes they had baked and decorated for him. They came to celebrate and take him out to breakfast. He wouldn't go. He wouldn't go, despite their pleading.

He wouldn't go.

I can only marvel at the kind of judge he stands before; the judge who sentences without mercy; the judge who'd deny a condemned man that least bit of comfort.

MEMORY'S THREAD MUST be made of spider's silk: It's so fine and hard to grasp. When I was a boy, I used to brush my father's hair. He'd come home from work, after commuting an hour each way (I wonder now if that time was precious to him, free as it was of the noise of family), and take a nap. Before he'd lie down, he'd sit in his chair in the living room and listen to music. Tonight he played the Schumann Piano Quintet in E-flat Major. It was one of his Music Minus One records. The string-quartet part was on the record. My father was supposed to play the piano part at home along with the record. I remember that you could adjust the turntable's speed so the recorded quartet was in tune with your piano.

I stood on the brick ledge in front of the fireplace, standing on my toes so I could reach over the back of my father's chair. The music seemed strange—buoyant and airborne—without the piano. It was lovely, but surely something was missing. My father sat in his undershirt and boxer shorts. I gave his shoulders a few quick karate chops for good measure and then, with his good English brush, the one with the fine white bristles, I began to brush his hair. I took a few of my mother's bobby pins and pinned up the front part so I'd be sure to get his scalp real good. His hair cream made my fingers sticky. And we stayed like that—him sitting and me brushing.

We had no words between us. Only knowledge. Knowledge that was elemental, unyielding, but nevertheless tender; but tender like a bruise is tender:

Here is my father. Here is my son.

KEVIN BENTLEY

Six Crises
of Bullmoose

My mother got leukemia the year before I turned forty, and the prognosis was grim. I hadn't been back to El Paso in thirteen years, and we hadn't been talking much for the last six, but now we talked—long phone calls about her condition, current events, and some awkward words of regret. "I'm sure you're going to make it, but I still want to come see you," I said.

"Wait," she said. "I have to talk to Daddy."

That had a sadly familiar ring. In the period after I'd first left home, when she and I were still in regular touch, she would call me from the back bedroom, her voice low so Daddy wouldn't hear. Critical conversations had often ended this way, with a follow-up call a day or two later to deliver the verdict.

No, my best friend couldn't stay over at the house during a brief trip home. No, they wouldn't loan me a modest amount of money against my dying lover's life insurance so we could afford cab rides to the doctor.

"Daddy says if we give you this money now it'll just be more next time—and then what if *you* get sick?"

I DID GO back that once, for a few days in the summer of 1982—a visit that made clear all I'd missed out on by making a life so far away. On my last evening we gathered for a backyard cookout. My older brother Randy arrived with his new, second wife, a peppy Filipina in a halter top and cha-cha heels, and popped open a Coors. My younger brother, who was still living at home, cranked up some country rock. Without warning, my father rushed out of the house, flushed, his fists clenched. "Turn down that goddam music!" he snarled, and knocked over the boom box.

"Fuck you!" Little brother abandoned the sizzling steaks, stomped to the driveway, and tore away from the house, tires screeching.

Randy slammed his beer on the patio, where it fizzed like a grenade. "You fucking asshole, why do you always have to spoil everything?" He headed for his truck, Tina wobbling after, her heels sinking into the grass.

My mother, who'd been making potato salad in the kitchen a few feet away, screamed, *"I hate you all!"* –which seemed a bit unfair, as I hadn't moved from my lawn chair or uttered a word—and slammed her bedroom door so loudly I expected to see the house collapse in on itself like a set in a Buster Keaton film. Flames were shooting wildly from the barbecue and I walked over and shut the lid.

Twenty minutes later, as I sat at the kitchen counter eating potato salad out of the serving bowl, and thinking about whom I might meet at the Castro Street Fair when I flew home the next day, my mother appeared, went into the garage, and returned. "Daddy's sitting in his car cleaning his rifle."

"I don't understand, is he going to asphyxiate himself or blow his head off?"

"You know I couldn't survive on just my salary, without his retirement," she said, loading the untouched dishes into the dishwasher.

DADDY. HIS RELATIONSHIP to us was more that of a spiteful and jealous sibling than the wise and heartwarming TV dads like Fred Mac-Murray on *My Three Sons* or Carl Betz on *The Donna Reed Show* that we watched in disbelief. "Bullmoose," my mother called him when we were little: "King Bullmoose has spoken." It must once have been a pet name; later it was uttered with sarcasm and resignation to the kind of bullying, indifferent authority he exercised.

I remember sitting, weeping, in a swing in our backyard while my father chased down the now-gangly Easter chicks we'd gotten at the dime store two weeks before and strangled them in their ludicrously half pink, half chicken-colored state, with pliers.

At Christmas, when the elaborately brown-paper-wrapped and twine-bound package arrived from his eccentric mother in Georgia, addressed to my brother and me in her loopy nineteenth-century handwriting, he'd open it up and smash or rip apart the contents. Granted they were oddly inappropriate gifts for children—chipped figurines, ancient sheet music— but still. Years later my mother told me, "Your father's mother caught him, you know, touching himself in the bathtub when he was a little boy so she whipped him with an egg turner and put Tabasco sauce on his thing."

Any remotely anthropomorphic toy I talked to, slept with, or tried to put outfits on mysteriously disappeared. Half my childhood was spent in a grim battle to get my hands on a doll. An aunt gave me a Cecil the Sea Serpent toy for my fifth birthday: He was essentially a bendable plush green tube with goggly eyes and a gaping mouth at one end and red felt scales down his back, but he came with disguises—Sherlock Holmes cap and pipe, Zorro cape. My father observed me carefully tying the red cape around Cecil's neck, and the next day the toy had vanished. "I don't know, are you sure you looked in your toy chest?" he'd say. "Maybe you left it outside and a dog carried it away." For a while puppets escaped his scrutiny. Soon I had a shelf full of hand puppets with which I privately acted out complicated soap opera plots: Dopey the Dwarf, Lambchop, a furry monkey. The best was a Mattel Dishonest John, in a black gown and villain's black hat, which uttered, at the pull of a string, "*Yaah*-ah-ah!" and a withering, "Go soak your *head!*" But someone was watching. When we unpacked after a move several states away to an army base in Alabama, not one puppet could be found. "Movers—those jackasses! They always lose one box!" my father said.

His occasional staged attempts at fatherly high jinks invariably went awry. He'd stretch his six-foot-four length down on the carpet and offer my older brother a quarter if he could make him laugh or say "uncle," and a rollicking wrestling match would ensue. Once, probably five years old, summoned to make the same attempt, I matter-of-factly reached for his testicles through the baggy slacks, and was angrily driven to my room in a hail of slaps and cuffs. "Don't you *ever* touch me there again!" he screeched, red-faced.

He used to poke his head into the bathroom when, as little boys, my older brother and I bathed together. "Be sure and use the washcloth and get it real clean—you know—*there*," he'd say in a weird tone, looking away but gesturing to indicate we should skin our penises back and soap up the glans. Why would he say that, when we were circumcised? He entered the Army at eighteen completely ignorant; what he knew of sex and hygiene he'd learned in training films. I don't think he understood this particular regime was meant for men with foreskins.

MAY 1960: WE'RE sitting at the kitchen table eating breakfast—Trix, Cocoa Puffs—Randy, aged seven; me, four; and my mother, reading the paper in her housecoat. We can hear my father whistling as he shaves in the distant bathroom. There's been more tension than usual in the last few weeks. I've seen my mother, wearing a cornflower-blue dress with a full skirt, wide belt, and large buttons I'll always associate with her unhappiness, standing in the dark hall, turned to the wall, an arm covering her face, sobbing.

Her favorite parts of the morning paper, which she turns to now, are the obits and legal notices. Her eyes scan a column of type, halt. She drops the paper with a bloodcurdling scream, sweeps her plate, cup, and silver-ware off the table and crashing to the floor, and runs from the room. My father's whistling pauses, continues.

I wouldn't learn the story behind this event till decades later. They'd been arguing about her third pregnancy. My father had secretly filed for divorce—it would go no further—and let her read it in the paper.

WE'RE LYING ON our backs in the shallow plastic wading pool in the far corner of the backyard, churning the water with our feet—Randy, our neighbor Cindy, and me. July 1962: I am six. Thirteen-year-old Cindy has only recently moved in down the block, and so far she has made friends only with younger kids like us. We kick to circulate the water in the hot afternoon sun, to shoo away the hovering bees from a neighbor's stacked hives, and to obscure our voices. My mother, who doesn't like Cindy and thinks it's odd she should spend so much time with two little boys, twitches the bathroom curtain aside to check up on us from time to time.

Cindy wants to see our penises. She'll show us her pussy, she says, if we'll go first. Randy grudgingly lifts the leg of his trunks and proffers a brief glimpse of puckered scrotum. Cindy peels back one side of her swimsuit and pinches out a plug of pink flesh. I am standing accommodatingly with my clammy suit around my ankles, when our father swoops down on us, shouting, and drags us both into the house.

We had done something so horrible it couldn't even be named. We'd been slapped occasionally for back talk or misbehavior, our legs and arms flailed at with the flyswatter by my mother, and, for the most serious crimes, subjected to the elaborate ritual of punishment with my father's belt. You had to unzip and pull down your pants, leaving underwear in place. My father loomed above as he silently unbuckled and swished his tooled-leather cowboy belt out of the belt loops. He began with the belt doubled over, but if you tried to straighten up or block the strokes with your arm, he'd become enraged and use the full length, which could mean getting hit with the buckle.

This time, shut in the next room, terrified, I heard the belt ritual quickly escalate to something more violent, with my father shouting angrily and my brother screaming with surprised pain. Even my mother was frightened, slapping her palms on the locked door and crying, "For God's sake, Hank, that's enough!"

"You'll be next," I'd been told. I lay huddled and trembling for the next several hours, expecting my beating each time footsteps approached the door. But when my father finally came to get me, it was for dinner. "You've had your punishment," he said smugly.

JULY 1967: WE'RE living in an army housing duplex at Fort Camp-bell, Kentucky. My father, who's never played a sport of any kind, informs me that I'm going to spend several days a week after school shooting hoops with Corporal Byrd, the young officer next door. It's my pudgy period. I hate PE and would sooner die than take off my shirt in public. My father has told us at dinner how, when their outfit had to cross a river on a wilderness survival course, Corporal Byrd stripped off his clothes and carried them across on his head. Corporal Byrd has a basketball hoop in his backyard. He's short and muscular, with a beaklike nose and a high forehead, and he plays basketball in a pair of black trunks with the white band of a jock strap riding up in back. He insists I take off my shirt. "What's the matter, are you a girl or something?" he says. When I throw the ball it goes nowhere near the hoop. It's a hot summer evening and I'm sweating; Corporal Byrd is drenched and reeking. He stands behind me, his body pressing closely, laces his fingers through mine, and ejects the ball out of my hands and through the hoop.

In this and other pungent and excruciating memories of gender awk-
wardness and homosexual inklings, why is it that my father is always present, lurking just at the edge of the frame, accuser and provoker, causing
precisely the opposite of the effect he intended? *His* body repels me, but
just to the side of him are those other enlisted men strutting in the shower
at the base pool or buying cartons of condoms at the PX; posing shirtless,
suntanned, and hairy-chested with their arms thrown over each other's
shoulders in his Vietnam photos; swimming naked across a river with
clothes piled on their heads. He leers from the periphery of these scenes
no matter how I try to scissor him out.

HAIRCUTS WERE CRITICAL to my father's authority. With the
advent of the Beatles our dislike of trips to the army base barbershop
intensified, but every three weeks we were ordered to the car and driven
to the Vitalis-reeking bastion of masculinity where, amid worn stacks of
Argosy and *Armed Forces Gazette,* a beefy bald man with woolly forearms
and tattooed biceps brusquely shaved our heads to tidy burrs. This routine required our being pulled from our sickbeds speckled and scabby
with chicken pox; my mother shrieked when we returned with open
sores on our scalps and blood trickling down the backs of our necks. On
one of these resentment-filled drives to the base barbershop when we
were thirteen and ten, he said, embarrassed and insinuating at the same
time, "Um, you may be waking up and finding your pajamas stuck to you
with something like Elmer's Glue." We remained silent; I was by that
time well acquainted with my older brother's glue.

Always, at any bus or train station, park, or movie theater, there were
his ominous warnings about the men's room, and the men in black raincoats—*fairies,* he called them, which conjured a conflicting picture—
who'd "do bad things to you." I dreamt often of these faceless men in slick
black raincoats abducting me, tucked into their pockets naked and hair-
less as a joey.

HE WAS SENT TO Vietnam twice, and then to Germany for two years,
and when he came home after the last of these long absences, his authority had irrevocably eroded. The first time he tried to make us get haircuts
my older brother ran out the back door, vaulted over a fence, and didn't
come back for two days. My father had taken an early retirement and
stayed out of work for a long, uncomfortable time, hanging around the

house drinking Carlo Rossi jug wine from colored plastic juice glasses, watching Spanish-language *Sesame Street* on TV and talking back to Big Bird and Cookie Monster.

IN APRIL 1975, age nineteen, after a jolting nine months of living with a gang of dope buddies at an apartment near the local campus of the University of Texas I was attending, I moved back home.

My younger brother had moved into my old bedroom, so I had to take the cheery canary-yellow study next to my parents' room. My doper pals didn't call, but then I'd turned my back on them. My few straight friends from high school had fallen away since graduation. Amid the pressboard furniture, dusty plastic flower arrangements, and gold carpeting, I tumbled backward into lonely adolescence. Several misguided crushes and grudging sex acts with stoned straight pals had taught me I was indeed queer; how was I going to make new friends now?

I was sulking in my room one night when my mother slipped in wearing the housecoat she'd sewn out of bright orange beach towels, and shut the door. "I just hate to see you so unhappy," she said, staring at the carpet and balling up a battered Kleenex in her fist, her voice quavering and soaring toward tears. "I don't *understand*. Is it drugs? Did Roy get you hooked on pot?" Roy was one of the straight pals I'd fallen in love with.

"Roy didn't do anything to me!" I wailed. "I love him, and he doesn't love *me*!" I cried inconsolably and my mother, who I hadn't touched in years, came forward and held me stiffly, patting my back, saying, "Hush, hush, you don't mean that...."

My father had always been a master eavesdropper. In this case, he'd listened at the door. As soon as my mother pulled out of the driveway the next morning, he appeared in my doorway, eczema-riddled jowls red and quivering, like some dense but dangerous bogey from *The Hobbit*.

"You'd better not bring any of your little queer buddies around here again, you got that? I won't have fairies in this house. If you want to associate with fairies, you'd better find somewhere else to live."

The last place I'd found to live hadn't worked out all that well. I didn't have my degree yet, and I was too stoned and thin-skinned to walk out and go to work at KFC. I would just have to kill myself.

My father was headed out for the day to attend a job seminar, but he waited to make sure I left for class. I got in my car and drove a few blocks away, parked, and waited till I saw him drive by, fussily adjusting his side mirror. Then I drove to a 7-Eleven and bought a bottle of Boone's Farm Strawberry Hill wine and a bottle of Extra Strength Anacin and returned to the house. I locked myself in my room, pulling the bed out from the wall and into the center of the room to make a sort of bier.

Contemplating death as I gulped down the grainy tablets, I searched for a Gothic feeling, and could do no better than the Styrofoam tombs and crepe-paper hell flames of *Dark Shadows,* the horror soap I used to watch after school in the sixth grade that made fatal love seem so stupefyingly turgid. I put my *Dark Shadows* soundtrack album on the stereo, swallowed the rest of the Anacin and wine, and sank back among the crashing waves at Collingwood.

That was the plan, anyway. Hadn't I seen umpteen public service commercials where absent-minded drinkers died in their easy chairs with brandy snifters at their elbows after mixing booze and pills? Wouldn't sixty Anacin and a bottle of wine be as deadly? I felt queasy and anxious, and my ears began to ring painfully. Instead of drifting off to oblivion, I felt my heart racing and skipping alarmingly. I sat up and started to gag.

"That was a pretty *stupid* thing to do. I oughta pump your stomach just so you know what it feels like—but I think I'll let you puke every goddam one of those aspirins up instead. What an idiot!" The intern walked away, stopping to say something to an orderly in blue scrubs, who glanced back over his shoulder, smirking. Randy, who traveled with a local rock band and was currently crashing in the little studio in back of our house, had driven me out to the army hospital after I banged on his door and woke him, weeping and retching. "There's always another sunrise to see," he'd told me, beating out a drum solo on the hot steering wheel. In the emergency room, I drained the paper-cupful of purple gel I'd been given, and began vomiting into a dirty mop bucket.

Later, I sat propped up on pillows in front of the TV on my parents' king-size bed, my mother holding cool washcloths to my brow and emptying my plastic bucket, counting the half-dissolved pills. My grandmother had come over, and she sat looking nervously away from me, tsking and shaking her head. She'd grown up on a dirt farm outside Abilene, wore faded wash-dresses, and always smelled comfortingly of Dentyne. "Why in the world would you want to do something like this to your mama?" she said mournfully, giving me a feeble pinch. "Why'd you want to go and be so *horsey?*"

Then I heard my father coming in the front door whistling, and I saw my mother's face harden as she rushed out to intercept him. I heard her voice rising angrily, and I let my head fall back while Grandma wiped my mouth with a clean towel.

I WAS REBORN, but it took two more years to fully kick off the chrysalis. Several false starts later, I moved to San Francisco, where, as my mother correctly pointed out, "there are other people like you."

THE NEXT TIME I called my mother in the hospital, the faint, ill voice said, "You better not come—Daddy says you can't. See, I'm immune suppressed because of the chemo, and Daddy says if you came I could get, *you know* ..." She died a few days later. My father dug up her garden, emptied the house of everything associated with her, and went to several mixers at a nearby church he'd never attended till then, where he met, and promptly married, a blond widow.

THE DAY BEFORE I hastily left home for good in 1977, my father tackled me in the bright orange and gold kitchen as I came sailing in from a night out with a GI from a South El Paso gay bar, the Pet Shop. He was squeezing me from behind in some kind of makeshift wrestling grip, a sickening echo of my previous night's grappling, trying to pry my car keys out of my clenched fist.

"Mom!" I yelled. "Dad's gone insane! Call the police!" I could see her through the crimped orange café curtains, aiming the garden hose at a bed of petunias, hearing, not wanting to hear.

That's where I'm leaving them now: my mother flooding the flower box, straining not to hear, wishing it would all go away; Bullmoose red and choking with hatred. That's where I've left them.

ERIC GUTIERREZ

Who He Was

The first lie I remember telling about my father was when he came to open house at Ranchito Street Elementary School with his boyfriend wearing matching dashikis. They both had mustaches and enormous Afros. The mustaches were real, the Afros, each the size of a beach ball, were wigs. They entered room 22, Miss Stein's classroom, and I could hear the shift in the air, the defiance of my father and his lover, the disdain of the other parents. While I had never before seriously considered the counterculture, in that moment I joined the marginal, the underdogs, the queers. "My father's a hippie," I declared with a pride I recognized only years later marching in my first Gay Pride parade as not pride at all but rather the shamelessness of exhibitionism, the insistence of the id to reveal, to act out, to love openly.

My father was never a hippie. He wore beads, hip huggers, gauzy shirts unbuttoned to his waist, and long sideburns, because he was a handsome, glamorous young man, with a legendary laugh and a deadly charm. In 1971, at my fifth grade open house David Gerald Gutierrez, my dad, whom everyone called Jerry, made his entrance as a gay man. And I was ten years old.

Even before that, without really knowing what *gay* meant, I knew my father was it. Despite his "friend" Larry's being imposed on us on every occasion, despite post-divorce Sundays spent in their driveway pretending to play while obscenities and dishes were hurled inside, I didn't pay much attention to the intimacies between them, the shared bed, the passionate outbreaks of temper, the matching fringed vests. It was unspoken information that didn't assume the contours and substance of knowledge until one Sunday when I was about nine. Crossing a supermarket parking lot with my father, Larry, and my brother David Jr., I tried to make them laugh by following two effeminate men to their car, mincing and waving my limp wrists until my father grabbed my arm gently, almost sheepishly. "Don't make fun of anyone because they're different," was all he said. That's when I realized what the difference was.

About the same time I began lying about my father I began lying about myself. I didn't offer my lies indiscriminately, like the almost pathological stream of whoppers told at recess by kids who had nothing to hide. I would lie only when cornered, or when the truth didn't seem like enough. Ugly and unathletic, I didn't lie to win friends but to make myself even more of an outcast. Rather than make up comforting details that would portray my flashy, gay father more like the hardworking, lawn-mowing dads that lined our street, I instead embellished his shortcomings, his weaknesses, his rage, into real perversity. Between the seventh and eighth grades, at a summer school for gifted children bursting with a happiness I did not share and so wanted to defeat, I enthralled my classmates with stories of how my father would tie us up or throw crystal goblets at my terrorized mother.

Jerry did throw and break things. But he never tied us up. We never owned crystal. Informed, quick, with a sideshow affection for freaks, I was an accomplished liar, building false identities for my father and myself by overstating truth on its own trajectory. I found myself lying when I intended to be honest and my lies began to get me into trouble. I remember writing a poem that gifted summer that was supposed to be my new leaf, my declaration of the truth and nothing but. It began "No thing was more still than we three/crouched in a bed of faded marriage linen/his fists at the door/his spit wanting in…" It was free verse vérité of how my mother and brother barricaded us in her bedroom, pushing the dresser in front of the door while I sat on the edge of the bed, too small and weak to be of any help even though I was six. Reading the poem in front of the class, I felt the same exhibitionistic rush as at the fifth-grade open house, the power of flaunting one's shame.

WHEN MY FATHER moved out David and I stood at the dining-room window and watched him leave. My brother cried with a soulfulness and an abandon that scared me, and so I cried, too. My mother knelt next to us, a hand on each of our shaking backs. She tells me that soon afterward I began jumping rope to one of my first original tunes, a little ditty called "The Mister and Missus Gutierrez have broke up." The entire lyric consisted of the title repeated over and over, accent on the first syllable of each noun, until my mother would scream at me to be quiet or simply stare at me in mute grief like a general wading through the aftermath of battle.

David, on the other hand, was inconsolable. He loved our father with a passion and a purity that began and ended with the declaration "Daddy." Nothing Jerry did, nothing he said or forgot or was in all the years to come could shake my brother's belief in that unquestionable bond. Because Jerry was his father, David was his son. A simple algebra, irrefutable but comprehensible only to those who know the meaning of X, who know how to be brave and openhearted. It's the reason he always had Jerry's phone number while I rarely even knew where he lived.

When my mother found out my brother was also gay, I was seventeen and living in New Zealand. Apparently she cried and lay in a dark room, less than prepared, but David was able to turn to our father at that time. David and Jerry wouldn't talk often, but they knew each other's boyfriends, they saw each other on birthdays and at Christmas. They weren't close but they managed to salvage a relationship. As an adult, I remained closeted to my family until I was thirty, sensitive to my role as the great brown hope who would carry on the family name, who would make up for other disappointments, who wouldn't go gay. Being out is a bond I never shared with my father. But even as a child I told myself I didn't envy Jerry's connection with my big brother, that I was just jealous of David's happiness in his presence and how easy it was for him to love. I wondered what was wrong with me, why I wanted to skip rope instead of cry. And then I'd be in the backyard playing, having fun, and suddenly, for no apparent reason—tears.

▪   ▪   ▪

EARLY SUNDAY MORNINGS right after the divorce David and I would wait at the dining-room window, watching the walkway out front for our father. In the beginning he was always on time, and we would go to the beach or the creek in Topanga Canyon to chase frogs the size of thumbnails and wade in the icy pools. As his hair grew longer and the patterns of his shirts grew bolder and more colorful, Jerry began to arrive later, sometimes not until almost noon. Still, David and I would be so glad to see him we would soon forget the hours of waiting and pouting, and welcome him with hugs and high, girlish screams. More and more often he would arrive smelling like last call and take us back to his place nearby, put us in front of the TV and go back to bed where Larry was waiting.

As they slept until two or three in the afternoon, David and I would watch Roller Derby, followed by Japanese science fiction movies. My favorite scene in *Son of Godzilla* is when the radioactive lizard teaches his offspring, as cuddly and puffy as a Ninja Turtle, how to breathe fire. At first the bloated baby can only belch smoke rings. But Godzilla is patient, and when the pneumatic little monster finally manages a lick of flame, the proud papa incinerates the sky. Together they will destroy Tokyo, two outcasts on a rampage, like father, like son. I can't remember exactly, but I think in the climactic, fiery finale, they turn on each other. I assume Godzilla wins.

One Sunday he didn't come at all. It was almost evening when my mother finally reached him. Even though she whispered, I had never heard her so angry and when she handed us the phone, my brother and I assured him it was okay, that we loved him, too, that we'd see him next Sunday.

Soon after that he stopped coming altogether. Sometimes he would call and promise to make it up, guarantee he would be there next Sunday at 8 A.M. sharp. And so we manned our station at the dining-room window. I remember, more than the beach or the zoo, standing for hours, forehead to the pane, chin on the sill. He never picked us up again. He never knew we were there, looking for him, waiting.

I SAW MY father four times the last twenty years of his life. The things I know about him for certain don't seem certain at all. He was a Taurus, but I'd have to look up his actual birthdate. I can't even remember what year he died, although I spoke at his funeral. Until recently, I thought of my father as a distant relative or someone I met as a child and was supposed to love, like the Santa who gave me a candy cane and made me cry.

What I know about him or have come to believe is mostly a composite of old photos, family lore, other people's stories or shards of memory I've stored. His contradictions impress me if only because they are real and incongruous, and can be used to verify both lies and dreams. The man who I'm told could make a family dinner into a party by force of his humor and charm alone was the same man who would lash at me and my brother with a leather belt until he was sweating and out of breath; the same man who I'm assured was adored for his kindness and manners also taught me how to swear by berating my mother in public. There are only two memories, two happy memories, that is, that I know are mine and not handed down from well-meaning sources, not tainted with prologues or epilogues of tears or curses or leather belts. My father, I can say, did this thing and I was there and remember it.

THE FIRST MEMORY:

The only landmark visible from any distance in Panorama City—"the Heart of the San Fernando Valley"—is the smokestacks above the General Motors assembly plant between Van Nuys and Woodman boulevards. It's a discount mall now, the food court offering greasy chow mein and Cinnebons tacky with sugar, a Penney's and Sears rafter-deep in boys' huskies and girls' petites. One block away, Lanark Street cuts through two-bedroom postwar homes made of stucco and cheap hope. The homes are painted enthusiastic, unlikely colors, like daisy decals. The hope here is still alive. It announces itself in the clean edges of the lawns where they meet the sidewalk, in the whitewashed bases of tree trunks meant to stave off bugs and decay, in the flower beds and kitchen curtains batting their ruffles flirtatiously in open windows. It is 1964 and there is no reason not to hope.

Jerry is on all fours, crawling backward, dipping his brush in a gallon of brick-red paint. The concrete steps, the porch, and now the walkway around back are glistening with a new coat. Jerry's four-year-old son is watching the progress silently—*I am watching*—and while I watch we talk, not often, nothing special, just the talk of a man painting and his preschooler watching. Nothing special, except it is only us and it is quiet and my father is happy. I see a garden snail begin to make its way across our walkway just where my father is about to paint. I expect him to pick it up, toss it into the street, like I've seen him do when working in the yard, grinning with satisfaction at the sound of the shell cracking on asphalt.

He picks the snail up and looks at me. Instead of lobbing it overhand, he dips his brush into the can of paint and daubs red onto the snail's shell and puts it gently down on the other side of the walkway. "There," he says to me, smiling. "Now you'll always know who your friend is in the garden."

AT MY FATHER'S memorial service a dark blond man, somewhere around thirty but with the gravitas of a teen, eagerly offered his condolences. "I'm Todd," he smiled, hand extended. I could see he may have been handsome, probably still was in bar light. "I was your father's favorite bartender." Approaching the door to the chapel, beside a plaster virgin inclined over magnolia blossoms singed by the heat, a man in a wrinkled suit handed out funereal trading cards. Printed on one side was the name of the deceased—David Gerald Gutierrez — with the dates bracketing his life and a verse from a scripture he never read, italicized to hint at a cursive grace and dignity to his fifty-six years. On the other side was a virgin, or a Joseph, or a Christ. I collected all three.

Dwarfing the spray of flowers sent by David and me was the display that came from The Oasis, the gay bar on Ventura Boulevard in Studio City where Todd poured my father his scotch. Jerry was a celebrity there, the silver-haired raconteur, once handsome, now a beloved regular whose staccato laugh and generous tips translated over the years into a lush arrangement of flowers and at least two pews of middle-aged men with gelled hair, pickled complexions, and narrow lapels. I didn't see Todd or any of The Oasis crowd at the family gathering after the service. They went back to the bar, raised their glasses in the direction of his empty stool, and downed a round in his name. On the house.

When people ask how he died I tell them in the starkest, ugliest terms possible: His liver disintegrated; he stewed in his own liquor. I'm not trying to shock by reciting an impromptu poem of domestic violence or playing out my melodrama of the gifted child for extra credit. But it's important that I remember this real thing I know for certain. My legacy is pretty slim— a narrow jaw and roman nose, a last name no one east of Santa Fe can spell properly, a garden snail—so whatever memories and knowledge he's left me I cherish viciously.

IN AMERICA THEY say a man is what he does for a living. My father died without having worked in more than fifteen years. When I was a child I never linked my father to an occupation like my classmates did.

They knew who their fathers were because they knew what they did, the mantle of their work. In our neighborhood full of accents and manual laborers, in the shadow of the GM assembly plant, sons took vicarious pride in the manly glamour of assembly-line workers, auto mechanics, and keypunch operators. For boys my age, those were identities you could count on, that defined a father on the asphalt playground and gave substance to our emerging apprehensions of what makes a man in the world.

My father never held a steady job. Even when he was young, he rarely worked. At different times, he was a garbage collector, a machinist, and, periodically, spread asphalt sealer on driveways and parking lots working for his father-in-law. I vaguely recall my mother once trying to reach him at the latest new job and being told he never went back after his first day. When she confronted him, he disappeared for what seemed like weeks. When he returned, my mother, who had dropped out of high school when she married at 16, was training at the Valley College of Medical & Dental Assistants on Lankershim Boulevard, a cinder-block vocational school near the 101 Freeway in North Hollywood.

I've never understood work in the manner that American men understand work. I've held jobs since I was a child, working for my maternal grandfather and great-uncle patching the cracks in asphalt so they could lay the seal coat, sometimes joined by my father and mother on the job. In the summer, my older brother, David, and I would fill brown bags we'd salvage from the Food King with apricots from our backyard tree and sell them door to door along the turns and straightaways of Lanark Street. But I didn't take to work. It was never my idea. The initiative came from the ethos of family business and family need. Or it came from my brother. David had always been a hard worker, beginning in junior high working long hours in a pet store after school for free. While David graduated to cleaning out cages for minimum wage and our mother made the four-mile round-trip hike each day to her job as a dental assistant, I read books about black stallions, boy sleuths, and Arthurian knights. My father was somewhere in the 1970s, being mistaken for the Marlboro Man with his glistening mustache and raw cheekbones.

In high school, my first experience of work, beyond the nepotism of the paving and asphalt industry and door-to-door produce sales, was as a busboy at a Howard Johnson's, a job like my father held at Schaeffer's Cafeteria in Los Angeles while he was still a teenager. We were the same age, sixteen, when we wiped down Formica tabletops, ferried glasses of water, and hoisted the sour stink of the bus tray onto our hips. I realize now that, despite my grandiose ambitions to be nothing like my father, this was just the first time I walked in Jerry's shoes. Schaeffer's had been closed for almost two decades but in the late '80s I would drive past the crumbling '50s facade still fronting Melrose Avenue every day on my way to my first boyfriend's place in Silverlake. Beside him in the car one evening, passing the boarded-up plate glass windows of Schaeffer's, I let romance get the best of me. I told him how my teenaged father had proposed to my schoolgirl mother there in the cafeteria, down on one knee in his stained apron and white paper cap; how she had dropped her plastic tray of canned peaches and Salisbury steak with a gleeful shriek; how the possibility of escape into one another's lives must have seemed like love. The truth is, he bungled the proposal, dropping the ring in front of my grandparents' bathroom, but saying he popped the question at Schaeffer's made me happy, transforming my father into more than an eternal busboy in a derelict building in a bad part of town.

When I learned years later that I had been mistaken, that the cafeteria on Melrose wasn't the same Schaeffer's at all, it reinforced how much of my father's story took place somewhere else, someplace I'd never seen.

In the hagiography of the American worker, my father is a failure. In the history of labor that explains fathers to sons, that gives one status and power on the playground and, later, in the job market, he is a cautionary tale. He never sought his fortune, staked his claim, made something of himself. This is a fact, not ugly in the way truth can be ugly, but just a fact. I knew my father only when I was a boy, and so he remains largely unknown, but even then he confused me. He wasn't straight like other fathers and he didn't work like them, either. Any child playing kickball on broken asphalt, witness to so little, unaware of so much of what makes his father a man, can at least boast, "My father works. He does something—he is something—for a living."

Aside from short-lived staff positions, I've been a freelancer all my life. Most of my twenties and early thirties were spent, like in my childhood, subsisting paycheck to paycheck. On my income tax returns under "occupation" the line has on occasion read writer, editor, screenwriter, public relations, and freelance journalist. Whenever I'd begin to make real money or real professional headway, I would take a month motorbiking in Turkey or follow a lopsided grin on a pale-cheeked boy to Australia. I resented work. I would make something of my life by living it, not through stock options or overtime. I held steady employment in contempt, like a pagan superstition to be exposed by the one true faith. Despite my own skirmishes with ambition and anxiety, I racked up stamps in my passport, wrote poems as if they were postcards, and ignored professional opportunities. Married friends envied my life from the hardwood prows of their hillside homes. Colleagues with national reputations and genius grants admired my work and valued my opinion. But potential has a shelf life. And time passes. I turned thirty. And then forty. And, like my father, it seemed as if I rarely worked.

Among the lies I told about my father is that I had no place for him in my life. My mother married a loving and supportive man who became my father in profound respects, but by the time I grew to love him the job description for "dad" had changed; the role had diminished. I would tell people my life was fully staffed. Jerry's long absences made his presence awkward, forcing an accommodation rather than filling an empty seat. And even when I had given him the job, even when he took it, soon, very soon, he would quit.

So when Jerry asked David to call me during final exams my senior year in college to ask how I would feel if he came to my graduation, I refused to wait by the window to see if he would come. "Tell him that if he wants to get to know me, there won't be time between the family and the ceremonies," I said. "And if he's just coming to be in the pictures of a Harvard graduation, then it's best if he didn't come." The role of father was filled. My stepfather, who had supported me literally and figuratively, who had not been the father I ideally wanted but became the ideal father despite all the resentment and resistance my brother and I could dish out, would be there. This other man called Dad was too confusing. He was a stranger and I was wary, on guard for the surprise, the betrayal, the theft.

It was then that David, whom I'd always refused the respect due his eighteen month seniority, introduced the concept of regret into my relationship with our father. Not regret at what was said or done between us, but regret at the fact of his absence, or rather what was to be done with it. "You'll only have one graduation," he said. "He's your father." I didn't care. That was David's algebra, where X is a chromosome and a lifelong bond, not mine. Jerry would get no rewards from me, no picture in the Yard, no son on graduation day. For that he would have to wait.

■   ■   ■

There is a second memory:

My father is home, sprawled on the sofa in his underwear. It is the middle of the afternoon and my mother is not at home. Is she at work? I am three, David is five, and our father gets up during the commercial break and tickles us. Unexpectedly, for no reason, he tickles us and we are so overcome with happiness and love that we scream and chase him around the living room and out the front door. Our father is running down Lanark Street in his underwear, laughing, and we are chasing him as fast as we can. He looks over his shoulder, a house length ahead, then three, then five. My brother is faster than I am but he begins to fall behind as well. Our father is still laughing and we are running as hard as we can, unable to keep up but still following, and as I see my father disappear around the corner I realize I've never been this far from home without a hand to hold. I am not afraid. I catch up with David who has stopped at the end of the block. Our father is gone. We are alone and no longer laughing. Suddenly our father leaps from behind a cinder-block wall. We scream and giggle, and as he runs past us back toward the house, our happiness is overwhelming. The chase is back on and I am giddy following his laughter. Falling farther behind, I see him round the hedge, disappearing into our house while I'm still half a block away. Soon my brother also disappears behind the hedge. I am out of breath, chasing my father, still laughing.

One of the lies I told about myself so often that it still sometimes carries the taste of confession is that I am like Jerry, like him in crippling, inescapable ways. In ways that hurt. My successes didn't feel as true as my failures. My fears often felt more real than my faith. I could not see how far I had come, how hard I had worked, how loved I was. I could not accept the truth of us. Not until I asked my father for his blessing.

As Jerry lay dying I watched him and my brother through the blinds from a neighboring hospital room. Standing in the dark, I saw David draw the sheet up, covering Jerry's bare chest. He arranged a wisp of hair on his forehead. He sat there on the edge of his father's bed and placed a comforting hand on his shoulder. Looking at them both, I suddenly felt foolish. I didn't have to wait like a child on a Sunday morning for Jerry to show up as my father. I was a grown man. I could have showed up as his son. When I went into the room I took his hand. There was no reason to lie about who he was.

▪ ▪ ▪

JERRY DIED AT Kaiser Hospital in Panorama City, just blocks from Ranchito Street Elementary and the house on Lanark Street. For three days he lay unconscious, his hair completely white, his skin deeply jaundiced and intricately lined around his eyes and the corners of his mouth as if made of cobwebs. At fifty-six, he looked like a very old man. He never knew I was there, just sitting with him, waiting. His brothers and sister came from New Mexico and northern California. Chris, his lover for sixteen years, was with him constantly. My father was loved. And I was a stranger here.

My regret is not becoming a man in time to be my father's son. There was no deathbed reconciliation of prodigals, no Hallmark epiphany, no shared forgiveness. We exchanged no words, his eyelids didn't flutter in recognition when I whispered in his ear, and when I squeezed his hand he didn't squeeze back. Our final exchange actually took place six years earlier at the funeral for my brother's partner. "I'm not a terrible person" were the last words I remember my father ever saying to me. That he felt the need to tell me so, that I may have given him reason to, is one of the great sadnesses of my life.

There is a common lie people tell about regrets. They say they are a waste of time and are pointless. They claim to have none. It's true that regret is wasted on the obtuse and those who don't pay attention. But for those willing to see and do things differently, there is redemption in choosing what might have been, a measure of wisdom to put in place of what's been lost or betrayed. It's one way to make sure the past stays where it belongs. It's one way to grow up.

My father's death did not transform me like I desperately wanted it to. I had to do that on my own. But when he died I began to tell the truth about who he was. It's the truth about both of us, of course, about the way regrets remain and the way happier memories survive, if we let them. It's a story of underdogs and queers, of fathers and their sons.

JEFFREY ESCOFFIER

Refusing
My Father.

FALL 1989, SAN FRANCISCO

"I'd rather have been sexually molested by my father than forced to play Little League." The magazine's editors—I was one of them—had recorded an editorial roundtable on sexual abuse and incest, and then published it. I had made its most notable comment. We used pseudonyms so no one attributed the remark to me. Many readers wrote in to complain; some even canceled their subscriptions.

It was a flippant remark—and not strictly truthful. I had wanted to stress the claustrophobic power of family life, that the family was an abusive institution. My father—my stepfather actually, but the only father I ever knew—had never forced me to play Little League. He was Dutch and had no interest in the game. He'd have rather I played soccer, but he never "forced" me to play it.

Sandra and I hadn't met for weeks to work on her book. The earthquake—it had lasted so long, 45 seconds—had flattened freeways, collapsed a section of the Bay Bridge, started fires, killed people, and made us all put off going about our everyday lives. We were both still a little jumpy. But right off, Sandra mentioned the roundtable and, although she hadn't signed the letter from a group of therapists who worked with incest survivors, she was close to them and objected to my remarks. I wanted to explain myself to her, but at the time I wasn't able to acknowledge the pseudonymous comments as my own. Nevertheless, as I thought about them and regretted the false notes I had struck, I tried to understand why I had said what I said and if there had been some truth to what I said that I wasn't conscious of.

SUMMER 1959, STATEN ISLAND

We were repairing an old steel lifeboat, riveting new plates on the bottom of the hull. In a corner of the Moran tugboat shipyard, I stood underneath the upside-down boat in the sweltering heat, holding over my head a large steel anvil pressed to the heads of the rivets that my father hammered down on with a riveting gun from the outside. It was grueling work. From early morning to late in the evening, my father never stopped working; he did nothing in moderation. Always mad to work and to perfect, he knew no limit except exhaustion. Physically drained, he then spent hours drinking and talking to gnarled old tugboat sailors while I sat in the car waiting to go home—wobbling between boredom and exhaustion, holding back tears of rage.

He always overdid things. That spring I was sixteen, and later that summer my father went sailing every day he could. We would leave early in the morning and never return before darkness had set in. "Susan" (a pseudonym), my fourteen-year-old sister—her father's true daughter, blond and physically vigorous—loved sailing. She soon became an expert sailor, but I hated to go. I used every excuse I could think of to stay home. In the end, I refused to learn how to sail.

My father's uncontrolled passion for sailing stirred all the smoldering hatreds in my family. My mother refused to go on those endless twelve-hour trips. Susan and I tried to bring our friends, but none of them wanted to go sailing from early morning to nightfall.

All that summer my mother and father fought over going sailing. Tangled up with that they also fought over Susan's first boyfriend, Richie. My sister was finally interested in boys, though she hadn't quite given up her passionate love of horses and other animals.

My father was insanely jealous of my sister's fifteen-year-old boyfriend. He could barely endure Richie's presence. Often, when Richie stayed overnight to avoid the long trip into Manhattan, we'd be woken up at three in the morning by my father screaming: "Get that faggot out of the house."

Rage seethed beneath the surface of our family life. My mother was passionate—and now, I see, almost reckless in her encouragement of Susan and Richie. She nurtured my sister's relationship with Richie as if they were Romeo and Juliet. On countless humid summer days I sat on the porch as Susan and Richie danced to Elvis Presley, Frankie Avalon, Connie Francis and Staten Island's own top-forty stars, The Elegants, singing "How Are You, Little Star?"—knowing that to come were those nightly battles that enshrined adolescent love and framed our sexual feelings.

What no one else knew was that by the end of the summer Richie and I started having sex together. Richie was a feisty Irish kid whose father was always drunk. Somehow he thought our family was nicer than his own. He really loved my mother. I was jealous of the attention my mother gave him; but I was not aware at the time that he was only a pawn in that summer's power struggle. My mother's move was to take him with us on our summer visit to our relatives in Baltimore.

On that trip he and I discovered sex. Twice on that trip we shared a bed, spoon fashion, my hard-on pressing up against his ass. I reached out and touched his cock. And then finally, when we got back home on Staten Island, in my room, I had my first orgasm with another person.

I remember claustrophobic Staten Island nights at dances on the local military post—Susan and Richie, me and my girlfriend Sonia. Long bus rides home late at night, and an impatience that we masked by sitting up with Susan and my mother talking even later into the night—an impatience to go to sleep (since he slept in my room whenever he stayed over) so that we could suck each other's cock and jerk off.

That summer my mother became curious about my sexuality—she often asked if I was a virgin. I bore my own queerness quietly—along with my betrayal of my sister.

Susan's first two boyfriends—Richie and David—were my own first two boyfriends. I had had sex with them while, I'm almost certain, she had not. But when she broke up with them, they left me. For years afterward I found my lovers among men attracted to my sister. I existed as my sister's double, my own desire a ghost image of hers. She was sexy, well built, blond. I was skinny, intellectual, and queer. Why would any handsome boy look at me?

That summer we all loved Richie—my mother, my sister, and me. My father hated him so much he was almost crazy with rage.

Starting that summer, I hated my father.

SUMMER 1962, CHICAGO

Three years later I was packing to go to Chicago and work for my father during my summer vacation.

My mother said she had something to tell me. Nine years earlier, she told me, she discovered that my father had been sexually molesting my sister Susan, who was then eight. She told of sitting outside my sister's bedroom door guarding it with a kitchen knife.

Now I knew (so I thought) the last and darkest sexual secret of my family. I was not only the secret sharer of my sister's boyfriends, I also knew my mother's secrets—her love affairs. Since refusing to follow my father to Chicago she—just in her mid-thirties—had embarked on her own sexual adventures. But when she told me about what my father had done to Susan, I was furious with her for telling me. I had only reluctantly agreed to go work for him. I lost all desire to go to Chicago. And with that revelation she bound me to herself all the more tightly. She destroyed him for me.

So, my father had broken even that taboo—incest. Fucking or sailing, he knew no limits. Politely he was known as a ladies' man, but later I heard that among the men at the boat club he was called "the whoremaster." All my father ever seemed to do was work and screw.

I went to Chicago with a renewed loathing for my father.

I took the Greyhound out from New York. It was an eighteen-hour ride through the night. My small overhead reading light was the only one burning as the darkened bus rumbled through Ohio. I read, excited and fascinated, *The City and the Pillar*, a novel about being queer, a story of self-acceptance and unhappiness. My hard-on ached when the hand of the man sleeping in the seat beside me brushed against my leg.

When I arrived my father was living in a room in the back of his office—a small rundown building on the Lake Calumet waterfront in the industrial wasteland of south Chicago. We shared an old-fashioned fold-out couch during the muggy summer nights. We worked ten- and twelve-hour days. Then I would sit for hours with my father in shabby old bars while he talked, querulously, on and on with longshoremen or tugboat crewmen. Waiting for the talk to stop I often dozed off sitting in the car—with the familiar boredom and exhaustion.

I was lonely, and I took the train as often as I could into the Loop. On hot summer nights I wandered around aimlessly looking for sex as I had in Washington Square Park before I had left home. Most of the time I was sick to my stomach with sexual longing.

My father's secretary was obviously queer. They often spoke to each other in sexual innuendos, sometimes quite flirtatiously for two men. I wondered if my father's libido had any limits. On weekends he went to Peoria to visit his girlfriend.

I did have one friend from school who lived in Chicago. He was quite an "obvious" fairy—not effeminate exactly, but he didn't (or couldn't) hide his attraction to other men. We had furtive, sweaty sex in parks and sometimes on the couch in my father's office. Once, during a rainy afternoon on a muggy day, I left my father behind in the office, and John and I drove out to an abandoned corner of a park in the vast and deserted industrial section of south Chicago. We took off all our clothes and started to make out when all of a sudden a cop was standing outside in the rain peering in and knocking on the car window, which was all fogged up. We begged and pleaded, "We won't do it again." And he let us go.

I remember once my father commented on a news story about the sexual molestation of a young girl. He said that anyone who had done something like that should be strung up.

Halfway through that hot summer I hated my father uncontrollably, and I hated myself. We were both filthy perverts.

SPRING 1990, SAN FRANCISCO

My father died that spring.

Years have passed. I am five years older than my father was when I spent that summer in Chicago.

I'd seen him only once in more than 20 years—for a few hours, in an airport bar late at night. A little drunk and clearly unhappy, he complained of my mother's coldness, of the divorce already 15 years in the past, of how we had all abandoned him. I longed to get away, back into the city. Instead I came out to him. Then he brightened up and said that he was glad that I was happy—unlike my mother's glum "How long have you been one?" But after that we talked on the phone only five or six times.

Just before he died my sister went to visit him. He was barely aware of who she was. I had no interest in going.

He was no father to me. Burning with resentment, I taught myself so much about growing up, work, and love. I'm still bitter at his crazy narcissism, his passion for sailing, and his promiscuous sexuality. He "chose" my sister; actually, both my sisters, but he never chose me, except in those strange late-night calls five years ago. He was drunk, raving—"You know, you're one goddam wonderful person," he said, over and over again. I didn't believe him—how would he know?—and told him not to call me when he was drunk.

When I remember him he is always naked except for a pair of baggy khaki shorts. He always wore as few clothes as possible. He liked to walk around the house in his underwear. He was muscular and fit—and each summer, burnt dark brown by the sun. He never seemed to be aware that his cock poked out of his shorts or underwear. I hated his nakedness, and I wanted him clothed. "He is one of the sexiest men alive," I was often told by the boy who was my lover at college.

In that summer of '59 we were all caught up in the passions of our family romance—my sister and I, in the middle of adolescence; my mother and my sister trying to escape my father's power. I wanted a man to love me, to want me sexually, to carry me away.

My sister forgave him. Perhaps because she is so much like him—driven, staking everything on her good practical sense, passionate about sailing. I still haven't forgiven him. He was neither father nor lover to me.

Instead I was forced to help my father build a boat; he would teach me sailing. I spurned my father's most deeply loved skill, the talent he most wanted to pass on to me: sailing. It was my sister who learned to sail.

Suddenly the pieces of this story fall into place. A parent's abuse takes place inside a tangled patchwork of love and domination. A father tries to force his son to become a real man—by playing baseball, or sailing. A mother uses sexual secrets and curiosity to bind her son in deep intimacy. A brother and a sister compete for the love of their father. A father avoids his son's sexual desire—answered only by a son's lifelong denial of his father's love.

JORGE IGNACIO CORTIÑAS

The Chronology of Events

I find the *Miami Herald* at an airport newsstand that sells papers from across the country. I look for the article about my father's arrest, and when I find it I cover his mug shot with my thumb so it doesn't distract me as I read. I am looking for the facts. My father is someone I don't know very much about. I read the article once, and then I start again at the beginning. I am on a stopover in Dallas, en route from San Francisco to Miami, to attend my father's trial. He is charged with smuggling cocaine. This is, for my Catholic, middle-class family, some sort of scandal. I am traveling alone.

I look for a pay phone so I can call my lover, now, though I don't have much to report, because I know my lover is at work. I live in San Francisco where I share a futon with a man who has blond hair and skin that smells of Ivory soap. We split the rent for a first-floor flat squeezed into the middle of a row of houses. I sometimes tell my lover that what I will remember most about him is how he always calls my mother by her first name. To him, my mother is never Señora, never even Ma'am. The rare times he and my mother catch each other on the phone he presses the receiver into the thin skin of his palm and says, Ignacio, Eugenia would like to speak to you. Those are all the words my lover says about my family. They speak even less of him.

Still, I leave my lover a long message on our answering machine in which I tell him I found the article in the *Miami Herald*. The Dallas Airport is enormous, the hallways so long I cannot see where they end. The article says my father was arrested at the house he bought his lover of seven years, a woman who is not my mother and not his wife. That my father lived with a woman, who was not my mother and not his wife, and that he had bought that woman a house, was something it seemed everybody in Miami knew. My father had probably had bank statements reflecting the purchase mailed to my mother's house, a house he still used as one of his mailing addresses after half a lifetime of separation. Or maybe he had used his accountant to finalize some details relating to the deal, the same accountant my mother uses. My mother says my father does these things on purpose. Your father wants to spite me, she often says, pacing in her yellow kitchen and holding the mail in her tiny hands, her bony fingers shut tight as beaks. He wants to rub it in my face.

I never say anything, but I think she's wrong. Whenever my mother confronts him with proof of the latest thing he did, the house he bought his lover, the secret trip to Santo Domingo, the wedding ring he hawked, my father always looks genuinely surprised that anyone found out. For him it's a miracle every time he gets caught, the last thing he expected even though it's what always happens.

I end my phone message to my lover by reminding him I'll be in Miami for a week or so and to please not pick up the phone if my office calls. I know better than to ask my lover to lie directly. To my lover, there's an important distinction between the two acts.

I lean against the chrome facade of a gift shop and watch the electric mini-shuttle carry the elderly and the overweight down the impossibly long concourse. As I reread the newspaper account of my father's arrest in the *Miami Herald* I learn the address of the house he shared with his lover. The address of the house where my father lived was one of several details I was to learn that year for the very first time.

▪ ▪ ▪

DURING BREAKS IN my father's trial my younger sister and I huddle in the cold hallways of the courthouse, the creamy fluorescent light clinging to our faces, and we tell each other stories about my father as proof of our competing theories of who he is. But in all the stories my sister and I tell each other, whether sympathetic to my father or not, his figure always fills up doorframes, and he always gets what he wants. There's one story I tell that no one else remembers. As I tell the story about my father operating on an elevator my sister stares at me politely and strains a feeble smile. My sister is a little reluctant to hear any new stories about my father, so I tell her, No, it's okay, this is a good story.

I was six that year. My mother had packed us all into the station wagon in our church clothes so we could go hear my oldest sister play at her piano recital. Her music teacher hosted the recital every year, at an old reception hall in the part of Miami we call the *sagüecera,* on the third floor. The place was crawling with grandmothers in dark wigs and screaming kids in lace dresses and white stockings that made too many layers for the suffocating weather. We sat in plastic chairs lined up in long straight rows on the linoleum floor. My father showed up five minutes after the recital started, all smiles as he handed us candy we were supposed to wait until later to eat. My mother shot him a look he knew better than to say anything to. At intermission he didn't even wait for the applause to stop, he grabbed me by the wrist and we were down at the corner cafeteria where they served you from the sidewalk through a small sliding window. He downed his Cuban coffee like shots of sour medicine.

Jesus, he said to the chubby man behind the counter, She's like an accountant with me. He rubbed his neck with a handkerchief and didn't pay me any mind. I was just proof he was spending time with his family.

My father waited till he knew the recital had started again, and then he pushed me back into the crowded elevator. He pulled the old steel doors shut, and the elevator started to jerk as it labored upward. In between the second and third floor, the car shuddered, then stopped. *Coño,* someone said, we're stuck.

Now, my father exhaled with finality, my wife is really going to kill me.

Hey, this is nobody's fault.

You, my friend, don't know my wife.

The elevator car was crowded. Over our heads we could see a line of light where the third floor started. Pressing your thumb on the emergency bell was like ringing a doorbell no one answers; nothing happened. I kept quiet, in the shade of my father's frame. Then he moved away from me and toward the console, saying, Hold on, let me take a look at this.

Two other men stood close to him, peering over his shoulder, encouraging him to do one thing or another. Cut here. Try this wire. My father worked methodically, at his own sure pace. He used his pocket screwdriver with the miniature light bulb on the end. He switched to his pocketknife, and he started to whistle. When the car started moving again, and the doors opened, he grabbed me, and we were the first ones off.

When I think of this story again I'm standing in the federal courthouse with its marble walls and windows so thin they look like coin slots. I think about my father's immigrant talent for moving himself and those around him through tight spaces. My sister says she doesn't even remember the day I'm talking about, but I see it like I'm still there. I am wearing the satin shorts my mother made me and my hair is pressed down so tightly it looks painted on. My father and I are in an overcrowded steel box suspended by a cable. People are standing shoulder to shoulder and sweating under too much makeup, too much polyester. We are trying to climb floors through a tunnel without dirtying our hands. My father is cutting bad wires, worn-out fuses, making the electric current flow with his big fingers. Then he does it, in front of a room full of strangers, he lifts me up into the reception hall.

MY FATHER'S TRIAL is the first reunion my family gets in a while. We're all there, except for my brother who keeps oversleeping and then muttering how sitting through the trial makes him feel bad, and isn't good for him. We show up because my father's lawyers say it will help his chances if the jury sees us together. But being together like this, every day for what turns out to be a three-week trial, from eight A.M. when it starts, through the one-hour lunch, to the five P.M. close, isn't something my family is used to.

On Tuesday two of my sisters, my brother, and I have lunch with my father. Inside a crowded sandwich shop our conversations are pushed up on top of each other. My oldest sister, now the mother of five, complains that the woman in front of her at the grocery store paid for her purchase with food stamps. My father explains how O. J. Simpson was framed. My brother tells the story of the day my parents returned a check issued to them by the Cuban Refugee Service of the State Department. My younger sister and I nod in polite agreement, unsure whose eyes to meet. The din is interrupted when a homeless woman, her hair matted and her red face covered with scabs, approaches our table and asks for change.

My father reaches for his wallet. He has promised Saint Jude Thaddeus, the patron saint of desperate causes, that he will try to be a better person. My father makes promises to saints not because he is exactly a superstitious person, but because he believes that every problem, every one of his problems at least, has an escape clause. My sister switches to Spanish. *No le des nada. Lo usan para comprar drogas. Estás dandole cuerda a esa práctica.* My father hands the homeless woman $5 and she shuffles off to the next table. Now, for the first time, we are all discussing the same topic, the morality of giving a beggar what she asks for. We are on a lunch break during the trial of my father, who is charged with trafficking in cocaine, and my older sister tells us it's rude to ask people who are eating for money.

My brother asks a question about the DNA testing during the O. J. Simpson trial and soon we are again pursuing our disparate conversations. This is what my too-large family calls talking. My older sister talks about Medicare fraud. My father tells a joke in which the federal prosecutor gets called a jungle bunny. My brother wonders aloud if it's too late to order another sandwich. I say nothing, but I think about the men I know in San Francisco who are on food stamps and publicly funded anti-virals. I think about the people I know in California who are healthy, healthy enough, and fond of staying up all night on speed and ecstasy pills. And I think about those big cloudless skies that early fall brings to San Francisco and how I associate the lightness of those long, mild days with not being too near my family. But I also think about the airiness, the quiet loneliness of that weather, and how that loneliness can so often feel like relief. I am freer in San Francisco, a continent away, even if I am sometimes in danger of floating away.

We leave the teal blue-and-white tile of this Miami Delicatessen (they serve ham on rolls, not pastrami on rye) and head back toward the courthouse. My father races ahead to meet his lawyers. My two sisters say goodbye at the parking lot; they need to pick up their children at school. My brother leaves me one block later. It will just be me then, with my father, for the rest of the afternoon. The shift to daylight saving time was a week ago and the shadows from the sun are already low and long. I am at the top of the marble stairs; my brother is at the bottom. He calls me back down and gives me a kiss on the cheek; he asks me if I'm mad at him for leaving early. I lie and tell him I'm not, that I'll see him later. He is crossing the street, he is turning to wave, my sister drives her car on the road between us, sees me, not my brother; she has one hand on the steering wheel, her other palm, with her fingers spread, against her side window and her silent face mouths the words Good luck.

THROUGHOUT MY FATHER'S trial the prosecutor uses phrases like *The evidence will show. The fact of the matter is. Clearly.* And the one he keeps coming back to, *The chronology of events demonstrates.* We hear over and over about this question of chronology. The prosecutor is telling the jury a story, and the story has a sequence. From the confusing testimony, from the disparate chapters in my father's life, the contradictions in his personality, the prosecutor hammers one consistent stubborn story. All the elements head in one narrative direction; the details are only damning. Who smuggled which drugs when, and who sold them to whom where. And then, for the self-righteous ending the jury already expects, he talks about the young people across this hardworking country who, innocently, were lured into using those drugs. I cringe at his ridiculous morality. The prosecutor means to imply that my father is threatening the children of the members of the jury; that my father, if left unpunished, will worm his way into their own homes and corrupt their children, squandering their precious futures in exchange for his selfish profit.

I remember the years the prosecution bases its case on, and my own runaway drug use. I was eighteen and had left Miami at the first chance I'd seen: college. I attended an Ivy League school in New England, wore black turtlenecks and smoked imported cigarettes. Twice a year, never more, I would visit my mother's house. When I got there I moved noiselessly over the carpet, picked up after myself meticulously, and rarely spoke. A strange boarder inside the house I grew up in. Over dinner I chewed quietly and excused myself before dessert. I would borrow my mother's car without asking, leave the banyan-tree–lined streets of Coral Gables, and hit Miami Beach.

I spent long nights with friends to whom I no longer speak. This was Miami in the 1980s and drugs were everywhere. Pot you didn't even talk about that was cheaper than beer. What everyone kept eyes open for was cocaine. We treated people we met with disinterest, as if we were all just partying together, but it was all about scoring. The minute you knew someone had cocaine, it was all pats on the back and where you been all my life.

Our hearts beat erratically and we went from bar to private party and back to the bars. We watched loud and tacky drag shows and snickered in each other's ears. We drove down a deserted Collins Avenue in convertibles that cut through the humid night, cars driven by men we had just met. If someone was dumb enough to hang over his balcony and call us noisy bums, it was Fuck you *viejo*, at the top of our lungs. We strangled our doubts inside the deep freeze of the cocaine; we were left with a cruel fearlessness whose limits we were always racing to find. We caused accidents on the expressway, scenes in all-night dinners, and, we convinced ourselves, aroused envy everywhere we went.

And we talked, a mile a minute. That we were right smack in the middle of it. That no, this town was dead. That we were moving to New York. Right away. That we would finish school early and never speak to our parents again. That the man in the blue shirt was fine and would he make it to the bar by the airport that didn't open till five A.M.

It's easy to look back and be embarrassed by our obnoxious hubris. But at the time, all that cocaine and all those bracing highballs and all those bright, form-fitting, designer shirts were necessary proof to me that there was another way of being in the world. That I didn't need to get married or open an IRA account or show up for Christmas dinner. That I was the architect of another kind of future, a scandalous future, entirely of my own making, and my future would have nothing to do with the suffocating suburb I came from.

I would make it back to my mother's house in time for breakfast, and then sleep till late afternoon in rooms with plastic Venetian blinds that the sun shone right through. My mother stopped asking me to take her to matinees, and took to leaving her car keys on the kitchen counter for me. Every scalding sunrise, on her concrete driveway patterned to look like cobblestone, I cleaned out her car, throwing away beer bottles, roaches, and empty matchbooks from bars that everyone knew by reputation. If my mother ever got a sense of what I did in her car, or where I went, she didn't say. Sometimes, in fitful daytime sleep, I saw her standing at the door of my old room, my ankles hanging over the baseboard of the bed, the *Star Wars* bedsheets thrown off me and onto the floor, my body covered in glassy sweat. When we passed each other in the hallway by the bathroom, the silence hung between us like the humming from the air conditioner.

If I ever saw my father during one of those trips to Miami, I don't remember it. He stayed away, leaving behind the pieces of his wardrobe that had gone out of style. Those old jackets and shirts hung in my mother's closet like the thin ghosts of other men. Sometimes I remember hearing he was out of town. In the Bahamas. Sailing. With whoever.

Maybe he was smuggling drugs that week, maybe he wasn't. I don't know what my father was doing. I know what I was doing, what I remember of it.

Maybe I snorted some of the cocaine my father smuggled in. Maybe it was the stuff I paid too much for, or maybe it was the stuff I got for free off that old Venezuelan guy who petted the back of my neck while I sucked up his lines as fast and hard as I could. Or maybe the stuff my father brought in went up north and was gone by the time I was in Miami again. Or maybe, I really had no way of knowing, this whole trial was a big mistake and my father was as innocent as he claimed he was. I tell myself I could find out, that if I did a little research I could clarify this sequence of events. But that would mean asking my father, so I don't.

ON HALLOWEEN THE judge announces his decision to recess court early. Four o'clock at the latest, and as the rhythm of cross-examination has it we are on our way back inland from downtown at 3:30. We take Flagler to Ponce de Leon then Calle Ocho to Coral Gables, inland, away from the afternoon puddles and glass skyscrapers of downtown, past the one-story storefronts of the sagüecera, till we reach the leafy canopies and the street signs made of coral rock in my mother's neighborhood.

There, eight of my nephews and nieces assemble. One panda, one lion, one vampiress, one Tigger from *Winnie the Pooh*, one ballerina, one clown, and two Supermen. Both of the boys old enough to walk come as Superman, one of their costumes complete with padded muscles. The younger of the two wears the same Superman outfit I wore twenty years ago. I do not notice that myself—my brother in-law points it out.

The children jump in place and scream when they run. They are an antidote. They have been told nothing about the trial. I let my two Supermen wrestle me to the ground and they pose for a picture with their feet on my chest, biceps flexed. Later I am walking by my father and think how he would never have played the part of the vanquished with us as children. He would have hoisted us up in the air, thrown us over his shoulder, growling with exaggerated victory instead.

His trial is the reason he is here with us. He has missed a lifetime of Halloweens, but this one, the one that may be his last, he dutifully makes.

Halloween comes the day before All Saints' Day and at one house, instead of giving out candy, a woman distributes cards of the saints bordered in gold leaf and wrapped in ribbon, addressed to Our Little Saints. My father is pushing a toddler in its carriage when he begins to talk about the mystics. He and I are at the rear of this small parade, our steps timid and measured. He speaks of the retreats of Saint Ignatius. I remember from Catechism that the retreats last forty-five days and are considered a rite for the truly devout, those men whose intellect and faith are completely offered to the service of God. I think: My father's talent for charming any-one and everyone is slipping. He is trying to establish common ground with me and missing by a long shot. He is confusing me with the altar boy I was when I was ten. But then it occurs to me that he is speaking to me the way a Cuban man of his generation speaks to a twenty-eight-year-old man who is still unmarried, which is to say, a man whose masculinity is suspect—my father is speaking to me the way I have seen him speak to priests. He is reaching out to me, in his way, and as I listen to him, respect-fully, dutifully, I begin to resemble the priest he imagines me as.

Under a suburban sky where it is difficult to tell a shooting star from the lights on an airplane, my father is still talking about Saint Ignatius. Founder of the Jesuits, an order dedicated to teaching and the upkeep of libraries and the war against Protestantism. Soldiers against doubt, against mass said in the vernacular. A saint whose five-hundred-year-old method of spiritual retreat my father thinks will save him. That's my term. My father uses the phrase Put me back in orbit.

When we are back at my mother's house and sorting candy, my father drinks Johnnie Walker and I overhear him speaking to my brother-in-law, a dentist who holds season tickets for the Miami Dolphins, making other plans for the future he imagines after his trial. He will live off his Social Security checks in the Dominican Republic, where, With those few coins, to use another of his phrases, he can live like a king, with a maid, a small house, and, he whispers into his in-law's ear, A nice skinny black woman.

I feel had. I feel my face turn red, as if I've been humiliated before a lover I've caught cheating. I go over the elaborate cultural explanation I had devised a half hour earlier to explain the private spiritual desires my father was confiding in me. I reprimand myself for forgetting that my father has spent a lifetime treating people around him like members of a jury whose sympathies he must win. Even now, perhaps especially now, he is trying to impress me, and so he made up a story he thought I wanted to hear, and he told it to me.

I am sitting on the carpet pretending to be the man two small Supermen can vanquish. I do not see my father get up and leave, I notice only later that he is gone. Two nieces are arguing over identical-looking plastic buckets made to look like jack-o'-lanterns. Give me that. That one's mine, says the vampiress.

No, the ballerina tells the vampiress, How can you can even tell the buckets apart?

Because I can. Your bucket is over there, the vampiress retorts. This one is mine. So there.

INSIDE HER HOUSE my mother makes herself sick. A week of clenching her teeth, of refusing food, of spending nights staring at her clock as it marks the minutes till just before the 6 A.M. alarm finally have an effect. On the ninth morning of the trial she announces she is too sick to go. For a few days she stays home and is spared having to hear strangers tell her about her husband, about herself.

Over the next few days my mother's heavy coughs can be heard day and night throughout her house. Her body struggles to push something out of itself, she covers her mouth trying to keep it in. My sisters and I call from the courthouse to see if she has eaten and we complain about the strict rations she allows herself, her excuses alternating between lack of appetite and nausea. She nibbles at crackers and sips apple juice. The chicken soup I buy for her sits in the refrigerator, untouched, inside opaque Tupperware.

When I accuse her of wasting her worries on a man who doesn't care about her, we fight bitterly. I take my father's photo down from the wall, she yells at me and fishes it out of the trash.

At night I use the pillow to drown out her irregular coughs, the deep whooping of lungs pushing instead of inhaling. In the morning, the house still dark, I hear her slide off her bed at 5:57, or 5:58. Always just before her digital clock bellows out its 6 A.M. alarm. Her body predicts the noise and gets her out of bed; she won't let herself be surprised.

My sisters ask me, because I'm the one with no children of his own, to baby-sit my mother. I stay at her house during the day and miss a few days of the trial. I try not to think. I bludgeon my body with too much sleep, too much food, too much TV. On the surround sound system my mother installed for her grandchildren, I watch science fiction movies that are deadeningly alike. When the enemy starships attack I see bodies splinter into crisp embers, entire cities obliterated. These movies are so loud they leave me with headaches that I cure by smoking pot, exhaling plumes of smoke through the screen in the bathroom window. Outside the locked bathroom door I hear my mother's dragging feet, her muffled coughing.

BEFORE WE GO in to hear the verdict, my father empties his pockets and leaves me with his things, just in case. He takes off his jewelry, gives me his wallet, his car keys, his handkerchief that smells of his cologne, the one that comes in a jar made to look like cut crystal. Afterward my sister, my mother, and I stand in the parking lot and see that we have one more car than we have drivers.

It would have been better if your brother came today, my mother tells me.

The trial was making him feel bad, I joke flatly.

My father calls me collect the next day from prison. He calls me because I have his things. While I stand in my mother's kitchen he gives me detailed directions. Some of the things inside his car are to be given to my mother; other things, including the car itself, are to be dropped off at the house he shared with the woman he lived with. My father asks me to call her, his lover, a woman I have never met, and in a voice low enough for my mother not to overhear I ask him for the phone number.

Inside my father's car I go through the glove compartment, through the ashtrays, through the seat pockets. If I am unclear if something should go to his wife or to the woman he lived with, I hand it to his wife, my mother. There are things I give to my sister, things I take for myself. Though no one has given me permission, and the man who owns these things is still alive, I take them. I give my sister my father's silver necklace. I take his handkerchief that smells of cologne. The cologne that comes from a bottle made to look like cut crystal. From inside his glove compartment I take a cassette tape when I recognize his writing on the label. It's a tape of old boleros and, as I drive his car to the house he shared with his lover, I listen to Olga Guillot sing hysterically of lost love, her voice straining to be heard over the overwrought orchestration.

I leave his car in the driveway at his lover's house. She's on her cordless phone when I knock and as I hand her the keys she covers the mouthpiece and says, *Gracias,* like this is something we do every day. She offers me a ride back to my mother's house. I tell her I don't think that's a good idea.

▪ ▪ ▪

THERE IS ANOTHER story about my father that comes to me three days after he's convicted. It's too late to share it with my younger sister— I'm on a flight back to San Francisco, a city that seems smaller and paler in my mind than when I left it. The blocks of painted Victorian houses seem untenable. A ridiculous toy. I haven't called my lover to tell him I'm coming back. He'll know soon enough.

The story I remember happened in 1980, during the height of the Mariel boatlift. I was thirteen. The newspapers were full of photographs of ships overflowing with people, refugees crowding the decks, people leaning over the handrails. Pages of newsprint given over to the listing of arrivals that my mother read every morning. She would circle some names in pencil, putting a question mark beside others. It was one of those weekends when my father was not around. This was not unusual. I remember nothing about that Friday or Saturday. What I do remember is my father and somebody else's husband swaggering into my mother's house late Sunday night, their bodies reeling like they were still at sea, their faces burnt ruddy, voices louder than usual, full of stories and the need to tell them.

What my mother knew and had not told us was that my father had sailed to Cuba to try to get his mother. He had sailed to that country, so often mentioned in our house but seen by me only in brown-and-white photographs. That country my parents had left and never returned to, that island that was impossibly far away, distant from us not because of geography, but because of bitter politics, there, to that place, impossible for anyone in Miami to get back to, was where my father had gone for the weekend.

In a voice salty and loud he spoke about the distance, the long day when they could not see land, before them or behind them, the storm, the waves, all of it made of water. That he was not able to get his mother was nothing compared with this: He had crossed the ninety miles I had always been told no one could cross.

I imagine my father sailing into the port of Mariel, dressed in a yellow raincoat, face burnt by salt and sun, beaming. I imagine him speaking to a man from the Cuban army who is dressed head to toe in olive green. The soldier holds a clipboard and a bullhorn; he steps onto my father's boat as if he owns it. The soldier argues with my father. There is something my father has not done, there is a procedure he has not followed. My father asks a question, and the lanky soldier argues. My father makes a joke, the soldier laughs, relents, gives my father his way. My father tells such beautiful stories.

This is the same way I used to imagine my father arriving in Miami for the first time. Laughing. Winning over strangers with a joke. Willing to sleep in his day clothes on a borrowed sofa, then brushing off the evening's wrinkles, pressing hard the hand of his host as he shakes it, then asking where he might find work.

Even now, that's the kind of man I still imagine my father was before I was born. Before his indefatigable ambition, before his desire to impress everyone, before a lifetime of polite white lies finally caught up with him. Even now, that's the way I can't help but imagine that my father was, somehow truly was, when I was twelve and sitting at the foot of the family table and listening, well after my bedtime, to the adults trade stories about the trip to Mariel.

I was young then, it's true. The young have that habit; we believe so much of what we are told. Maybe I should stop making excuses; besides I think you can tell. I imagine you know that when I was twelve I believed everything my father told me, and in those places where his stories left off, I made the rest up myself.

JAMES M. SASLOW

Daddy Was a Hot Number

All gay boys are in love with their daddies. This affectionate, confused, and artistic little fellow was about eight when he began to notice that his handsome beefy father, then only twenty-seven himself, was sometimes mistaken for Marlon (*sigh*) Brando. If Freud hadn't been such a latent homophobe, he would have spotted that psychological archetype and named it the Orestes complex—after the Greek myth of the handsome prince attended by his inseparable sidekick, Pylades. Orestes, who along with his devoted lover was held up to Athenian schoolboys as the paragon of male intimacy, offers a gay mirror image of the straight son Oedipus, who got so much more press for killing Papa and bedding Mama. In the epic dramas of Aeschylus and Sophocles, Orestes' struggle with his scheming mother, Clytemnestra, over the affection of his murdered father, Agamemnon, ends in her violent death at her son's hands. Which is just what little gay boys fantasize when they realize, as I had, that Daddy was a hot number, that everything about him attracted and fascinated me, and that my main rival for his attention was Mommy.

Unlike Orestes, I didn't want to kill her—I wanted to *be* her. An ambition full of ironies: I could never, by definition, be enough of a "real girl" to lure his erotic attention, but I was in fact so "feminine"—lousy at sports, bookish and creative rather than an outgoing salesman like my macho old man—that our chances for relaxed male camaraderie were slim. Therein the gay son's inescapable dilemma. At least straight boys cut their Oedipal teeth on desire for a heterosexual woman, who could, in theory, respond—Jocasta and her kid had quite a thing going for a while. But gay children get the same hetero parents as their straight siblings, and that kind of father couldn't possibly love his little Orestes in return. Not the way *I* wanted, anyway.

Though doomed to perpetual frustration, I found Daddy irresistibly beautiful. Beauty is the common gene shared by eros and art, who are twins in the psychosexual womb. And not coincidentally, eros and art have been the twin seeds of my own personal and professional identity, as a homosexual and a historian of the visual arts. During my childhood, our relationship swung from cuddly to stormy to distant, and it was not until many years later that we started to grope our way back from an uneasy truce toward mutual amnesty. Only then could I appreciate how he had guided me through the family boot camp by both positive and negative example, and taught me two lessons indispensable for a gay man: how to feel desire, and how to survive disapproval.

Basic training in sexual attraction was easy—he was the classic football-hero hunk. One of my fondest childhood memories is the "minnow and whale" game we'd play in the pool of our 1950s suburban New Jersey swim club. I would duck underwater and try to swim between his widespread legs, and he would try to catch me in his "jaws" by scissoring his legs together. It was fun to make it through, but even more fun getting caught. To lose a round was to win the reward of his furry thighs' brushing against my neck and arms, to feel his massive warmth stoking the flame of summer sunlight dappled across the pool bottom, and then to burst upward for air, grappling past his crotch and up his bathing suit into his arms like a wee monkey happy for a hug.

I wouldn't have understood the term "intercrural intercourse," but it's from a boy's father that he drinks in his introduction to the male body, which is doubly important for gays. It starts when daddy shows us how to shake our peepee after making number one—the *Ur*-lesson in the body as a site of desire (and a skill that later comes in handy for playing well with others). We learn lust literally at his feet—or, in my case, his legs—and gay boys often take a furtive seminar in the hypnotic allure of body hair, and shaving, and locker-room physicality. Toward puberty, when the other guys would giggle at the half-naked mothers and sisters we sometimes glimpsed through chinks in the wall between the men's and women's bathhouses, I couldn't see what the fuss was all about. We were with our daddies, who were stripped to their tanned and muscular flesh, and there was plenty to drool over right here.

Survival training in disapproval, on the other hand, was not so pleasant at the time, however much I learned that later proved an essential coping mechanism. To give the old man his due, from where he stood there was a lot to disapprove of. I was unathletic, precociously intellectual, and displayed an alarming propensity for taking my mother as a role model. Like her, my talents ran to painting, theater, and dance—not the sort of career goals to boast about with his weekly poker buddies. Nor did Orestes earn any bragging rights for Agamemnon by trying to outdo Clytemnestra in the kitchen. I once dragooned my little brother into helping cook a surprise breakfast, complete with fresh juice and flowers on the table. Daddy padded down the stairs, stared at the spectacle in groggy shock, and muttered sarcastically, "You'll make somebody a fine wife someday."

The two paternal comments I heard and resented most were "You're too sensitive" and "You think too much." "Sensitive" was code for both artistic and homosexual, then considered more or less identical. And "thinking" meant questioning meant commie pinko—a type supposedly in bed with homosexuals, politically if not erotically. By fourth grade I fitted perfectly into the most dreaded stereotype of postwar *Father Knows Best* culture: the fruitcake/egghead/nonconformist who made a favorite target for the House Un-American Activities Committee. My classic jock dad just didn't know what to make of his classic sissy boy. He coached Little League, but I couldn't make the team if I tried, so I ended up as the scorekeeper—where my math skills, otherwise the stigmata of a nerd, at least had some practical use to offset the humiliation. When the acting bug bit me, he came to the plays with a forced grin; when I danced in a Christmas *Nutcracker* in tights and ballet shoes, the grin disappeared altogether.

In many of my most vivid mental snapshots of those days, I am gazing up at him as he squints sideways at me with a little backward cock of the head that signaled a puzzled incomprehension. It communicated without words that whatever I had done or said was so far outside his experience as to seem literally uncanny, and therefore to remain unmentioned, avoided with silent distaste from an emotional arm's length that amounted to a McCarthy-era version of today's schizoid military policy: "Don't ask, don't tell." The few occasions when we tried an awkward game of catch would usually end with his shaking his head, "You've got a great eye and a great hand—you could be a terrific pitcher— why don't you want to *try?*" I didn't yet know, because no one dared mention such possibilities, that hand-eye coordination also makes good painters. Or that the ultimate compliment to an art historian— also decorators, dress designers, and assorted visual occupations stereo- typically rife with gay men—is, "He's got a good eye." I only knew that once again, I didn't measure up. I cringed from the look, and shriveled at the tone of voice.

All children suffer that aching stab of inadequacy when Papa turns his face away; it's just twice as sharp when he's your object of desire as well as your mentor and role model. Only mother love is unconditional— very comforting for heterosexual boys, I would imagine. But fatherly love is also about licking the child into shape, in two senses: nurturing, as in the legend that bears tongue their featureless newborns into the phys- ical form of a cub; and punishing, as in "I'll give you a licking you won't forget." Fathers challenge and then judge us—their role in socializing the next generation. In this mythic battle of wills, persuasion and example are the preferred weapons, but if they don't work, the drill sergeant may have to unleash the A-bomb of familial warfare: rejection.

The urge to honor tribal demands before personal feelings, and to train or bully your children into obeying the same code, must be hard- wired: Abraham consented to slaughter Isaac just as Agamemnon regret- fully executed the gods' order to sacrifice his own daughter, Orestes' sister Iphigenia, to ensure victory in the Trojan War. Now mythic parallels only stretch so far. Daddy wasn't about to turn my brother into a burnt offering—though at times he must have been sorely tempted to ditch *me* on some faraway altar, since by the only criteria he knew, the raw recruit he'd been given to work with was unpromising and exasperatingly unco- operative. But only once did he go so far as to stop speaking to me: when I finally came out to him. Before disappearing on a three-week drunk, his sole comment was, "Don't take out an ad in the paper." Translation: I'm throwing in the towel, sorry I couldn't lick you hard enough, now just keep out of my world so you won't embarrass me.

So I learned the hard way: disapproval may be a chronic disease, but it ain't fatal. Useful toughening for a member of any minority, sexual or otherwise. All the same, such unkind cuts leave scars, or at least bad habits. Sometimes, when my companion, Steve, and I get into some domestic tiff, I catch myself turning distant and judgmental; hey, Daddy showed me just how effective that tactic can be. But then I remember that term of exile with a shudder, and his admission, after he felt able to lift my excommunication, that it was the biggest mistake of his life. And I try harder not to inflict the same crap on the man I love.

Keeping that distance not only hurts Stevie—it also hurts me. As I grew up, I realized Daddy, too, had suffered the pain of failure, both as son and father. As much a victim as a perpetrator, he had been rejected by *his* old man—Grampa never bothered to hide a chronically unsatisfiable crabbiness—and it burdened him all his life with an unshakable and defensive self-doubt. Unshakable, at least, without the kind of unflinching self-examination and cathartic expression of emotions that "real men" didn't indulge in—no matter how much your old man reproached you for siring a faggot grandson. Not that the '50s insistence on repressed, stoic masculinity was all that different from most of history. We males have passed this vicious cycle "man to man"—oh, loaded phrase—down all the generations since Adam left Eden and raised Cain.

No wonder he drank. Another lesson taught by negative example. I watched him knock back the booze—a much too regular occurrence about which everyone agreed to "don't ask, don't tell"—and I ached over how uptight he was when he *wasn't* drinking. My brother and I would joke about the extravagant protestations of affection that blurted out when he'd had a few, and rue the promises that he never quite made good on after he sobered up. Which opened my eyes to another coping mechanism: sour grapes. The Holy Grail of heterosexual normalcy, which receded ever farther beyond my grasp as I matured into a semi-flaming drama queen, looked more and more like a toxic chalice, tarnished by alcohol and seething with denial. Faced with every generation's question—whether 'tis nobler in the mind to suffer the slings and arrows of paternal misfortune, or to take arms against a sea of troubles and, by opposing, end them—I swore to lance my emotional boils rather than poison myself to numb their festering throb.

When he died at fifty-two of lung cancer, after decades of two packs a day and far more bourbon than is good for the liver or the soul, some in the funeral congregation expected my eulogy to slap him for his self-destructive excesses. But in the end I couldn't bring myself to reproach him, having come to appreciate that, for all his troubles, he had the gusto—some would say foolhardiness—to pursue whatever gave him pleasure, waistline or worse consequences be damned. And he told anyone who criticized him to butt out. From that example, splendidly over the top as it was, I learned that if you have a passion, go for it. It wasn't a long life, or a wise one—but it was fun while it lasted.

So he was gone too soon—we were just edging around to a mutual respect, and I was touched to hear when he bragged to the hospital nurse that his son wrote for an "important" gay newspaper. I'll always regret that I never got to speak to him of understanding, and forgiveness, and gratitude. And memory—for he will always be with me. He lives on in the universal way that fathers are bodily present in their sons: It's his lips I see in the shaving mirror, his hairline that's receding on its DNA-driven death march. But he's also in my mind, in a way that's unique to gay boys: as the very stuff of my desires, and thus of my capacity for happiness. Take the lithograph I made in art school, when I was just coming out. It showed a worm's-eye view from the bottom of a pool, and a hunky male figure floating over me, limbs invitingly splayed—testimony to the enduring magic of those halcyon childhood days when, as I wrote in the caption that coiled up and around him, "I flewswam through my father's loving legs." If I swim through Stevie's now, it's because Daddy left me a priceless legacy: a vision of love, and the courage to act on it.

He also just plain left me. When I started writing this, I was the same age my father had been when he died; now I've got a couple of years on him. Losing him was hard, but outliving him is my vindication. So: You thought I was too aesthetic, too femme, too introspective to make it? You gave me a licking, metaphorically if not physically, for not being enough like you? You got one thing right—I *did* make somebody a fine wife someday, and he and I are pretty happy that way. I'm still in reasonable health, a tenured art professor living in a big Upper West Side co-op with a nice Jewish doctor; at my age, *you* had moved into an urn. So whose instincts made better survival equipment? By now I've even got your incipient little belly, sign of a comfortable middle age you'll never see.

Maybe there's something to be said for thinking too much and being too sensitive. And maybe revenge has finally helped close the books.

When I played the piano at his funeral, my mother asked for a song expressing her feelings, from the Broadway operetta *Showboat*. When all is said and done, it would have been my choice, too. Once each Orestes gets over the stage of rivalry with his personal Clytemnestra and finds his own Pylades, then he and Mom have a passion in common and, like I said, she offers the closest model for how to feel and act toward the men of our dreams. My own mother views life more as a musical comedy than a Greek tragedy, but some ideals transcend theatrical genres. In Mom's signature song, the leading lady laments that her fella drinks and stays out late, but her devotion remains unconditional: Just as "fish gotta swim and birds gotta fly," she confesses that "I even loves him when his kisses got gin." The Greeks didn't know gin—or bourbon either—but they did know that such a tie may also bind male to male, father and son. As Orestes might have said, "Can't help lovin' that man of mine."

DOUGLAS SADOWNICK

My Father, My Self

Coming Out Inside as the Next Stage of Gay Liberation

A year after I recovered from the major depression that followed the breakup of a 14-year-long gay domestic "marriage," I proceeded to fall in love again, this time with a much younger, needier man who allegedly wasn't going to leave me. But I was wrong. Two years later, I was destined to replay the entire drama of abandonment, divorce, and emotional devastation, as if I had learned nothing from its cathartic wisdom the first time out. This reenactment forced me to confront the fact that my romantic problems with men seemed to point to a familiar pattern that predated adult life. It occurred to me that I was ironically dating men who bore some disturbing emotional and vaguely physical resemblance to my biological father. I began to open up then to how tragically unresolved my childhood romantic ("Oedipal") feelings for my now-dead father actually were. I saw that working these traumatic emotional states through ongoingly in the here-and-now offered the only realistic way to break free from the addictive pattern of romantic hell—what Freud calls "repetition compulsion." A more gay-centered, psychodynamic approach to the ubiquitous predicament plaguing gay men like myself, it seems to me, has revolutionary implications for our personal well-being as well as for the next stage of gay liberation.

To get to the heart of the classic drama: All my life I've struggled—as I think all gay men do perhaps, whether they are aware of it or not—to come to ultimate terms with the troubling childhood experience of father (or father surrogate). But we need an entirely new, gay-centered outlook if we're to outsmart amnesia (and forestall unnecessary tragedies) and open our eyes fully (homosexually) to the neglected narrative of this long-forgotten First Great Romance.

The key to initial understanding can be found in the radical Freudian hypothesis of Oedipal infantile romance with one parent or the other between the ages of four and six and attendant murderous rivalry felt for the other, a childhood "Oedipal crisis" resolved through the sacrifice of the incest wish and the eventual identification with the formerly hated parent. This highly charged episode takes place, according to psychoanalysis, before awareness, and informs seemingly-aware adult choices in love, sexuality and personality development. No wonder we fall into folly. For like Oedipus, all human beings suffer a tragic blindness about this oracular truth, a severely inhibiting myopia exacerbated for us gay men by the all-too-often minimized problem of internalized homophobia and toxic shame that we repress rather than redeem.

What can we do about historic short-sightedness? Synthesizing Freud's theories of past sexual and emotional trauma with Jung's veneration for archetypal meaning and purpose in a gay activist way, it seems to me, provides gay men like myself finally with the necessary vision to see how the mental image of the straight-acting, homophobic dad (or other versions of him) can be transformed though ongoing "inner work" into a shamanic guide and erotic initiator.

Having the tools to change from the inside out is one thing, but using them consistently and heroically is another. Perhaps if I tell you a little about the man I am more inclined to forget than recall, you will see why the avoided pain of homosexual childhood becomes an insidious block that, in my personal situation, undermines my capacity to love and within the larger gay community, holds gay liberation back for us all.

My father was an anomaly for a Jewish man, eccentrically macho, and, in that respect, not dissimilar from the men with whom I tend to fall in love nowadays: implacably sexy in a paradoxically shut-down kind of way. When I was a child the thinly disguised contempt my dad aimed at me resulted in a terrorizing feeling of abysmal alienation that I covered up with straight As at school. He handled his envy for my boastful intellect with happy-go-lucky alcoholism and a cigarette habit. He looked an awful lot like Humphrey Bogart, especially when he lit up one casual Lucky Strike after another. He hunted, fished, and golfed. He worshiped nature despite my mother's operatic complaint that she needed more money to move from the once Jewish now black Bronx. Although we lived in a concrete high-rise, he did what he could to convert the small, four-room apartment to a neatly organized quasi-back-yard, filling each room up with houseplants, half-finished new closets, fancy new blinds, and bubbling fish tanks. He made no bones about favoring my brother. Both of them celebrated a love of the body beautiful and the gravid world of sensation, in contrast with my adherence to my mother's investment in intellect.

As I look back on my childhood, however, I sense that my father had an aching need to be close to me, especially when I became about sixteen. By that time, I had become something more of a man because (unbeknownst to him) I had been kissed by blue-collar young adults, and their working-class ease with getting off in their Brooklyn apartments when their mothers were at church had rubbed off on me. That's when he took me fishing, six or seven times. We spent Sundays casting into the Long Island Sound and he would sneak me a sip from his flask. I once felt so close to his conditional love that I almost asked him why he had waited so long to extend it to me. But I was terrified of his temper and how he could take his hatred of women out on me, if I provoked him by acting sensitive.

The epitome of this dynamic—how he identified me with my mother because I identified with her—took place right before my bar mitzvah. We were at some extended family Passover Seder and it disgusted me how, with each gulp of whisky, my father badmouthed his wife to her relatives. She was no fun, she didn't like to drink, all she cared about was work. Unable to tolerate this drunken litany of self-mockery another second, (in part because I lacked, as he did, the ability to temper my emotions), I rose from my seat and demanded in front of dozens of uncles and aunts that he stop his boozing. My mother tried to silence my shocking outburst, but it was too late. He sneered at both my mother and me, blind with humil-

■ THE MAN I MIGHT BECOME

iated rage, covering it up with apologetic smiles to the tittering relatives, as we said our goodbyes. But once we got in the car, he inflicted his reign of terror. Speeding down the New England Thruway at almost 100 miles per hour, he screamed the words "bitch," "goddamn bitch," "ball buster" and "party pooper" for at least twenty minutes. He was ostensibly cursing my mother. She sat stonelike in the backseat between my brother and myself, gripping our pinkies, asking her husband for forgiveness without lowering herself too much in front of her children. But I think everyone sensed that the word "bitch" was really meant for me.

It worries me now that my romantic relationships seem, in many respects, a tragic replay of that night. For a very long time I wondered whether I could ever fall for anyone who didn't in some ways secretly— very, very secretly—get off on hating me, much less his own homosexual feelings. I did not believe that any therapist could help me come to terms with the insidious shame I felt for how my love and hate wires had been inextricably crossed. No other gay man could suffer the kind of internalized homophobia I did. I wasted valuable years in my twenties failing to turn to a therapist because I transferred my hatred for my father blindly onto any potential Fisher King crossing my path.

I'VE DEVOTED MUCH of my life to trying to figure out this conundrum, first, in chiefly "extroverted" ways, as a journalist writing about gay and AIDS issues, then as a gay activist, and later as an author. In the early `90s, however, my gay activism took a decisively "introverted" turn when I became initiated by gay liberationists linked to Mattachine Society co-founder Harry Hay into the inner world of gay psyche and entered a serious gay-centered analysis and eventually became a therapist. I learned I could stop poking my eyes out, if only I would but see the naked truth: At the heart of my potential and capacity to love like a warrior materialized the slyly deprecating image of my alcoholic father, mocking the ritual way towards a greater and more heroic gay self-realization while also pointing the way, like a wounded healer, towards ultimate psychological freedom. The situation was therefore not entirely hopeless. If I related to this arrogant masculine force through internal, tough gay-activist means, and didn't just surrender addictively to being his bitch, or repress his image and thereby drive it further into the unconscious, his manner of drowning me in bad feelings could be alchemically transformed. A homosexual archetypal truth could be discovered and redeemed from within the crushing father complex, a mysteriously incestuous figure possessing the incorruptible and immortal buried treasure of gay love.

Some of what I am saying may strike a well-intentioned but cut-to-the-chase reader as unnecessarily impractical. Part of our oppression, it seems to me, is that we gays are as extroverted in our approach to our psychological problems and potentials as our enemies; we don't see psyche as the watery source of all life in which we all swim, containing inner personalities and transformational substance. I know about this blindness from personal experience: Even though I have been doing inner work consistently as a gay man for more than ten years, I am as caught in my unconscious complexes as the next shark. I act out my greedy sexual needs rather than struggle with the underlying infantile feelings motivating them and still pick men who correspond too closely to my arrogant father, rather than struggle with my dissociative tendency to mask psychic pain and inner violence by acting out. Only tears can make the fish of the soul swim again, but who wants salt when there are mostly wounds?

I suspect that I will be writing and thinking about these existential challenges for decades to come in part because the sad feeling of failure that comes with trying to write well about gay liberation helps to expose and redeem the massively toxic homophobic devaluing rooted in my childhood. Here I can only try to suggest the outlines of the rich psychology and mythologies of human development outlined in scientific terms by Freud and Jung (but in my estimation first discovered by queer alchemists and philosophers) and that can be reshaped and revisioned in modern gay-centered terms so that they make practical and revolutionary sense for gay men's lives today.

The fundamental starting point for me is the radical vision pioneered by gay-centered psychologist Mitch Walker. A gay-movement activist and organizer since 1972, Walker has been researching homosexual psychology and gay archetypal truths for over 30 years and was the first openly gay writer to be published in the Jungian literature. He is best known in the gay community for his groundbreaking sexual liberation book, *Men Loving Men, A Gay Sex Guide and Consciousness Book,* and *Visionary Love: A Spirit Book of Gay Mythology and Transmutational Faerie.* He also co-created the first gay-centered spiritual movement in 1979, the Radical Faeries, with Harry Hay, which is now a worldwide phenomenon.

In an unpublished paper, "Father-Son Incest and the Oedipal Complex in Gay Men: A Reconceptualization," Walker integrates classical Jungian terms to gay liberation thought to describe how gay boys at the tender age of four or five fall inexorably into romantic-erotic love with their fathers. "For a gay boy," he writes, "it is the father who is loved and yearned for as the expression of libidinal striving, in the way that the heterosexual boy 'falls' for his mother." He tells us that for gay men, "the mother serves as the competitor and the one who is identified with in pursuit of the father," and that "gay men seek through romance and sexuality to regain symbolically a father-son union."

My own internalized homophobia and toxic shame allows me to hear and identify with the gasp of revulsion I can imagine being experienced by gay male readers at the suffocating thought that we wished romantic merger with our fathers. But consider the fact that our straight male counterparts have had more than a century to accept as received wisdom the idea that they were, for a fantastic time in early childhood, in passionate, erotic love with their mothers. Gay men do not have a well worked out version of Freud's and Jung's discussions of Oedipal theory to help us relate empathically to the imperishable primitive mind of gay childhood. This tragic lack of basic theory and practice not only thwarts our capacity to understand and "work" the creative alchemy of romance to its fullest and heavenly potential, but in fact contributes to the worst forms of self-sabotage that are all too ubiquitous in our community. Without an indigenous homosexual "myth of meaning" to inform our worthiest goals and libidinal yearnings, we are unwittingly and suicidally entrapped within the enemy's value system, floundering, so to speak, like fish out of water.

Attending to the crisis, Walker begins his discussion by grappling with the homophobia of traditional theory and gathers together voices criticizing it. We learn that both Freud and Jung view "mother-son incest," in which the straight male child falls in love with mother and fears the castrating father, as foundational to their theory-building. The healthy mother, in the ideally normal situation, frustrates this naturally-occurring drive. When thwarting is done lovingly and intuitively, it helps the libidinal process along to take its next dynamic action: According to Jung, the blocking of the incest wish magically brings forth an Inner Beloved in the psyche of the heterosexual boy a "ghostlike presence which has objective reality" and is felt as "the source of life, the prime mover." The father-son paper tells us that "this clearly demarcated functional complex can be best described as a 'personality' in the unconscious." This is the "intangible living presence" within each and every one of us that Jung has termed the "soul."

Walker's paper starts from the assumption that homosexual libidinal attraction is inborn and constitutional, a natural variation for some boys and girls, and reworks Freud and Jung's theory to account for the incipiently gay child and gay-identified adult, and the creation of a homosexual inner experience as entirely separate and apart from heterosexual interiority. What makes the paper so vitally urgent for our community today is that it charts in a step-by-step fashion the development of a homosexual soul-complex emerging from the father-son incest wish and its transformations in practically transcendental terms. For the first time, gay men can resuscitate a "gay soul figure" analogous to Inner Beloved (the anima) that Jung has described for heterosexual men. Quoting from Jung's analysis of heterosexual soul figure dynamics but in a gay-centered way, the father-son paper amplifies how this inner homosexual figure moving in the depths emerges as our one-and-only True Love, personifying our "inherent creative power" and our "self-creating tendency." He is a "mystical brother within, "a secret sharer," a "figure with the all the erotic and spiritual significance attached to anima, but of the same sex, and not yet a shadow." Here's what we find: The man with whom we want to fall in love is nothing but a projection of a transcendental image whose erotic and energetic source is located within.

While this articulation of an inner Mr. Right offers to gay men a Copernican Revolution in our world view, it can not be felt as inwardly real and erotically satisfying without great internal struggle (and much therapy). I can feel my own defenses reacting violently to the idea of the gay soul figure and I have been trying to "make him" feel real inside myself for many years. I imagine readers groaning at the implication that the most embodied and satisfyingly transcendental of lovers is to be located not outside (where most of us normally look) but rather inside, within the unfathomed, shamanic depths of the numinous psyche. I can feel the toxic shame pooling inside myself the moment I start to seriously animate the soul figure. Is this yet again another repressive line telling gay men that they shouldn't have sex and love in an outer-directed way? What good does it do to imagine, amplify, construct, meditate on, or dialogue with a homosexual "ghostly male lover, moving in the depths," when one is lonely or broken hearted or in the delighted throes of romantic infatuation?

There is a natural resistance any person is bound to experience before diving into the phenomenological waters of the living psyche. Nothing could be more scary. What makes initiation into soul-figure dynamics all that much more challenging is that the gay male Oedipal experience is no doubt profoundly more traumatizing than the equivalent for heterosexual boys, due to the added assault to the gay self experienced by gay children pre-Oedipally (namely with their mothers) and the homophobia afflicted on them by their fathers. So the unresolved pain of homosexuality's childhood, and the defenses that are installed to protect us from excruciating inner experience, become an invisible prison in adult life, locking us unwittingly into extroverted answers to what are essentially internal dramas.

One reason for this understandable defensiveness lies in the way the Oedipal wish unfolds for the gay child. Although most mothers may seem to play the role of understanding their child's Oedipal pull toward them and can help let the child down easily, many fathers are at best mystified and at worst utterly repelled by their sons' attraction, and react with veiled anger and sometimes outright hostility.

The paper turns to the psychiatrist and gay Freudian Richard Isay, whose work "places this new understanding of the father's role for a gay son at the center of his study on gay men and their development," to explain what might happen for a proto-gay boy vis-à-vis his Oedipal love object. Isay says why it is that gay men have a special rapport with both the feminine and the masculine, and outlines how the "rivalry with the mother for the father's affection" leads to "an underlying bond with women that is based on a mutual attraction to other men" such that a homosexual child of four, five or six, "may assume some of her attributes" in a wish to be "daddy's little girl." I suspect that most gay-identified men can relate in one way or another to Isay's observation: "These boys may be more sensitive, have more aesthetic interests, may not be involved in competitive activities and may be more seclusive than heterosexually inclined boys." He adds that this dynamic "may lead both to the father's withdrawal and to his favoring an older or younger male sibling." This problem "is invariably experienced as a rejection," resulting in poor self-esteem and often difficulty as an adult "in forming loving and trust rather than angry and spiteful relationships." As Isay sums it up, "ubiquitous in the love life of adult gay men is the persistence of an early erotic attachment to the father and a need to defend against these feelings."

While I myself don't recall the "early erotic attachment" per se with my father, I can free-associate to memories that symbolize the dilemma, such as the moment when it dawned on me consciously that my father preferred my brother to me. My first memory of my father's unabashed partiality toward my brother takes me back to when I was ten and my brother eight. That's when the Bronx public schools closed for a week due to race riots and Vietnam War demonstrations. My father and brother transformed the slip-covered living room into a putting course, with plastic tees, old golf balls, and fake pieces of plastic green grass littering the matted-down shag-carpeting. I wanted to feel my father's calloused, tobacco-stained mailman's hands around my delicate piano-playing own just as he taught my wiry, wise-cracking little brother how to grip the club. But I was also acutely aware that both of them felt repulsed by my awkward presence and I detected my father sneering at me through his pursed lips.

In the past, I would have resorted to the feminine wiles adopted unconsciously from my mother to win his approval, and I think I recall my father's experiencing that giddiness as cunning and cute. That day, I felt that I could no longer rely on such bait. I recall hopelessly dying inside. I shrugged my already hunched shoulders and retreated into the crowded kitchen. That's where my mother and her sister, over Sanka and coffee cake, discussed joining the anti-war demonstrators marching past our six-story apartment building down the Grand Concourse, because they were sick of keeping company with their loser husbands, who used the excuse of social unrest to take the day off from delivering the mail to drink.

My mother took my hands in her own to warm the chill off them, and I felt alternately rescued and poisoned as she asked my opinion as to whether she should march or not without waiting for a response. Years later, I experienced the same kind of nauseated stuck feeling when I'd let myself get fucked by men in the hope of winning their sadistically ambivalent love. I think this is the kind of dynamic—father rejection; mother entrapment—that would have led me to becoming seriously ill with one STD or another had not stronger impulses to re-create my nuclear family dynamic in the form of gay "marital" life with a long-standing lover (and dog) had not taken over. It has taken years for me to break the cloying grip this unholy triangle still has on my homosexuality, where a rejecting masculine complex pushes me into the arms of a seemingly kind but ultimately raping maternal force. I want to be a gay man in the radical core of my existential feelings and actions and not a mother-dominated "nice" assimilationist, casting for her approval at the expense of his.

The closest I come to setting a limit on my warring internal complexes is when I make a choice to mindfully attend to the inner racket, take a breath, and make a moral and embodied effort to train my mind continually on what could be more erotically beneficial than internalized homophobia. At such moments, I can sometimes feel my father's son coming alive inside of me, energized into sensuality through the sincere and urgent request for help made by my gay ego, called into conscious collaboration to suffuse my mind with amazing images of being loved by a swarthy stud so as to help me fight my demons and reach toward fuller gay potentials.

I can't tell you how my father's erotic "son" got birthed inside my gay psyche by the creative will of Homosexual Libido in "the constellation of love towards the father" when I was about five or six. But a certain knowing tells me that the nativity of a homosexual "ghostlike presence which has objective reality" absolutely happened; I can feel its procreative legacy to this day. All my life I have felt the demonic erotically charged spirit overtake my conscious ego state every time I develop a crush or fall in love—or look at a naked picture of a hot guy. I am not myself at those times. This electrical jolt of inspired yearning feels both godlike and infantile. I stop thinking, act impulsively, and feel driven toward a calculated surrender. The men to whom I gravitate bear no real resemblance to my father. But without exception each comes at the world from his body like my father did, has a defiant earthiness, and often struts and strides, or so it seems to me, even while just sitting still. I often find myself when I am in the presence of such irrational physicality thinking about fishing—even drinking—even though these are not experiences I generally value consciously.

When I am holding hands or driving or eating or breaking up with such a man, I can confusingly feel at once both the sometimes harsh, something endearing personality of my father resurrected from the oceanic depths of my soul as well as the attendant internalized homophobia trying to regress me violently into being a bitch for loving a masculine man. If fact, you can say that the soul figure may echo aspects of my father's fishy manner of loving and may be poisoned with traits that are not what you would call gay positive. In this way, it would be more accurate to term the inner figure a "soul complex" for the ways in which its own internalized homophobia has yet to be fully analyzed and worked through and thus rendered a more purely apprehended and loving figure. Another way of putting the problem is that the psyche is asking the ego and the soul-figure to go into a kind of couples counseling to work through the internal and unconscious domestic violence. Dialoguing with inner figures—what Jungian thought calls "active imagination"—stands as the fundamental intervention bridging the sightlessly violent gap between the ego and the unconscious and restoring masculine homosexual wholeness to the neurotic split effected by the repression, hatred and devaluing of homosexuality.

One way the unknowing pain of the unresolved father complex compels gay men to defensively act out is through idealizing a fantasized hot stud on the outside and then chasing or rejecting him (or both) in endless cycles of pursuer-distancer fun and games lacking a modicum of insight. However, if a person, either through broken-hearted fatigue or sudden illness or unprecedented intelligence, wakes up to how relationships fall into self-negating patterns, a new inner attitude can shine through the blind spots. A more loving and capacious homosexuality can come through encounter with what Jungians call the "shadow," and what we, in our community, can entitle, the "gay shadow," a personification of the hurt, crushed gay boy inside.

THE CONCEPT OF the shadow extends a helpful metaphor to every ethical person willing to take responsibility for the most inferior, hidden and deeply shameful aspects of personality. Humanity's current political/spiritual refusal to confront its shadow problem, according to Jungian psychology, renders so-called individuals into prehistoric barbarians pretending self-knowledge but really acting out from the blindly controlling group mind, a fascist situation in which inappropriate shadow feelings are managed through a rapacious and exploitative "us versus them" scapegoat mentality destroying the world's peoples and natural resources. Most of us are split into opposing halves not unlike Dr. Jekyll and Mr. Hyde. But yet, as "nice" people, we don't recognize this violence of the inner splitness until the shit hits the proverbial fan, such as in the form of a serious malady or break-up or breakdown or worse. This out-of-control and yet simultaneously repressive organization of personality, according to the Jungian world view, is speeding us as a people and a planet to the point of extinction.

One way of getting a handle on the gay shadow is to meditate on what transpires in unbridled romance and infatuation. When I fall in love, I become mad with need (which I try to hide) and return cinematically and operatically to my Oedipal crisis without being aware that I am doing so.

THE MAN I MIGHT BECOME

As if I were a five-year-old child all over again, I throw the great treasure of the soul figure inside my mind towards a "daddy" (no matter what the age) in a process called "projection." And since the projection is pretty much at full-throttle, I am left swimming about with little more than my woundedness, the effects of internalized homophobia, an assaulted and enraged self.

Regression to this anxiously-attached child who would rather cling for dear life to a violent father-substitute than try to stand on his own wobbly two feet provides me with three existential choices, if I would but face then: (1) murderously repress the feeling child; (2) identify with his hidden masochistic agenda and act it out; or (3) try to "partner the feelings" via a newly-developing sort of gay activist empathy. How, you ask, can this dynamic and historic gay love unfold? By way of a provisional answer, I will first tell an embarrassing story.

Shortly after the breakup described above, I found myself jerking off to the fantasy of my ex fucking his new boyfriend, while I looked on plaintively, the two of them literally getting off on purposely neglecting me. In this midst of the violent fantasy, it dawned on me that the childhood Oedipal triangle was taking place in my own erotic mind *right now*, with me as the little gay boy on the outside looking in, while my mother and father got it on—or, more likely, given my mother's frigidity, when my father and brother grew closer during my teenage years. Either way, I was always excluded, the odd man out.

Once I opened my eyes to how the fantasy was serving two purposes— leading me via an erotic dissociation from the true infantile source of my pain while also trying to return me symbolically to its shocking Oedipal Primal Scene—I snapped out of my delusional state. This is what I thought: *This is how I might have felt at the age of four, five and six when my dad repudiated the magical experience of homosexual incestuous love I projected onto him all the while preferring my mother or heterosexual brother.* This realization amounted to one of those decisive moments where I pledged to take over the job of parenting myself from my parental complexes—a pledge I would soon forget.

Having a more-loving paternal attitude gives me the choice of intervening on the fantasy and calling a truce between the bitch-boy and the sadistic father, and offers the opportunity of directly encountering powerful forces of oppression and freedom within my own psyche and working with them. The uncontainable feeling experience of the little gay boy is hard to tolerate, so acting out offers a weak and fragile personality a kind of temporary heroin to keep a wounded ego from its underlying feelings. But if I harness all my ego strength, I can cordon the gay boy off from internal hell and relate to his catastrophe with an unprecedented intensive care and thus strengthen him and my ego through a new kind of healing and empathic separation between ego and complex.

For help in this matter, I must silence if not crush my negative father complex, whom at his worst is a remorseless homophobe, and, at best, emerges as a containing figure promising me the precious secret inherent within incestuous homosexual libido. Additional help in fighting toxic shame comes from him his "son," a being who personifies "essentially the life-breath" of homosexual eros into "spatial and corporal form" organized along homosexual lines. He is available to me in the secret hiding place of my frozen heart, felt as "the source of life," "of all our good and hopeful flashes of insight," "the springs of life felt as a ghostly male lover, moving 'in the depths.'" I can make an alliance with this gay soul figure to help me struggle with annihilating toxic shame. The generative activity of gay soul making, however, will trigger my mother complex who inhabits a large part of my shadow. Fighting her regressive "comfort" amounts to a great challenge for many gay men, who often identify too much with their mothers at the expense of the getting in touch with the more intimidating masculine. However, if a strong gay activist ego attends to the inner feminine problem, she can emerge as a sisterly aid offering a gay-positive feeling relatedness to soothe and nurture a wounded inner gay boy. All the inner figures can help me in the process of drawing the boy, venting his feelings, witnessing his pain, screaming it out, and transforming his ancient hurt. This vision of gay erotic redemption and self-realization is what the father-son paper points to and what is sorely missing in gay life. "Individuation as gay," says the paper, "in essence, is a process of *gay soul making*, and through gay soul" the promise of homosexual self-realization "is made fully actual."

The inability or refusal on the part of our movement leaders to see gay liberation primarily as an effort to liberate the homosexual mind and to foster "the reclamation of gay soul and its making," in our relationships and in our aloneness and in our movement, it seems to me, stems from a violent, community-wide defense against feeling the painful truth of our unfinished family business, in particular (for us gay men) our unresolved relations to our father.

It is due to the current "soul-sickness" and lack of an introverted vision besieging our community, despite our significant political and cultural gains, that I draw the reader to the seminal statement made by the father-son paper. "In the development of gay male personality," says the paper, "initiation into the masculine by working-through the 'erotic problem' of homosexual romance enacts the redemption of the inevitably lost father of early childhood and leads to the androgyny of the Self." The ongoing process of gay-soul making intervenes in the visionless extroversion manipulating gay minds today and "liberates homosexual libido to follow its own course based on a homosexual archetype" of phallic masculinity, so that a gay man today can discover inside his own self-making mind "a homosexual father who is creative" and completely redemptive. With the partnership of our "soul-double" a gay man can "return to the primal wholeness of father-son union" and thereby "'win to immortality'" and reach towards "completion of his soul."

But embarking on the inwardly-directed path of coming out inside can be challenging, to say the least. My own internalized homophobia, for example, has stymied the writing of this paper in a hundred ways. I am sure its nefarious agendas are sabotaging gay liberation in a variety of fashions I still lack the eyes to see. But I would contend that there is a greater force behind homosexual alchemy than its opposing power. That psychic power, I'd propose, is our true "father," it is the purposive libidinal motor driving gay identity, the coming out process, gay liberation and ultimately the successive, transformational processes involved in the further stages of homosexual self-realization than those of which we currently can conceive. This "intelligent' dynamic has been fathering humanity (and in the case of Lesbians, dynamically mothering), since the dawn of historic time. It is awakening with increased intensity in those people called to proclaim a gay-identity in postmodern times.

In actual fact, through much of human history, homosexuality has been seen as the father of philosophy, democracy, free thought, creativity and social transformation. Plato espoused homosexual love as a superior form uniting the "heavenly" (i.e. psychological) form of marriage that fathers "children of the mind," thus setting the foundation for Walt Whitman's celebration of the "dear love of man for his comrade, the attraction of friend to friend" as the "base of all metaphysics" and the development of a true spiritual democracy. Harry Hay grounded his own efforts in these ideas to initiate a political movement based on the concept that gay people, in contrast to heteros, have the tendency to treat others like subjects like themselves (i.e., in an empathic or loving way) rather than as patriarchal paternal competitors and objects to dominate and kill, thereby modeling a new masculine attitude desperately needed by a violence wracked society.

These newly revealed barbaric times demonstrate what happens when bad heterosexist fathers rule the world and compel us gay people to an awesome challenge to transform the homophobic father inside of us through ongoing inner work. Our unique homosexual relationship to the erotic aspect of the gay soul figure—our father's "son"—provides us with a crucial edge in the task of transforming the duality of warring aggressors into a new transcendental psychological-political attitude, making us natural messengers for a vitally needed fathering attitude amidst the current decline of the decadently patriarchal social order. This is why we might consider taking the visionary call of gay love named by Plato, Whitman, Hay, and, now, Walker, to its next logical step: to confront the tyranny of our own inner father complexes, lift our own repression to engage the inner figures of gay psyche, and come out inside our own minds to further actualize the revolutionary potential of our ancient homosexual wisdom in today's world.

Perhaps homosexual love is meant to mirror the possibility of a loving relationship with one's own psychology, and the outer lover references an inner teacher and guide, our father's son. To bring this new understanding of the father-son wish-fulfillment as the royal road to political freedom to bear, then, we might question our outdated addiction to exclusively extroverted answers and instead begin the introverted effort to open up psychologically and confront Father (and the legacy of 1000 years of brutal homophobic hatred symbolized by his presence), We should do this not to demonize and destroy, but, through ongoing inner work informed by empathy and a gay fathering attitude, transform the ugliness of Father's rejection into the radiant power of gay spirit love that births an entirely new form of creative and empowering Gay Self. Through this modern form of homosexual alchemy—a political attitude that aims to defy the source of fascist thought via our unresolved father issues—a completely different alternative to the monumentally hubristic and unjust patriarchal epoch can finally take seed and grow.

ALEXANDER CHEE

Self-Quiz

After my father's death, eighteen years ago, my mother divided his things between my brother and me. My brother and I each got a watch. My brother got the cuff links, the fly-tying equipment, fishing rods, and guns, all of which fit him perfectly. What I got, what fit me perfectly, was a bit unnerving: the tailored suits and the handmade shoes. I remember when she suggested I try them on I had a premonition they would fit. I'd never worn anything tailored when I first tried the jackets, and so at first I thought they were too tight. When I looked in the mirror, though, I saw the suit fit me perfectly. I put on his evening opera coat over that, and the handmade shoes. I had the sensation of slipping into a space my father had left, but, too neatly, in a way that felt airless and shut out the distinctions between us. And, for that matter, I didn't want to fill his shoes and suits. I wanted him back, so he could do so.

Whenever I moved, I brought them with me, for years. I wore the shoes tentatively but took the unopened bags of suits from apartment to apartment. And the times I wore the shoes, I usually ran home to take them off, frightened by how I could feel the way he walked, walking through me, the print of his steps in the concavities of the shoes, the ways they'd worn. It felt like summoning him too closely, almost an act of necromancy. Wearing his shoes seemed unlikely to help him to rest or me to move on, and so I stopped.

Later that same year, I went to Korea to visit our family there, on a pilgrimage to the family shrine. Everywhere I went, people I'd never met wept on seeing me and said I was the image of my father.

I DIDN'T SEE it then. Not for years. But over time the resemblance has increased, externally and internally, until I couldn't deny it: On a visit to my mother's sister several years ago, when I was procrastinating with my writing, I reorganized her bulging pantry and made a list of things she purchased repeatedly because she couldn't find them on her disordered shelves: dried bulk basil and cinnamon, lard, microwave popcorn, herbal tea. Afterward, my aunt called my mother, amazed at how I had repeated an act my father had done for her nearly two decades before.

AT A RECENT panel discussion of Asian American men and masculinity, I was the only one of nine panelists who had a positive male role model in my life. My father: the teenage tae kwon do champion, rocket engineer, oceanographer, deep-sea diver, college Rugby captain, my dad. I have a photo of him that I love, taken during a martial arts demonstration, flying through the air, hands and feet both forward, a deadly human horseshoe, all focus. On either side of him are two students each holding the boards that are splitting against his feet. Precision, applied force, this was my father: Life was targets, force directed at the place it would have an effect and nowhere else. Aim was only economy. He had trained hard, starting as a child, until he could run on his bare feet in snow, do push-ups on his fingertips and break bricks with his hands. And so when, at the age of forty-one, he was in a head-on car collision in the middle of a winter storm, he survived. Although the driver of the car he was in was injured less severely, he died and my father lived, his doctors disbelieving, but not any more than he when he awoke from a four-month-long coma to find himself trapped, paralyzed, all down the left side of his body.

We would read to him daily during his coma, at the urging of his doctors, to lead him out of himself and into consciousness, as if his head were a forest he was lost in. He dreamed the whole time of his accident, and remembered it all too clearly. Shortly after his waking, my mother and I walked him in his wheelchair. It was a cold April day and my mother walked ahead as I pushed him from behind, a blanket over his legs. My father gathered everything in himself then and very clearly asked why my mother had let him live. And everything in my world began to change.

My father's body's neocortical will to live was larger than his desire to live, and for the three years that he survived after his accident he was alternately bitter and depressed. While occasionally he would make small gains, he would return always to his suicidal despondency. My mother had been asked by the doctors, that awful first night, about whether to perform the experimental procedure that saved him, and my mother, tutored in my father's aim, said yes. Now, alive, he was caught in mid-flight inside the broken cage of his body. The night he finally died of complications from his injuries, I remember, it was snowing, and I felt him slipping through the air, continuing on his way.

My mother was shattered. I watched, frightened, as the years after his death passed and she went from first working every extra hour to avoid her empty bed, to moving away from Maine, where her family had been, for more than three hundred years, on the same farm. She and my father had been lovers, best friends, business partners, co-parents, and co-conspirators, had gone against the wishes of both their very old families from two very different countries and married. Both their fathers skipped the ceremony in protest, both were eventually won over by the depth of their love for each other, and the commitment they showed to me and my siblings. My mother spent the first three years of my life in Korea with her in-laws, the only blonde there for miles, in 1967. My father was the one who couldn't walk, but she was broken, too. And I wandered the ruin of it all again and again, moving her first out of the house we'd shared with him, then to another, and another, selling or storing the furniture, the photos, the South Pacific carved wooden fish, the hundred relics, things that had once been memories of love now made into memories of what was lost.

THREE YEARS AGO my sister married and my mother remarried and my brother became engaged. And so a couple of years ago I became serious about "finding a husband," in the way of someone who actually doesn't know what it will take and who will probably fail—a woman's magazine sort of way. I even read them for clues, bought books about gay relationships, took self-quiz after self-quiz and tried to accumulate information. I made a list of attributes I was looking for and of things I wouldn't accept. I went on dates that were more like interviews and even dated men I had no physical attraction to, in the hopes that it would come later. Prior to this, I'd had a series of bad relationships with men either already involved with other people or unavailable because of past emotional damage from long bad relationships with other people. First on my list of rejected attributes: being in or just out of a relationship.

And then I met someone and fell in love, someone who had just gotten out of a relationship but met all the other criteria, and to whom I was overwhelmingly attracted. I felt I'd be missing something if I let him go. I allowed myself to be reassured by him that he was serious about me, and so we were together nearly a year, during which time we struggled with that one thing I'd let slide, which turned out to be a room inside his mind full of the unacknowledged accumulated injuries from everyone who'd come before me. He had let it all sit, untouched. In the course of the year, I watched as everyone else in his life found themselves shut out and then eventually let back in, and then, within the week I recognized this pattern, he left me, with very little ceremony and no discussion, on an April afternoon.

I realized, in the days after, that I had assumed I was different. I let myself know I wasn't. I found myself, in the first month, whether I was at work or out with friends, having to run into the bathroom to burst into tears, and sometimes wouldn't make it in time. I had silent dreams, apparently a symptom of nervous shock. I began going to yoga classes, eventually every day, rigorous Ashtanga classes that left me sweating, empty and light at the end. And as I lay in what's called final relaxation pose, or corpse pose, on my back on that yoga mat in my lower Broadway classroom, eyes closed, room silent, I heard something very disturbing in the quiet early dark. I heard someone screaming for help—inside me.

My friends were dumbstruck and soon worried. The devastation I felt outweighed the event by so much that I was left with no choice but to look past the situation, to whatever it was that lay in me. Why was I screaming for help, for myself, from myself, inside? The experience always left me shaken but I continued with the classes, which were transforming my physical health. I wrote long, angry, sad letters to my ex and didn't send them, and eventually concluded I had to be projecting or transferring something onto him. I tried a variation on an exercise I'd learned in college, a racism exercise, where you look at someone and change his race and ask yourself how you feel about him. I took one of the things I'd written to him and changed the pronoun from *you* to *I*. As in, from *You are shut down*, to *I am shut down*. *You took advantage of me* to *I took advantage of me*. *You live isolated from love* to *I live isolated from love*.

I stared at the odd jackpot under my pen and remembered something he'd said to me near the end. I feel like we're right on top of each other's issues, he had said. I feel like that's why we fight. And, we had fought, regularly, but, I had thought, because it mattered. A strange light seemed to emanate from that notebook page across the days of the previous year with him.

I then thought back to the list of attributes and recalled one item that had, in retrospect, made me laugh—that this particular ex had reminded me of my mother, and that I had decided this was a good thing. But it wasn't my mother he reminded me of, at the unconscious level, I saw some months after this exercise. All my math was wrong. I had the wrong parent in the equation.

IN THE TAE kwon do demonstration photograph of my father, his face is partly visible but his legs in his *gi* are the most visible, and are the exact image of my legs. My sister, looking at the photo, marveled at it. Those are your legs, she said.

I think of those legs quite a bit when I look down at my own. My dad and I used to compete at swimming, racing each other in fifty-yard sprints. I remember when I was beginning to win. It was in the months before his accident. I'd been swimming competitively, and at age thirteen regularly swam miles a day. We had two types of contests, one above the water and one under, and I don't know if I was winning because he was slowing down or I was speeding up. His body seemed as tough as ever. But it was a significant contest to me because of how he had taken me out of tae kwon do lessons a few years before. He'd pulled me out, saying he didn't like the instructor's style. No discussion. I didn't know what to think of it at the time but trusted that my father knew what he was talking about. At the time, if I ever worried about not knowing the physical discipline my father had mastered, I simply thought of myself as unequal to it, and unequal to him.

Now I do know why he removed me: Tae kwon do isn't just a martial art, it's an embodied history of the Korean people, and this wasn't what I was being taught. All the forms of tae kwon do are organized into *hyung*s, patterns of fighting that are named after figures in Korean history, an important battle or place or general. For instance, the first *hyung* is called Chon-Ji, and refers to the sacred mountain Paektu, the birthplace of the Korean people. The second is Dan Gun, and refers to the mythological first Korean. In training in it, you become a fighting history, protecting yourself and the culture at the same time. None of that was being taught to me. I learned it only recently, in doing research for my next novel.

Instead, what my father told me that day as I left the martial arts studio for the last time was something that seemed innocuous then but that has grown in force to stand as the single guiding moral force of my existence: The best fighter never fights. He always finds another way. This was the road he set me on after he took me out of class. As I now swing my body in and out of the different yoga *asana*s, the patterns in which yoga is studied, I think of that now and then, and of him. One of the precepts in yoga is nonviolence, and it begins, for me, by not hurting myself. Violence is the observable child of unanswered pain, a connection made by thinkers as varied as Simone Weil, Thich Nhat Hahn, and Adrienne Rich. What I saw in my notebook that day was that the struggle I had engaged in with my last boyfriend was in part about us, but came in part because I had someone screaming inside me for my attention, who turned out to be me.

That summer after the breakup I went to two different yoga retreats and looked around inside for clues. In the woods around the Buddhist temple in upstate New York I ate vegetarian meals and did yoga twice a day. I tried to find compassion for my ex and was still failing, and then I began to understand what compassion actually was. It started with admitting to yourself all of what you felt. I couldn't feel compassion for him, anyone, until I had some for me. I had been struggling through these yoga classes, fighting the limits of my body and wearing myself out, and then in the middle of one of the classes I saw how by pushing my body so hard I wasn't actually admitting to myself what I knew: that I was in pain. That pushing so hard hurt. And that pushing hard was weakness, not strength, if it meant denying what I felt.

When I came out of those woods, I finally took that mythic time off from dating mentioned in some of those women's magazines, determined to be alone until I understood what I had seen: that I hadn't really let myself grieve for my father. The pain I was now feeling was that pain. In psychology it's called transference experience. The power of what I felt for my ex was not entirely dishonest: He was a genuinely good person, with some of the best qualities I'd ever found in another man. But in the time I knew him, he went from being like my father before the accident to being like him afterward, at an emotional level. He'd left a job he hated with a lifestyle he enjoyed and headed to remote places to look for a sense of meaning in his life, and returned, with few answers. The struggle proved too much for him, and in the end he returned to a job not very different from the one he'd left, and turned his back on everything he'd tried to welcome before. Including me.

My previous serious exes had also been like this: men who were shut down, wanting out of an emotional paralysis, depressed and hopeless. Point me to the saddest boy in the room, I used to joke with my friends. I wanted to fix and heal them, instead of me, and this was because inside me was an emotional charge I'd decided not to face back then at age sixteen. With my father, I'd set a task for myself above the capacity of a love expressed for another. I know now love's work is human, earthly, made of things people can do with and for each other and for themselves. And I didn't think much of that work for years, because what I wanted then was for it to be magic: to heal the sick, bring back the dead, a spell to storm heaven for my father's return.

Now I know: I am the way my father returns, am that spell I sought, the DNA/RNA that began with my birth. Each day my father's return deepens, and my heart also. All this time I had been asking love to do all that it could not do, had been running after people, trying to press my wounded heart to theirs. It was no surprise that it hadn't brought anyone any healing.

I am dating again. And as I do I see the pattern that kept me cycling through one broken man after another. I see it, as if it's a *hyung* in a personal tae kwon do, with each new insight named after the men in my life, starting with my dad. The lessons come at odd times, but they arrive when needed, and I feel myself avoiding previous mistakes, these new men flying past me now. I meet men full of problems, but now I don't date them. Sometimes I wonder if I will find a lover, but I don't worry too much about it. I am on the journey my father made for me, on these legs that look like his legs. And he found my mother with his legs, a woman with an extraordinary capacity for love, and, with her, broke with tradition, marrying across the racial boundaries that existed in his family and hers at the time they met. Boundaries that had been legislated in the state of California, where they found each other, up until a few years before their marriage. My ability to acknowledge my own love for men is the child of that radical love, and so I don't worry about it anymore. It's in the next pattern, ahead of me.

DANIEL MENDELSOHN

Paternities.

Until 1970 my father doggedly kept—and kept repairing—the 1957 Chevy Bel Air that was his first car. It was black and silver, and had fins. This car was always up on concrete blocks in our garage, bleeding a dark and satisfyingly shiny pool of oil that was to leave a permanent stain on the floor, which my mother tried for a long time to obliterate with jets of water from a hose, and if you ask me what visual memory I retain of my father in the 1960s I will tell you that I remember parts of his body—arms and legs sticking out from under this recalcitrant automobile—but no head, which is strange for me now since my father is a scientist, very cerebral, a great problem solver and dogged crossword puzzler, and as he has gotten older he seems to be becoming all head, the way babies do. (Like Rose, the mother of the child I have tied my life to, my father is a mathematician by training, and I am sure this has something to do with my connection to Rose—as if I, who have little sense of the practical, of the way things add up, instinctively attach myself to those who know how things work, how to make things.) Like a tangle of computer cords, the veins at my father's temples stand out from his flesh, pulsing with the data they carry to his brain.

As a child I hated the car, since my father's refusal to give up on it meant that we wouldn't have a new and more attractive one, like the ones that appeared every year on the driveway of our neighbor, who was (I knew from my parents' whispered conversations) a vice president of something. At the time, and a long while afterwards, I ascribed my father's persistence with this old Chevrolet to a miserliness that even then shamed me, my mother's child and the heir to her family's grandiosity and avidly curated sense of noblesse oblige, left over from a lost life in a dead empire; but I now see this is wrong. My father is, after all, someone who knows how numbers work, sees rigidly ordered connections between things in a discipline that, he insists to us, who do not believe him, is ultimately an aesthetic one; and I think his refusal to give up on things—his various cars, the Friday *New York Times* crossword puzzle, my mother, us—stems from a need to believe in the orderliness of things, as if any thing or person were merely the sum of its component parts, which, if you could only find the instructions, the theorem, you could identify, remove, fix, clean, and finally reassemble to create a better and more enduring whole. This is why I can still conjure the muffled sound of his voice, gruff with the effort of staving off inevitable failure, as he asks my older brother for some tool or another, and I can still see a grease-blotched arm, hairy and threatening to me, thrust out to receive it. A hierarchy of status and taste is already in place among us children, and I am never asked to hand him tools. Instead, I help my mother fold laundry as she watches Bette Davis movies, mouthing the dialogue to herself a moment before the characters utter it.

When my father drove this car, or any of his subsequent cars, it was his shoulder that would catch your attention, since it was the only part of his body that moved. My father drives with the severe concentration of the intolerant, as though the grim force of his own intellect were keeping those other, less alert, more foolish people from driving off the road and into one another, or us. His face, while he drives, registers little more than a screwed-up frown. But it is his right shoulder that moves, every now and then, suddenly upwards, in a kind of tortured shrug, as though he'd been trying to solve something while driving, some crucial question about the direction that his car or his life was taking, and had given up.

In the early 1970s, after the Bel Air is finally hauled off to the town dump and replaced by a flimsy British car whose interior panels start falling off soon after he buys it, my father starts building colonial furniture from kits. These kits arrive by United Parcel or APA in confusingly small boxes, and the wood, when he carefully pulls it out of the boxes, smells clean. In the garage, which is empty now except for the oil stain, newspapers are spread on the floor where my father assembles these kits, a process that inevitably culminates in the weaving of straw seats, a process he clearly hates not because it is difficult—he enjoys difficulty, since it justifies his flinty brand of stoicism—but because the instructions are inadequate and leave him confused and angry. "There is no way that this piece is supposed to reach *that* corner," he would snarl, tugging at a piece of straw and glaring at the instructions, beads of perspiration standing out from his smooth bald pate like condensation on a cold glass. As often as not he is wrong, and has merely misread the instructions, but he will not admit this; as often as not he ends up inventing his own weave, which I suspect makes him happier anyway. Nearly all of the woven rush seats on the chairs he has built have an oddly shaped, small but noticeable hole in the center, the irreducible trapezoidal shape of my father's obstinacy, which you won't find on the store-bought versions.

The furniture phase culminates in the construction of a harpsichord in 1975, which, after months of laborious construction by my father, my mother, much to everyone's dismay, decides to paint blue. Blue is my mother's color. Her house is filled with blue things: blue glass, blue china, blue Delft ashtrays; huge blue glass vases are stacked in front of her spotless windows; she has lined the shelves on which she keeps her immaculate unused dishes with blue adhesive-backed plastic. Blue faience beads hang at her ears, the Museum Shop necklaces around her throat are as likely as not to have some bit of blue enamelwork. Whenever I return from trips abroad I am sure to bring her something blue, a piece of glass or ceramic that disappears into her passion. Her eyes are blue, as are mine, as were her father's.

So when my mother announces that she will paint the harpsichord blue—an absurd, a willfully wrong color for a musical instrument—no one argues. My father's province is construction; my mother's—and, by tacit and uncomprehending agreements on everyone's part, mine—is decoration. It is a paradigm I still find hard to discard. In anticipation of decorating the harpsichord's soundboard, I have spent a few months reading huge illustrated books about ancient instruments. When the time comes, I begin by tracing the outlines of delicate flowers on the soundboard in a wash of turpentine and raw umber. But at a certain point not long after I've begun to paint, my mother, who had studied art in high school and who had been an accomplished draftsman herself before marrying, decides that my flowers aren't vigorous enough, and adds her own impasto zinnias and dahlias to my weary blooms. (This is before she decides to paint the outside of the instrument blue; I think my weakness emboldens her, gives her the courage to demand more blue.) This curious hybrid of styles can still be seen on the harpsichord, which stands in my parents living room, pristine and unplayed throughout the twenty years since my older brother, the pianist, went to college.

I think it is soon after the harpsichord is finished that my father turns his attention to barbecues, perhaps because they need no decoration. He will spend the next few summers designing and constructing a bizarre series of Rube Goldberg-esque funnels meant to hold lighted charcoal briquettes. "It's a simple law of physics," I remember him saying; the words make an impression on me, perhaps because the idea of physics, or of simple laws, terrifies me. "They'll burn hotter and faster if they're all bunched together. *Then* you spread them out." When my father makes pronouncements like this, about lighting barbecues or bundling newspapers or driving on expressways, it is with a tight self-satisfied flourish, as though each one were a point won in the silent and ongoing argument that is his life.

Some of the funnels my father makes are made from old cans of chlorine we'd accumulated when we had an above-ground pool. The pool no longer exists: we'd shared it with the neighbors whom my mother has stopped speaking to, and the pool is one of the more visible casualties of that rupture. My father makes vents in the sides of these drums with an old can opener, from the inside out, and the pointed peels of metal sticking out give them a sinister, weaponlike look. My mother, who fears chemicals and has regular conversations with the people at the poison control center, is convinced that the funnels will explode. But they don't. I think my father secretly relishes her fear; it fuels his eroded sense of authority. I can still see his face, eyes screwed up in concentration, as he watches the flames shoot out from the tops of the funnels, his eyes following the charcoal dust and burnt paint as they float upwards. The charcoal is, as he promised, very hot; the flames at the center are a pure liquid blue. My father stares into the fire. He is pleased with what he has made.

THE BODIES YOU see up and down the streets of Chelsea, on Eighth Avenue, parading at the Intersection of Desire, are the result of many hours of hard work, but it would be a mistake to say that they are all the same: there are swimmer's bodies, which are "defined" but not huge; gym bodies, which are big, but still reasonably proportionate; and body-builder bodies, which for all their extremeness always seem oddly unfinished, as though the clearly demarcated hunks of muscle were waiting to be made into something else—dog food, perhaps, or sausage. Looking at them, you can't help sensing the effort that went into them. There are other bodies, though, that you occasionally notice as well. These are the bodies of young men that have begun to fail. The skin on these bodies, which is the same wizened orange that my great-aunts in Miami Beach had, seems eager to part company from the flesh beneath; the skulls are already visible beneath the faces; the hair is lank and thin. The limbs are, anomalously, covered. As different from each other as they are, though, both kinds of bodies seem more generic, somehow, than the kind of body you used to think of as being "normal": they have come to belong to the realm of the symbolic. When you see them, you're less apt to think of the people—or, rather, the personalities—that inhabit them than you are to think "gym" or "sex" or "AIDS." It's as if the extremes of strength or disease have squeezed out any space for the particularity of personality, or history. All that's left is bulk or wasting, excess or lack.

I have lived here so long that it seems odd that, when I think of a "normal" male body, I think of my father's body as I used to see it when I was a child: neither tall nor short; less attractive than functional; and, at least on weekends, often covered with a mixture of sweat and motor oil, or sweat and grass cuttings, sweat and sawdust, sweat and charcoal dust, or just sweat. It would never have occurred to me to describe it; it merely was. The well-muscled gay man's body today seems, by contrast, like something decorated, embellished. This is ironic because, in a way, this body seems clearly to be an attempt at recuperating masculinity, a visible sign of adequacy and power and legitimacy to be displayed proudly by those who, as children, may have been taunted for being too thin or too weak or too clumsy. Once, when I was about eleven, on a very hot summer day, I was ordered to help my father cut some shrubbery. I couldn't lift the electric hedge cutter; misinterpreting his laughter—or perhaps not—I was humiliated. I waited till he'd gone in to eat something, and then, with a pair of clippers, stood in the sun and hacked away until I fainted from dehydration. Not long after I secretly bought something advertised as a chest expander, and I worked with it at night, with the door shut carefully behind me.

Gay men's bodies are the bodies of men who do not want to feel shame before their fathers. But there is no way to get one of these bodies without assiduously working at it, which is of course something our fathers would never have done.

JOSEPH HANSEN

Flapjacks

I am in my eightieth year, my father has been dead for half a century, and this means that what you are about to read comes not just from another time but from another world. In that world no one thought coming out was a moral imperative. Coming out was tantamount to self-destruction. And for only one reason would you come out to your father: Because you hated him and wanted to give him pain. Two or three young fellows I knew had done this, it had worked, and they were smug about it. My father never hurt me, I never wanted to hurt him, and before fate let me come out to all the world, he was long dead. He would have been embarrassed by the novels and stories that earned me my small measure of fame. They are almost all about gay men and women and the lives they lead. For my take on how he would have reacted, look into my books. None of the father figures you'll find there—insurance tycoon Carl Brandstetter in *Fadeout* and *Death Claims*; Whit Miller's jokey dad in *A Smile in His Lifetime*; the stern attorney sire of actor Oliver Jewett in *Job's*

Year; the droll musician Frank Reed in *Jack of Hearts* and *Living Upstairs* —is comfortable that his son is gay. That was how the world was then. I spent a lifetime writing books I hoped might change that.

MY FATHER HAD a sweet tenor voice. "It was music that brought us together," my mother used to say. She was remembering a spring Sunday in 1905, when she was eighteen and Henry Hansen was twenty. Why Alma Rosebrock, of Owatonna, Minnesota, was visiting Des Moines, Iowa, and how she came to be seated in the parlor of Bertha M. Hansen I can't say. But that parlor also held a piano, and Alma Rosebrock played the piano beautifully, so that at some point her hostess rose, went to the kitchen, and called out the back door in her Norwegian accent, "Henry, come in here, now. We are going to have a little art." To which Henry replied, "Aw, Mama, I've got Art out here." He was tossing a baseball around with a friend, Art Sutherland. But his tiny mother was not to be denied. He came inside and sang while Alma accompanied him. They were to go on doing this for another fifty years.

Sports meant as much to him as music. My mother kept a sepia photograph of him at maybe eighteen and no more than five feet five inches tall, running with a football. The uniform was quaint. But it can't have been from any school. He'd left school at eleven. His father had died in a blizzard in 1888, and Henry had to help his brothers put food on the table. Jumping ahead to the 1920s, and a couple of degrees west to South Dakota—my brother, Bob, nine years my senior, was keen on sports and played them all to a degree that almost killed him, since he, too, was only five feet five.

Just when it dawned on our dad that sports held no charm for me I don't rightly know. If a ball came toward me, I would shut my eyes, hold up both hands, and the ball would hit me in the face. I swung a bat with equal success. I threw without accuracy and never far. But I suspect he at last got the message on the day he tried to teach me to swim. My screams of panic must have roused the whooping cranes from the sand hills of Nebraska. Since he loved swimming, my reaction must have puzzled and saddened him, but he never bothered me with it again. My brother did, my mother did, but never my Dad. For him, being a good father didn't entail tormenting his offspring.

We rented a spindly house across from a fly-blown livery stable in Aberdeen, a South Dakota railroad town surrounded by farms that, in 1923, when I was born, were producing bumper crops of wheat, corn, and hogs. My father, with a partner, operated the H&H Bootery, a shoe store on Main Street. And business was good. We had enough to eat, beds to sleep in, and clothes to wear—shoes in particular. We even had a wind-up phonograph and records by John McCormack. But we had no car, our water came from a hand pump, and the kitchen range burned wood. He wanted a better life for my mother, my sister, my brother, and me.

The stock market in those years was climbing up and up. All over America, in small towns as well as in cities, plain folk, who until then had regarded Wall Street as a rich man's preserve, took their savings out of the bank and bought stocks. Henry Hansen had no money in a bank or anywhere else. But there were other ways to get in on the action. You could go into business without investing a dime. How he learned about this, I don't know. But it was not his lucky day.

He left his partner and on his own opened a small store down a side street. The Brown Shoe Company of St. Louis supplied the stock. All he had to do was pay the rent, sell the shoes, send Brown its cut, and keep the rest of the money for himself. I was five years old, so all of this passed right over my head. Except Buster Brown. This comic strip smarty, with his bulldog, Tige, was the Brown Shoe Company's logo. Which meant that twice a year, at the bidding of Brown's publicity division, a midget appeared in Aberdeen with a bulldog in tow. And since my dad was the Buster Brown dealer, the midget came to dinner at our house. Not in the red knee pants and Tam o' Shanter Buster wore in the Sunday funnies, but in a regular suit. Naturally, these tiny men, hardly bigger than myself, charmed me.

When we got a car, a spiffy black and tan Jewett with wood-spoke wheels, Dad liked to take long drives on Sunday afternoons. And if, by chance, beyond the alfalfa fields arose a Ferris wheel and a cluster of faded carnival tents, he perked up, and headed straight for it. Before the dust settled, he was out of the car, asking directions from the nearest roustabout or freak, and with me by the hand, flinging aside a tent flap, and in the hot, sawdust dimness inside, among clowns and waddling dwarfs, tiny dogs in pointed hats, baby pigs in nighties, locating one, or, with luck, more than one, of the little men who had graced our table as Buster Brown. These reunions were always cheerful and garrulous.

The shoe store never earned enough money for my father to buy a house. But he got one, all the same. In 1928. So new it still smelled of pine sap. Out on the edge of town, across from an apple orchard, an improvement on the pungent stables we'd faced at the old place. It seems one of my father's brothers had formed a company, in those heady, high-rolling times, that was buying lots and slapping up houses helter-skelter all over the West. And he made my Dad a gift of this one, on a corner lot, complete with two big cottonwood trees. All Dad had to do was pay the taxes.

And so began our fifteen minutes of prosperity. My mother bought ghastly new furniture, all mohair and fringes. A piano. A radio that stood on a green woven grass carpet among wicker chairs on what we called the sunporch. Outfitted in new clothes, she widened her circle of women friends, so that her name began appearing in the Aberdeen *Evening News*—Mrs. H. H. Hansen (married women in that place and time were strictly adjuncts). The closet of my grown-up sister's pink bedroom held silly shoes and pretty frocks. My brother's room, which always smelled of Absorbine Jr., and which I shared, no doubt to his joy, was strewn with baseball gloves and football jerseys. I loved dressing up and making believe, and was given a cowboy outfit, a pirate outfit, and a drum major's uniform with a busby fashioned from an old caracul coat and a Quaker oats box. At his workbench in the basement, my father built me a little drop-leaf desk with a bluebird painted on the front.

What did my father have? Gray suits and a felt hat for winter, a lightweight white suit (he called it his ice-cream suit) and a straw boater for summer. Two-tone shoes. White or pale striped shirts with detachable collars and cuffs that fastened with little gold studs. Nondescript neckties. Silk socks. A gold wedding band. A ring set with a bloodstone (black with little veins of red). A stout orange and black fountain pen. A slim pearl-handled penknife to trim his nails. I loved his smell, a blend of talcum powder, cigars, and peppermint. In the way of possessions, he didn't have much. He was the kind of father who when there was chicken for Sunday dinner served the leg parts to my brother and me, the breast to my mother and sister, and claimed he preferred the back.

HALF A DAY'S drive from Aberdeen, the James River (my dad called it the Jim) meandered toward the wide Missouri. Somebody with more enterprise than sense had built a few flimsy cabins there among the stream-side cottonwoods and willows, and with a little money to hand, for a couple of summer weeks, we rented one of these, usually sharing with another family. I hated the heat, the mosquitoes, the bloodsuckers in the stagnant elbows of the river. Seeing that I wasn't happy, my father, bless him, took me on walks. Just the two of us. Which was how I liked it best.

There were sparse woodlands of gnarled old tick-infested oaks. Red-wings whistled in a cattail marsh. And suddenly a blue heron (my dad called it a shitepoke) rose on stately wings and flapped lazily away over the treetops. I was awed. Crouching, my dad parted brittle wild grasses to show me a wonderful little plant with small brown paper lanterns that, when you tore them open, revealed yellow fruits he called chokecherries. Very tart, they were. Half hidden in the grasses also were pasqueflowers and shy wild roses, wonderfully sweet to smell. We drank from a gushing artesian well, the water gaspingly cold, with a strong bright metallic taste the mouth never forgets.

Another time, among barren hills, at a sun-struck lake called Enemy Swim, he took me fishing in a leaky shiplap rowboat. But only once. I cried when I saw the shining fish he'd caught, gasping and flapping as they died at my feet. He'd brought along a little bamboo fishing pole just for me, so he must have been disappointed. But as with the swimming lesson, he never put me through that agony again.

IT WASN'T THE stock market crash of 1929 that ruined my father. It was the drought. In 1931, and the year that followed, and the year after that, the rich prairie topsoil got no rain. Grasshoppers swarmed by the millions to eat the shriveled crops. Winds picked up the topsoil and blew it away. Day after day, dust turned the sun to a red fireball. Cows died in fields of only dust. Farms died. And the banks that held the loans on those farms died also. Credit died. All over the Dakotas, Kansas, Nebraska, Oklahoma, businesses large and small went belly up. My father opened the Buster Brown shoe store every morning, and dusted off the stock, but no one came through the door. And soon the company sent a truck and hauled the shoes away.

My brother had a few dollars saved at a dime a week in a schoolboy bank account. This financed Bob's Fruit Stand. The new-built plywood hutch looked nice on its corner of fresh white gravel. Every day Bob and my Dad set out the stock in trade in bushel baskets there, and at sundown glumly stowed the baskets back inside. Nobody bought. I ate enough apricots and peaches, grapes and melons, bananas and tangerines that summer to ruin my digestion for life.

Then the plywood hutch vanished, and my father was out on the road, in the forlorn hope of trying to sell dress shirts to cracker-barrel stores in the little faded, no-hope towns scattered across the prairies. Within a few weeks, he arrived home late at night, dusty, weary, and thinner than I'd ever seen him. And the next morning the dealer came and towed the car away.

That was bad. But worse was to follow. The house was seized for back taxes. And suddenly we had no place to live. My father left to tramp the bleak streets of Minneapolis, looking for work. My brother hiked off, sleeping in barns and haystacks, hoping for some rinky-dink college to take him in on a scholarship. None did. He had the talent, in music, in drama, in sports—but not the grades. Nor did my father find work. He was fifty years old. For the few jobs to be had, younger men got hired. Which meant he sent us no money. Which meant my mother and I never stayed long in the spare rooms of any white-haired widow who took us in, and grocers started chasing me off when I said, "Charge it, please."

Somehow we survived until July 1933, when my father found a job and sent for us. It wasn't much of a job, and it didn't last long, and we were hardly settled into a couple of half-empty upstairs rooms before he lost the job and we had to take refuge under the roof of my mother's sister Anna. Minneapolis was hell for him, but it was good for me. An amazing place, a public library, became my second home. There were free symphony concerts for school kids.

My father's father had come to this country from Norway wanting to be an artist, had ended up a day laborer, spent his last pay packet getting roaring drunk, missed the bridge that would have taken him home through swirling snow to his wife and four little kids, and staggered down into the Des Moines River, where he froze to death at thirty-four. But even luckless fathers leave legacies, of talent, or unfulfilled ambition, or both. And I guess this must explain why, one startling day, my father took me with him on a streetcar downtown to the Walker Art Gallery.

No such place existed in Aberdeen. The glossy splendor of the massive old paintings in their gilded frames, row on row, in room after glorious room, left me big-eyed and breathless. Did my father teach me artists' names, the towns and times they lived in, their tricks with light and shadow, how to tell a Velásquez from a Rembrandt? I don't think so. I don't think he knew much more about such stuff than I did. But he taught me a lesson without which all the rest are nonsense—how simply and truly to look at a picture.

STILL, THE MOST amazing thing to happen in Minneapolis was that on Christmas morning, 1934, I mastered a sport. My father had a steady job now, stoking the furnace of a towering, stone-cold downtown church. We had our furniture back, including the piano, and were living in a decent apartment. This still didn't mean there was money to spare. And why my father would give a proven loser like me a pair of ice skates defied reason. But there they were under the tree with my name on the tag.

And soon there I was, wading through the snowdrifts of Powderhorn Park, bundled in sheepskin coat, muffler, knitted cap, to the edge of the frozen lake. There he sat me down on a log, removed my boots, put the skates on me, and walked off across the ice. My heart thumped. What was happening? Was he abandoning me here? But no. At last he stopped, turned, and called out to me to stand up and skate to him.

"I don't know how," I wailed.

"It's just like walking," he shouted. "Stand up and walk."

I stood up, took a step, and landed on my butt.

"You're not hurt," he called. "Get up and try again."

I did. And this time I did not fall. This time I walked. And after a few shaky steps, I skated. Why or how I can't say, but as jumping hurdles and shooting baskets had come naturally to my brother, so skating came naturally to me. And all that winter, and all the following winter, skating was my passion. I lived for it. And if my joy in it eased my father's misgivings about my daintiness, it eased mine as well. Bullies, who had ragged and punched me at school, I could skate rings around on the ice, and they left me alone after that.

WHEN SCHOOL LET out in 1936, I was sent without explanation to stay with relatives in Duluth. I was uneasy. And my uneasiness grew when, after a month, they sent me back, not to Minneapolis, but downstate to Owatonna, my mother's little tree-shady hometown, where my aunt Edie still lived. There my dad met my bus, an unfamiliar dad in a purple nylon polo shirt. He led me to a regal old Marmon automobile. Where had this come from? He and Mom had sold the furniture to pay for it. My sister had invited us to come live with her and her husband in California. This was too much for me. In my aunt Edie's bathroom that always smelled of lavender soap, I threw up. And I went on throwing up for days.

The summer of 1936 set records for heat that still stand. But the shortest, and hence the only, route for us was through the sun-blasted Southwest. Bob drove all the way. My father never took the wheel. This wasn't my dad. He loved to drive long country miles. I see now what I was too young to see then—it was a silent protest. He did not want to make this trip. He'd been argued into it. Beside him on the backseat my mother moaned and sweated. I'd never seen her so miserable. Nights we slept, all of us in one room, in shacky cabins, or half-ruined old hotels. What the others ate on that trip I don't remember. I ate ice cream, the only food I didn't throw up.

LOUISE AND JOE Hubbard lived on ten acres of dying fruit trees at the foot of hulking brown mountains above Pasadena. At night, deer came down and peered in the windows. The house was no more than one long room, a kitchen, a bathroom, and a screened porch. Two daybeds stood on the porch. My parents slept on one, my brother and I on the other. Louise and Joe slept on a sofa-bed in the living room.

She worked in a bank, he in a steel mill. In her pretty head, it wouldn't be long before Dad and Bob found work. Meantime, bringing us all together under one roof made sense. But my mother loathed Joe Hubbard. He was coarse, he was common, he drank, and he was too old for Louise. That he loved her so much he'd opened his house to her whole ragtag family meant nothing. There were bitter quarrels.

My dad looked for work, week after week, but without luck. My brother, trying to patch up his education, registered at the local junior college and took part-time jobs. But these didn't pay his keep, let alone the keep of his parents and kid brother. So Joe Hubbard found him a full-time job at the steel plant. Joe was in the right, of course, but Bob wasn't about to slave his life away in that blast-furnace hell. There was a shouting match, and Joe threw him out. Plainly, he was fed up with Louise's dream. Living off the man's charity had always galled my father, and the next morning, in fog and cold and drizzle, we climbed into the creaky old Marmon, and left that place for the last time.

THE SUMMER AMONG Joe's beehives under the scraggy fruit trees had been lonely for me, and my dad, combing the classified ads as he did every morning, came across a notice that boys were wanted for a church choir. Like his other seedlings, I had always sung. So, figuring it would give me something to do, he took me there. The cheery, handsome choirmaster took a fancy to me. Soon, I was sleeping over at his house on weekends. He played a lot of piano recitals at the homes of wealthy parishioners, which meant I was sometimes alone. I didn't mind. In his room at the back of the house, stretched out across the sunny bed, I spent hours poring over his stacks of art books, blissfully happy. His record collection was enormous, and when he found time, he played symphonies and operas for me. At Christmas he heaped me with gifts. Convinced, who knows why, that I was a genius, he put me into a fancy private boys' school, where I failed at everything. If they'd offered a class in breathing, I'd have failed it.

We lived the rainy winter through in rooms of a wisteria-covered cottage rented out by a tiny old woman called Miss Criss. Paid for how? Maybe Dad sold the Marmon. Anyway, the money was soon gone, and we were sleeping catch as catch can in the houses of desperate widows again, met by my mother at a nearby church. My father took what he could get in the way of work, a day here, a day there. We ate oatmeal for breakfast, peanut butter for lunch, and Campbell's tomato soup for supper. The ritzy school, unable to wake me up, dropped me. The choirmaster, off in Rome studying Gregorian chant, had no comment. I started in a public school, made some new friends, and slowly woke up on my own.

Nineteen thirty-seven was the worst year yet for my dad. He was gray and quiet as a shadow, reading the paper, drinking coffee. I'm sure I chattered at him all the time, but if he spoke or smiled I don't think it was because he heard me. He certainly never joked now. I did my lessons (except arithmetic), drew pictures, tried to put the Psalms of David into modern English, sang in an all-boy staging of *Pinafore*, composed an operetta (well, the first page of an operetta), and wasted afternoons with my friends, playing back-porch poker, or knocking together go-carts out of orange crates and the wheels of discarded coaster-wagons.

Eventually I rebelled against arithmetic, and ended up in a different school where the subject was never mentioned, at least not to me. Here I began to act in plays and to write for the school paper. I won medals for acting, and a prize for a short story. My voice changed, ending my choirboy phase. Suddenly I was six feet tall, towering over my father. And sex, a subject I had cared about even less than arithmetic, began pestering me for attention. During all this, if I'd taken a moment to look around, I would have noticed that my father and I had drifted apart. I was too self-absorbed to look around.

TO PUT INTO a few words the years that followed is not easy. Who was going to look back at me from the mirror when I got up in the morning I never knew. Everything fascinated me. Everything bored me. I had no patience with things as they were. I was into religion one season, singing my head off for Jesus. The next I was feverishly trying to find a friend to jack off with. My academic classes droned and inched along. I skipped them for weeks at a time.

I wrote poems. I wrote plays. I had fun acting at the school radio station. And onstage. My grandfather's genes led me to a class in freehand drawing. At a rare rational moment, I decided a marketable skill might help me scratch out a living till I was acclaimed as a writer, and I took a course in touch typing. I wrote all the time for the school paper, but the minute I was offered an editorial post, I turned it down.

I read Thoreau's "Civil Disobedience" and Emerson's "Self Reliance," and grew ornerier than both sages put together. When I turned eighteen and the Army came after me, I told them I was homosexual. It was true. So it couldn't accept me. It was against its own rules. Now, such information was supposed to be secret. But some woman on the local draft board, moved by maternal feeling, patriotic fervor, spite, who knows?—rang up my mother and told her.

My father said nothing. He probably couldn't find the words. The subject was far outside his ambit. Could a man discuss this with another man, let alone his own son? But my mother raised instant hell and would not shut up. She even tried to beat me with a broom. Which made me laugh. Which made things worse. I stayed overnight on the butt-sprung sofa of a couple of young would-be writers I knew at school.

And next day, when my mother was out and my father was at work (by this time he'd been selling shoes for years at good, gray, Mather's department store), I collected my books, records, typewriter, and a few clothes, and headed for dowdy old Hollywood. There I got a bookstore job at eighteen dollars a week, paid seven to rent a room (bath down the hall), tacked a Van Gogh sunflower print up over the desk, and sat down to write a novel.

AFTER THAT, I seldom saw my father. I married, and when our baby was born, at my gentle wife's prompting I took the baby to see her grandparents. When she was a toddler, I took her more often, on the rattly old interurban bus, but my father wasn't often there, and things were always edgy between my mother and me.

She telephoned me when Dad got jaundice that wouldn't go away, and I went over and arranged for a doctor I'd known when we were both in school to come have a look. Diagnostics was his specialty. But it was too late. When surgeons cut my father open, they found pancreatic cancer they were no match for.

I went to see him in the hospital. His room was on the top floor with a wide window looking for miles over the orange groves and farmlands east of town. The sky was blue. He lay small and gray and old in the high white hospital bed.

"Beautiful view," I said.

"Yup," he said. "But I'd like it better if those doggone vultures would stop circling." And he laughed.

He died soon afterward. The year was 1954. He was seventy-one.

HOW AM I like him? I'm bald. Most of my life I was poor. It has been said that I am witty. He certainly was. He loved to sing, and so did I. From Christmas 1951 to Christmas 1953, I sang folk songs on the radio every week. I don't know how good he thought I was. He had high standards. But I'm pretty sure he listened. And I hope he wasn't ashamed. When I buckled down to painting for a while in the 1960s, I sold a couple of pictures, and I guess that would have pleased him, though my pictures are nothing like those he showed me so long ago at the Walker Art Gallery. He'd have called my pictures posters, and maybe they are.

While he couldn't have been proud of my books, it might have pleased him that his youngest son's name was known in London and Paris, Berlin, Rome, and Tokyo, and points between and beyond. Foreign places attracted him. During our brief prosperity, he bought a small globe of the world, and spent happy hours musing over it. But of course he never traveled. Only as far as Califonia. And once he got there, he often said he'd like to go back to Dakota. He missed the long summer twilights.

His finest quality was constancy. My mother could be difficult, sometimes downright impossible, yet he stuck with her, no matter what. She needed him more than he needed her. Though it may sometimes have seemed she was the strong one, he was the strong one. Even when his luck (or judgment) was at its worst, he hung in there doggedly, and did his best for us. He loved his children without question or reserve, cheering us on in whatever we chose to do, and keeping faith with us when life knocked us down. He knew how to love. He showed us how. Our marriages lasted for life. That was his best legacy.

But this is solemn stuff, and he was never solemn. Grim sometimes in the grim years, but never solemn. I'd rather close this remembrance with a moment from as far back as my memory reaches. We're alone in the sunshine of an early-morning kitchen. I sit giggling in my highchair, and my dad is at the stove, singing "Fiddle-dee-dee, fiddle-dee-dee, the fly has married the bumble-bee," taking nifty little Charlie Chaplin dance steps, and cooking flapjacks. Not ordinary, round flapjacks. Never. Each of these is shaped like a different animal, elephant, camel, giraffe. With raisins for eyes. I thought my dad was great then.

And I haven't changed my mind.

BRIAN MALLOY

Things I Never Told My Father.

In 1976 I attended my father's funeral. I was fifteen years old, dressed in my first suit. I remember that my girlfriend was there and that I drank a beer in front of my mother at the reception. The rest is just a blur.

Those of us who lost our fathers young will never know what it's like to test the bonds of family by coming out to Dad. So we use our imaginations to tell our fathers the truth about our lives. We play out little scenarios that usually end with a heart-wrenching coming to terms that permanently cements the bonds between father and son. I do this routinely myself, in spite of the fact that it's about a million-to-one shot that my father would have hugged me after I told him the news.

More likely, he would have threatened to put his foot up my ass.

He had talked about doing it often enough while I was growing up. My bad grades, sullen attitude and inability to see through a commitment of any kind left him so frustrated that he'd bark, "Brian, I'm gonna put my foot up your ass if you don't do as I say."

In reality, he did it only once and it took us both by surprise. I was eleven or twelve at the time and giving him some particularly nasty back-talk. Instead of scolding me, or giving me *the look*, he kicked me, right in the ass. He seemed as shocked as I was. Even though my father was a man of his word, neither of us actually believed that he would ever make good on this threat. I remember thinking at the time: *Jeez, he really did it. He really put his foot up my ass.*

It changed things, at least for a little while. I was nicer, more compli-ant. He was kinder and maybe a little scared by how angry I could make him. My ability to make him so mad that he lost control was one that my brother and sister didn't possess. It makes me wonder if he had seen the gay me coming even before I did. If I made him crazy not because I was a brat, but because he suspected my difference from day one.

Of course, I'll never have the opportunity to ask him what he thought. He's been my dead father now for twice as long as he was my live father. He's frozen in time and I'm frozen there along with him, my young, immature, self. Dad missed the graduations, the shaving lessons, the first time I ever drove a car. He wasn't there to yell at me when I came home drunk or reeking of weed. He never saw me in love. He didn't get the chance to watch me grow up and witness my becoming an adult male who can look after himself just fine, thank you very much.

I find myself looking at photographs whenever I try to piece together what kind of man my father was, when I wonder what kind of relation-ship we might have had if he were still alive. I've learned not to trust my memories entirely of our life together; I think it's human nature to fill in the gaps with some self-serving imaginings that create a new, more impressive history. So I try not to think about anything as I gaze at his image. I don't try to recall which year the picture was taken, or where we were living at the time or which grade I would have been in. I just look. In every photo I have, he's smiling, or there's a content expression on his face, one that assures me that whatever problems our family faced, he was the one who could fix them.

These are the only times—when it's late, my partner is asleep, and it's just me and my father's picture—that I talk to my dad. Even as I age, soon to be older than he ever had the chance to be, he will always be my sen-ior, the final word. I can't imagine having children as young as he did, I can't imagine carrying around the knowledge that I would have to leave them while still in my prime. How brutally unfair it must have seemed to him, to receive a death sentence in his forties. Of course, I can only appreciate this now that I am in my forties too.

I tell this man, a peer now, that I'm gay. The look on his face doesn't change. His expression remains confident, even in this unfamiliar territory. He's concerned that my sexual orientation is a liability waiting to be exploited by a mean world. I say to his photo, "It's not as awful as you think it is." He looks at me, all the while quietly deciding whether it will be his disapproval or his support that stands the best chance of straightening me out.

And that's when it hits me all over again, the realization that he will never know who I am any more than I will ever truly know who he was. We are outlanders to each other, and with the passing of each year, time moves my experience of having a father further into the past.

To discover what sort of relationship we may have had as I grew into adulthood, I have to look to my older brother, Tom, for clues. Tom had a full seven years more of opportunities to shock my father and test his parenting skills. A big test was Tom's hair, which he grew down to his shoulders. Dad chased him all through the house, yelling at him and his *goddamn hair*. But then Dad stopped, his face red, his breathing hard. He sat down. He said out loud: "That was ridiculous. I'm not doing that again."

And he never did.

Tom was stopped by the police twice when I was growing up. The first time, the cops took him down to the station. They called my father and ordered him to come and pick up his son. Is he drunk? my father asked. No. Is he high? Dad asked. No. Well, then, he told the officer, you will have to drive him back to his car so he can make his own way home.

The cop did as my father said.

The father of my brother's friend, however, went down to the station and ripped his son's license into little pieces. He then took him home and shaved his head (in those days long hair was reason enough for police to stop white males). My brother, on the other hand, got to keep his hair and, whenever he crossed paths with the cop who had hauled him in, the policeman would simply ask, "So, how's your dad?"

The next time Tom was stopped—and searched—he was again with a friend, although a different one. This friend, who had been driving the car when the sirens went off, had made the mistake of being black. When Tom and his friend showed up at our house, shaken up and more than a little pissed off, Dad took the friend aside and told him, "You shouldn't be seen with my son if you don't want trouble with the cops." The friend laughed and so did Dad. I think they both understood it was their only option.

After Dad's long and painful death, Tom became a much larger part of my life. He helped me pull myself together—I had convinced myself that I was such a rotten son that I had driven my father to an early grave. Tom was the one who taught me how to drive a car, how to shave. He took it upon himself to mentor me into the man he had become, the man my father had been. Which is why it was so painful when we didn't speak to each other for months after I came out to him.

Actually, I made my sister do it for me. I told her first, because I was confident she could handle it better than he could. I knew she wouldn't take my homosexuality as an indictment of her own skills as a role model for a fatherless boy. She accepted the invitation to visit me in D.C.— where I was living at the time—even with the warning that I had something serious to tell her. She assumed that I was in trouble with the law or had gotten some girl pregnant. I wouldn't call my being gay a relief for her, but it seemed to beat out the other possibilities she had feared.

When she got back to Philly, she invited Tom over for pizza. When she told him I was gay, he said, "Jeez, it can never just be a pizza. It always has to be something else." He went home, thought about what my sister had said, and called me. He was abrupt and to the point. Gay men are promiscuous. Gay men are effeminate. Gay men are not happy. He offered a warning just before I hung up on him: *"Whoever you wind up with better be just like you."* We took the summer off from each other and rebuilt our relationship slowly, my sister serving as the family's diplomat.

Fourteen years later, after receiving a terminal diagnosis of brain cancer, Tom asked my sister, "Remember when Brian's being gay was a big deal?" I like to think that it was our father speaking through him. It was a funny thing to say, but wistful, too, as if life had escalated to the point where coming out belonged to a simpler and more innocent time. With my brother's death, I lost an important link to our father. But stories and memories can comfort as well as sadden, and the following one still makes me smile when I miss my father. My brother, sister, and I were still small when we were packed into the car and taken to Yellowstone Park. My father, a kid from South Philly, wanted his own children to experience the natural world. A world denied him when he was a boy, growing up in Malloy's Bar at the intersection of Point Breeze and Mifflin Avenue. The consequence, of course, was that he was unfamiliar with wild animals. So when a large bear decided to scavenge our campsite, my father took out his camera and had his children pose with the bear in the background. Then he grabbed a log, one end still smoldering, and chased the bear back into the woods.

My mother didn't sleep at all that night, terrified that the bear now had Dad's scent and would sneak into their tent and eat him. He, on the other hand, slept like the log he had so recently charged the bear with. The latest crisis was over. Dad's breath was deep and even, his eyes rolling behind their lids, enjoying a dream only he could see.

Papa.

NOTE: *For the benefit of the living, and the dead, I've changed all the names of people and locations. Everything else is true.*

I am back in the house my father worked so hard to keep. It's a little white stucco box with black trim on a tiny yard, beneath a big Baldwin apple tree; a couple of hours away from New York. Dad and I were very close, and during the sixteen years we had together, we treated each other more as friends than parent and child. I think about him often, now that I have taken on his responsibilities at the house, and help my elderly mother after the stroke she suffered. Mom mentions, every once in a while, that she knows "our papa" is still here—twenty-nine years after his death—watching over us.

Down in the basement is an ancient battered trunk, locked and strapped shut, which touts, "The Wonderful Webb Brothers! On Tour!" Straight out of high school, Dad and his three older brothers worked the fringes of vaudeville. I'm not certain what made the Webb Brothers "Wonderful," but it might have been my dad, a modest prodigy not afraid to perform on eight different instruments: guitar, banjo, sax, trumpet, accordion, organ, piano, and was it the drums? Did he switch from one to another, to another to another, to wow the audience?

My favorite family myth is that Dad played in the Warner Bros. orchestra for *The Jazz Singer*, in 1927 the first "talkie." He was twenty then. Even when I lived in L.A. in the '80s (as a film student and screenwriter) I didn't try to track down the roster. Some myths are just too delicious.

The Webbs worked the circuits till there was no more vaudeville, then they called it quits. Although Dad and I were close, and he told me many things, he was silent about his years in show business. After he died, Mom showed me the smaller instruments, neatly packed away in the attic. I always knew about the trunk in the basement.

Dad had put music behind him—boxed it and strapped it shut—along with what else? Then he had forty years of jobs with his lifelong partner, Larry. They were movie theater managers, coal sellers, car dealers, and clothing store owners. And what else? Their partnership ended abruptly: I never learned why. Over the years, Mom and I, each in our own way, have come to speculate: Was "our papa" gay? Like son, like father?

Mom, despite her extreme conservatism, has been supportive of me, her gay son and only child. But every time she voices those questions I tell her what I believe: Papa loved us as much as anyone could, and he was a truly good man.

He never had an easy life—early poverty, bad health, business frustrations—but I never heard him complain. (But then, silence played a large role in our family.)

From birth he had a severely deformed back; he must have suffered many taunts for being a "hunchback." Family legend says it was caused by a drunken midwife, the best his parents could afford. Dad's body is maybe my earliest memory: scrambling all over him, on the shore of a lake. I remember his red-plaid trunks and his big belly. He was so slippery. But lots of places for handholds and toeholds, to climb onto his shoulders, with his help. Maybe that's why, from earliest childhood, I felt a special connection to certain monsters, like Dr. Frankenstein's creation, the lovelorn Phantom of the Opera, and of course Quasimodo.

Dad had other health problems, too, including a malformed esophagus which forced him to choke down every bite he ever ate. I remember only one occasion when we ate in a restaurant: The stares and grimaces kept us from ever trying again. I often wondered, What must it have been like for him, living on the road in his youth? Did he have the condition then?

Later he lost his right eye, which was replaced with a glass one. Beautiful, but unsettling. It reminded me of the marbles I played with.

Mom, to this day, sincerely believes that "he was such a handsome man." I think so too. Not just the dad I remember, but the man I see in old photos. My favorite shows him in his twenties, dressed up in a nice suit, hair brilliantined, holding a guitar. He must have been alarmed at my lackluster music grades in elementary school. He never criticized, but asked if I'd like to take piano lessons. Yes!

I remember him sitting next to me on the piano bench—not playing, just helping me along—and the tangy scent of Old Spice, sparingly applied. Me banging away at the keyboard: No, those weren't "tone clusters." I wish he had made me practice more diligently. Even so, music opened so many possibilities. When I turned twelve, Dad began taking me to Broadway musicals and the opera whenever I asked (the rear balcony was ten dollars in the 1970s). Before going, I liked being "prepared"—so Dad, who never had much money, encouraged me to buy all the books and recordings I wanted. They came to life on the stage, and opened me as much to the pleasures of reading as to music.

The first opera I saw was a Saturday matinee of Gounod's *Faust*. Just before Dad and I entered the New York State Theatre, a solar eclipse turned the sky pitch black. Who could wish for a more striking backdrop? And I remember Dad's subtly swaying during the performance. I could feel him feeling the music.

Dad and I didn't just go to highbrow events, we also spent time stargazing, playing catch, flying kites, walking around the woods which, then, began right at the end of our street, and fishing.

The first time I caught a fish with Dad I was five. It was an early spring day, gray and freezing; and the catfish must have been very small. From movies, I knew you were supposed to hit it over the head with a rock before you scaled it. Dad watched silently as I found a stone and began whacking away at the flopping fish for a long time. When it refused to die, I gently put it in a pail of water and we took it home. Dad watched as I dug a "grave" and buried it. But I could not sleep that night, thinking about what I had done. The next day, Dad and I dug it up. Dad was even more surprised than I was that the fish was still wriggling, although just barely. He took my hand as we carried it back to the pond and let it go. I remember the water felt like ice.

My memories of discovering grown-up books are tied to cold. I would read for hours, sitting on top of the freezer in the storage room at his mom-and-pop grocery store. Dad's tastes ran exclusively to mysteries, but at an early age I discovered the Classics. His store had one tall book rack, and along its bottom rows—easily within reach—were the Airmont Classics: Shakespeare, Stevenson, Scott. Microscopic print on pulpy paper, but I didn't care. Since no one ever bought the Airmonts, I wonder if he stocked them just for me.

Next to the freezer I found—early on—a hidden stack of thin newspapers. I never saw Dad come back for these "under the counter" tabloids, but I now know I missed a lot. I can still see haunting images of smooth young men tied up in chains, some of them dangling in harnesses suspended from giant hooks. (Years later, when I came across bondage imagery, there was a moment of recognition and understanding.) And I knew about such hooks from Dad's butcher department. One of my daily jobs (every day after school Mom picked me up and drove us to the store) was scraping blood and viscera off the meat block with a big studded brush. Now I wonder if Dad looked at those tabloids; and if he did, what he felt about their world of bound desire.

For the last eight years of his life, Dad was proprietor of the Lakeside Mini-Market. "The store," as we all called it, was near the shore of an erstwhile resort lake which had fallen on hard times. I cut my feet on submerged glass and cans whenever I ventured into the water, but somehow managed to avoid tetanus. Eventually I learned to wear sneakers, even when swimming.

Dad worked at the store obsessively his last eight years: sixteen-hour days, beginning at dawn, seven days a week, open all holidays. Not even one full vacation day per year. Even after becoming sick, he kept himself at the store as much as he could.

In the nightmarishly conservative postwar years, a small businessman, especially one who never fought in a war ("4F" because of his health) and who wanted to fit in, had to marry. Mom "chased him" (her words) for eight years before they tied the knot. Was she the only woman who wanted him, a man who fit no conventional stereotype of manly beauty? Of course he was strong, and silent.

I never remember seeing Dad and Mom touch. Not even hugging. The only kiss a peck on the cheek, reserved for birthdays and the major holidays. It took them eight years to conceive me. By then he was fifty.

He was more demonstrative with my dog, Cleo, a nervous little beagle who loved the many car rides my dad took alone with her. She would stick her nose out the window and wag her tail with delight as they drove off, late at night. Maybe that explains why Mom was jealous of the dog.

I can never forget what Mom told me the night my father died, when I was sixteen. Her confession began not long after we saw my father's corpse in the hospital. The nurses had not even covered his face—his glass eye looked more alive than his natural one. Blank, not peaceful.

That night, for the first and only time, Mom unburdened herself to me. Her story helped me understand much more about her, and my dad. She grew up in a poor, rural family, born after her fifteen-year-old mother was raped in 1920 while scrubbing the steps of her employer's estate. Never happy in school, Mom was herself sexually attacked —and became pregnant—twice. After her first abortion, then illegal, the doctor brought in a shoebox with a bloody, mangled fetus and made her "look at what you've done."

Two nights later, he fell asleep smoking in bed and burned to death: My mother still blames her "wickedness" for the good doctor's demise.

The second man to assault and impregnate her was Larry. After which, my father married her. But that child was lost.

DAD AND LARRY: I have so many questions about them—together from childhood, inseparable friends, drinking buddies, partners in business. I know so few details of their relationship; and they—and the people who knew them—are dead. What did they feel for each other during the forty years they shared together? Was Dad able to connect with Larry through Mom—her body some kind of commonality for them? What kind of life might Dad and Larry have had if they lived today, in a society more accepting of all kinds of partners?

Dad and Mom: What did he think about this lonely, high-strung, naive woman—who saw herself as "illegitimate" in so many ways—who "married a father" (her words), a man the same age as her mother? I wonder if Dad felt relieved that he had found a wife who professed to hate sex.

When Mom and I have driven past the old justice of the peace office where she and Dad were married, she always—always—asks why no one from his family came to the wedding. I say nothing. (Our family was so fractured that the only time we ever heard from Dad's three brothers was at his funeral. I'm sure they are all dead now.) And Mom cannot forget the excruciating wedding night at Niagara Falls: Her husband suffered a massive attack of asthma and had to be rushed to a hospital. Mom "confessed" so much the night dad died—but there was only that one quick mention of Larry.

Other than that, not one word about her husband's partner, although Mom still accuses the woman Larry married (they had no children) of having cheated Dad out of money over some failed business venture.

But I remember feeling a connection between my dad and Larry—although I was only a child then—which was not there between Dad and Mom.

My earliest memory of Larry is at his and my father's clothing store, which they ran together for many years. I remember crawling on the floor under the clothes racks, a jungle of suits and coats blocking out the light overhead. Larry lured me out with an offer: He held up a shiny new football and a $25 savings bond, and said I could have my pick. Easy! I took the bond (my father had already instilled sound financial values in me). Larry and Dad laughed, saying that I'd made the smart choice. I remember Larry's picking me up, as he always loved to do, and spinning me around. I connect that dizzy feeling with the smell of Larry's cigars. Larry paid a steep price for them: A few years later, he died of throat cancer.

My father never spoke about Larry's death. He went to the funeral alone, while Mom and I stayed home. Or maybe she kept me there. When Dad came back, he said nothing.

A COUPLE OF years after Larry's death, Dad became sick. He never told mom, or me (I was fourteen), about the doctor's diagnosis: colon cancer. He died a slow death. Mom still cries sometimes, saying, "Why didn't he tell me?"

Dad's last months, I remember him drinking a lot more. Tears running down his face while he sat alone on the sunporch, holding a beer, a TV baseball game playing on and on. One operation after another. And the smell from the colostomy bag. Then the night, not long before the end, when he went outside naked and walked around the house. Crying, I begged him to come in. But he wouldn't. Just kept walking around the house. No one called the police. He never said a word.

What did all those silences mean? How many different things were hidden there? Do I want to know? Yes, to understand the father I love.

I strive to be like Dad in many ways: honest, fair, decent. But I don't like silence and secrets; it's too easy for lies to fester and spread. Since my mom likes people to "keep their mouths shut," she'll never see this piece. She does not need to read my speculations about Dad: She has enough of her own.

The Wonderful Webb Brothers' trunk is still there, down in the basement. One night a few years ago, I finally moved the pile of boxes off it, undid all the locks and straps, and opened it . . . to find it stuffed with Mom's fabrics. Waiting to be made into quilts. But behind the trunk I found a little black rubber ball which Dad had gotten me, when I was very young, during one of his business trips with Larry. I started bouncing the ball on the floor and off the wall, catching it and throwing it faster.

Then I threw it too hard, and it disappeared. I looked everywhere— under tables, behind chests, in dark corners—but could not find it. Since I was near my file cabinets, I decided to look at an old film project.

Five minutes later, suddenly, every hair on my arms stood up. I didn't know why. Then I turned around and saw—from across the basement, by the trunk—very, very slowly the ball was rolling straight toward me.

I'm a skeptic, but I had to wonder: Was Dad playing catch with me one more time?

Does our papa benignly watch over the house, as Mom believes?

Could he know how much things have changed for his son—and other gay people—since his death?

Does he know that, even more than speculating about the secrets of his life, I love him?

I picked the ball up and put it back inside the trunk, under Mom's fabrics, then fastened a couple of the straps. I saw no need for the lock.

BOB MOSER

The Ghost
of My Daddy

First came the Supremes incident. On a Sunday night in 1967, when I was three or four, Miss Ross & Co. sashayed their way onto our black-and-white Zenith, sporting form-fitting gowns that glittered through the fuzz and chanting, if memory serves, "Love Is Here (And Now You're Gone)." It took approximately one verse and chorus to convince me: I wanted to be—no, I *had* to be Diana Ross.

My big break came a couple of days later. After picking me up from Ardmore Methodist preschool, my mother had followed her usual routine: Drive to the L'il General store, send me inside to fetch her a candy bar, then head home and collapse on the sofa for the afternoon. Somewhere in the middle of *All My Children,* I looked up from my Legos and saw that she had fallen dead asleep, Heath Bar wrapper dangling from one limp hand.

I tiptoed into her bedroom. Within thirty minutes' time, I had donned a sleek pair of cream-colored low heels and ditched my North Carolina basketball T-shirt for a silky red blouse that I slung capelike over one shoulder. Perched in front of Mother's low-slung makeup table, I had just begun to apply a carefully selected shade of pink lipstick when everything came to a crashing halt.

"Lord!" Mother bellowed, so suddenly, so loudly, so hugely that the word rang through me like the booming cry of a fairy-tale giant. Before I knew it, the hand that had been languidly dangling the Heath Bar wrapper had a fierce grip on my wrist, yanking me out of the bedroom, across the den, through the living room, along the kitchen floor and finally into the bathroom, where it released me and twisted on the hot-water faucet with a vengeance. Then it seized a washcloth that scoured my face and fingers for an awfully long time.

Mother hollered and hissed the whole time, but the only words that stuck in my addled brain—aside from that giant "Lord!"—were "Never!" and "Boys do not do that, do you hear me? Do you hear me?"

That is my first memory.

Soon came my second. The next Saturday morning, I woke in the near-dark to muffled crashes from the basement. My daddy's feet clomped up the rickety steps. My bedroom door squealed. His head poked into view as the overhead light switched on. He held up two skinny sticks with wires. His flat North Carolina accent mimicked enthusiasm. "Come on, gotta go."

I knew where we were going. A night or two after Memory No. 1, Mother had bellowed into the kitchen while Daddy was cooking supper. "Hey, isn't it time you taught this boy how to fish?"

He mumbled something we couldn't hear. That always set her off.

"Do you hear me? This. Week. End. Take him out to Tanglewood and show him how to fish. Boys need to learn how to fish. That's what fathers do with their sons. Isn't it? Do you hear me?"

So Saturday morning we puttered down the highway in Daddy's old Volkswagen, headed for Tanglewood, whatever that might be. We drove through huge trees and jerked to a stop by a muddy pond where they rented paddleboats. We lugged everything to a shady corner and found stumps to sit on. Daddy brushed off the red dirt before we sat down. This is what boys do, I thought. Pay attention.

"Look here," Daddy said, poking a curvy pin through a purple worm. "Watch," he said, flinging the worm out over the muddy water. He poked another worm and handed me the short stick. It felt splintery, like it might crack apart. After a couple of tries, I tossed the worm a few feet out and watched the ripples spread and fade. "That's real good," he said.

We fell quiet and stared at the people in the paddleboats. They yelped and giggled. "Sticky day," Daddy said. He caught something dinky and threw it back. "Can't fry that," he said. The sun hit the bristly little hairs on his knee for a few minutes, then moved away. I wondered if his knee would burn. We each ate a pimento sandwich and a bag of Fritos.

My stomach turned flips the whole time. We'd never gone off together before. Daddy was like a ghost, there but not there. Mornings he would wake up me and my sisters, cook breakfast, visit Mother in her bed, drop me off at preschool and go to work at the R. J. Reynolds World Headquarters. At supper time he would come home and cook. He never asked for help. He'd clean the dishes, stack them in the drainer, go to the bathroom upstairs and slip out to the back porch, where he kept books for people as his second job. He would work out there till after I was asleep.

"It's almost my birthday," I finally blurted out.

"Before you know it," Daddy said. "Be old before you know it too."

After a while, he looked at his watch. "Well," he said, "about that time." We loaded everything back in the Volkswagen and drove home in quiet. Skinny Carolina pines blurred by. When we rounded the exit that led to home, Daddy cleared his throat. "So. What you think about fishing?"

"It's all right, I guess. It's kind of boring."

His face loosened a little. "Well," he said. "Don't have to do that again."

I couldn't agree more.

OUT OF THE blue, the summer I turned eight, my oldest sister got married. Mind you, Dianne wasn't just any oldest sister: She was, with the possible exceptions of President Richard Nixon and Cher, my favorite person in the world. While Mother had languished in bed with her fourth and final case of postpartum depression and Daddy worked his fingers to the bone, it was Dianne—thirteen when I was born—who had changed the diapers, rocked the cradle, read the pop-up books and done her best to buffer me from the sharp eyes and fingernails of my mean other sister, Cathy, who narrowed her eyes and spat "Weirdo" any time I so much as flipped a wrist or launched into my rendition of "Gypsies, Tramps, and Thieves."

Dianne was shy like me, with the same milky face, the same wispy blond hair and pale eyes, the same hint of a double chin that no diet could ever erase. When she went away to college, I felt that all I had to live for was the next summer's long vacation. Now summer had come, but hardly according to plan. For weeks Dianne had barricaded herself in her upstairs room. Sobs, sighs, and long, hushed phone calls filtered through the living-room ceiling to where I sat in front of the TV, anxiously building one Lego nation after the next. Mother left her perch on the sofa and took to her bed. The next thing I knew, I was being fitted for a mini-tux and taught the rigors of ring bearing.

Before the wedding, I was confused. After the wedding, I was distraught. Who was this dark, hairy boy from N.C. State who'd swooped in and taken away the only normal person in the house, with the possible exception of Daddy? And the one person who surely loved me? I couldn't be sure about Daddy. Was he keeping to himself, or keeping away from me because I stunk at the sports he was so good in?

Still in the tux, I dashed upstairs when we got home and bundled myself into a ball of misery in the cramped hallway between Dianne's room and Daddy's. Everything was hopeless. I wanted to die right then and there. I sobbed and moaned and sobbed some more, wiping my snot onto the rough surface of the tux sleeve. When that didn't help, I kicked and screamed and threw a fit. Surely somebody would stop me. Nobody did, for what seemed like hours. Not until I'd been reduced to exhausted weeping did my father's footsteps start creaking up the stairs. Finally, I thought, ratcheting up the volume of my cries to stoke his pity.

"Hey," he said, looking down at his crumpled heap of a son with his lips drawn into the same tight smile he was wearing when he walked Dianne down the aisle. "Scuse me." He brushed past my pants leg into the bathroom and closed the door behind him. I muffled my cries and listened to him pee and squirt out farts, then wash his face and brush his teeth.

Downstairs, I knew, my mother was sitting on the other toilet, smoking. That's because I could hear, echoing up the stairs, the familiar sound of my remaining sister's banging on the door, coughing an exaggerated cough and screaming, "Do you think we don't know what you're doing in there? Don't you know I'm allergic to smoke? Are you trying to kill me or what?"

My stomach felt like it had been stuffed with a boulder. I heard Daddy sigh a little sigh, then open the bathroom door. His face was ironed flat, still wearing its tight smile.

"You OK?" he said.

"Um-hum." I stifled the urge to grab his pants leg, to cling and cry and ask questions. I hugged my ribs tighter instead.

"Hush now, it's all right." I felt the light brush of a hand on my shoulder, a second's shuddering touch, then watched as his shiny black wedding shoes turned to tread down the hallway to his room. The door clicked quietly shut behind him. "'Night," he said.

"'Night," I said.

That was the end of my crying. I began to watch my daddy carefully. I watched the way he ironed his face. I watched the way he walked deliberately, peacefully, out of a room whenever my mother or sister started acting up; the way he bent over his desk every night, making things right and tidy in the spartan bookkeeping office he'd created on our back porch. I found a sport—golf—and cut out the Cher imitations. I had someone else to imitate now. If I worked at it hard enough, I could be the other normal person in this house.

A COMPLICATION AROSE when I was 16, in the devilishly pleasing form of doe-eyed Andy Dillon (whose name I've changed). A few weeks after we met in the cafeteria of R. J. Reynolds High School, Andy and I were tearing off each other's jeans in the hatchback of my sister's hand-me-down Vega, admiring each other's lips and nipples and buns and balls as if they had been lovingly sculpted by Michelangelo. We fogged up the Vega's back window every chance we got, spending the rest of our nights cruising around Winston-Salem in search of new, suitably dark places to park and spark.

I felt both giddy and terrified. Things had been going so nicely. I had made the golf team, earning a big gold "R" that I could put on a jacket and wear around to certify my normalcy. I had a girlfriend, though we had not yet technically kissed. I was, outwardly at least, nearly as sedate as my daddy. I worked hard at my golf, hard at some of my studies, harder at calmly dismissing my mother's occasional outbursts. In a rare moment of eloquence, my father had once said, "Idle hands . . ." and I had filled in the blanks. I tried to keep too busy to think, or—much worse — feel. But I had always known, deep down, that something was wrong. The same something that put me in those cream-colored heels. The same something that made me queasy and achy around even halfway cute boys.

Two years before, I had scoured every reference to homosexuality in *Everything You Always Wanted to Know About Sex*. I came away with the small consolation that this queasiness, this aching, was merely a phase that many a young man goes through on his way to normalcy. But this Andy Dillon business felt a lot more scary than any mere phase. I could not stop my stoic self from giggling into the phone with him every night that we weren't fogging up the windows.

I tried desperate measures. I kissed my girlfriend. I went to my sister Dianne's fundamentalist church, where her soul had finally been saved after its own teenage wickedness, and solemnly answered the altar call at a Sunday night service. I nodded yes with genuine fervor and tried to ignore the bulge in my pants when the minister's huge hand rested gently on my head and he whispered huskily, "Do you want to renounce your sins? Are you ready? Are you ready for Jesus in your heart?"

Salvation lasted only until the next ring of the phone, until the next time my father said, "It's that Andy again," only until my next visit to the toilet. I had taken to pulling out Salems from Mother's hidden stash of cigarettes while frantically jerking off, thinking about that hatchback.

Still, I clung to the idea (written by the world's most renowned expert on the subject!) that it was all a phase—maybe even one that my father had gone through. Which was probably what motivated me, one afternoon in the spring of my uncontrollable lust, to sneak up the stairs while Mother snored on the couch.

In our house, like most proper Southern houses, you did not open the door to another person's bedroom. You would no more do this than you would hug a family member or say "I love you" out loud. You certainly did not take long looks around this other person's bedroom, noticing how dark it was with the late-afternoon sun shining on the other side of the house. You did not see how everything inside the room was brown: pine-paneled walls, tile floor in checkerboard squares of tan and sienna, high walnut chest of drawers, mud-brown bedspread. Nor did you walk inside this person's bedroom, click on a ship's-wheel lamp that added a lurid yellow glow to all those tones of brown, and start rooting through his closets and drawers.

But I did, that afternoon, with no idea what I might be looking for—or what I might find. The closet yielded nothing but a few boxes of my brother's childhood toys stashed amid military rows of white and tan shirts, midnight blue slacks and fat clip-on ties. The drawers of Daddy's walnut chest revealed nothing more than a Giant Print Holy Bible, covered in blue leatherette, and an impeccably organized series of brown and blue socks, white T-shirts with tantalizing sweat stains, and frayed Hanes briefs that I dared not study too closely.

Under the bed, nothing but dust bunnies. On the built-in shelves, nothing but stacks of *Sports Illustrated*s. I stood on the tiny mud-brown rug that Daddy had laid at the foot of his bed and looked around. Only his trunk remained. It looked scary, old and eternal-looking, like something you'd find on an ocean floor. Opening it would be the ultimate invasion of privacy. But there were higher matters at stake. I jimmied my fingers under the lid, braced for a good hard yank, but it weighed next to nothing. The lid flew back against the bed rail, sending powdery dust smoking toward the ceiling through the lurid light of the ship's-wheel lamp.

I pawed through the trunk's dim, deep innards. Old blankets. Unopened packages of clean T-shirts and unworn briefs. A rusty box of old coins. A small blue sweater made of big nubbly loops. What's that? I shook it open and saw a big "L" sewn into the middle. Gold, like my "R." Daddy's letter sweater, from Lewisville High. I ran a finger over the big blue loops, wondering if his mother made it for him, wondering if he had a mother who did such things. I buried my nose in the sweater, sniffed, suppressed a sneeze. It looked way too small for Daddy. It would fit me fine. I laid it on the bed and kept digging.

Under another unopened shirt, a yearbook lying flat along the trunk's knotty bottom. Lewisville High School, 1941. I pulled it out, sat back Indian-style on the rug and started flipping through. I stopped on a page where a poem had been written, slantwise above the office staff, in the most flowery script imaginable: "I think that I shall never see / A boy as lovely as S.T. . . . ." An ode to my daddy from a girl named Frances, borrowing from Joyce Kilmer's "Trees." I rocked back and laughed. Imagine. My graying, slump-shouldered Daddy, a heartthrob!

I skipped to the sports section. First came soccer. Mother had once told me how Daddy captained every sports team at school, but I figured it was just another one of her exaggerations. My eyes scanned two rows of solemn-faced farm boys with crew cuts, kneeling and standing in their impossibly short shorts. See? He wasn't there. He wasn't even on the soccer team. Unless—could that be him? The handsome one standing on the left, easy-shouldered, tousled blond hair, the corners of his mouth turned up in a snarky grin?

It was him. I turned over more thick, slick pages. The handsome face peered out from an old leather football helmet. From under a baseball cap.

From the kneeling row of the track-and-field squad. From one side of a tennis net, poised for a forehand. From a free-throw line, underhanding a basketball.

In spite of the different settings, they all looked a lot like me.

Spooky. I snapped the yearbook shut, placed it back on the bottom of the trunk, closed the lid and sat on the rug in the yellowy light, wondering what it all meant. My daddy at sixteen didn't look a thing like my daddy at fifty-four. Somewhere along the way—when he came back from the war and married Mother?—he had transformed from a cocky, handsome heartthrob into a stoic, slump-shouldered man.

There had to be a lesson in this for me. It didn't take me long to realize what it was: If my father had remained a cocky, handsome heartthrob, he could never have kept our family together. He could never have put food on our table, put up with my mother and sister, given me an example of quiet rectitude to model myself after.

I would follow the example he had set. I would put a stop to this Andy Dillon thing. My own yearbook pictures would end up looking tight-shouldered and impassive. Nothing like my father at seventeen. A lot like my father at fifty-four.

"LORD, BOB, THEY'VE sent him to the hospital." Mother's voice quivered through the receiver. She had caught me at my newspaper office, working late on a Friday night. "They say it might be—oh!" She stretched the word into a moan.

"Might be what?"

"They taught us never to say the word, you know. But cancer. Cancer! You know how that man refused to go to a doctor. Stubborn as a goat, wouldn't step foot in that office until he got so he couldn't swallow a morsel of food, and I told him! I must have told him a million times! I told him, I told him. What will I do? What is going to happen to me?"

"I'm coming."

But what I did first was spend another hour at the office, emailing meticulous instructions to the other editors in case I couldn't get back by Monday. Then I drove home and did my daily workout: sit-ups, push-ups, forty-minute run. At thirty, my life was a series of checklists. I worked 14/7, exercised religiously, dated women. Whole weeks went by when I didn't sleep. I was too freaked out by my dreams.

I showered, fixed a quick dinner, washed the dishes, and put them in the drainer. I packed carefully, then set off down Interstate 40, keeping my fuel-efficient Nissan precisely seven miles above the speed limit. Daddy had once told me you didn't get tickets that way, and he was right. I sang along with Neil Young, mouthing words so familiar they'd long ago stopped registering. "Old man, look at my life, I'm a lot like you were."

The words registered this time. I felt like throwing up. I thought, holy shit. Your father is dying. You are crying. I didn't know which was weirder. I hadn't cried since I was eight. It felt like a boulder was turning flips in my gut, dolphin style.

The next morning, the boulder still flipped as I went to the hospital to wait with Daddy for the oncologist's verdict. "You know I can't stand hospitals," Mother had said, her lips trembling. "You go."

At 6 A.M., I walked into a beige cinder-block room that smelled like piss cut with Pine-Sol. Daddy was already sitting up, arms folded over his chest. A strand of his starched gray hair stuck up and out, like an hour hand at two o'clock.

I edged around the bed, plopped down in a square orange chair by the window. Daddy looked drawn, sharp-edged and shriveled. He had chin stubble. How much weight had he lost since Christmas?

"Hey," I said.

"Hey."

"Well. This is the pits, huh?"

"Mm." His tongue flicked his lips. "But you know, if this is it, that's okay."

The words floated in the close air of the room, mixing with the smell. I glanced at him. He gazed blankly at the TV hanging from the ceiling.

"You want to watch something?"

"Mm."

The martial theme of the Gomer Pyle show had just struck up when the oncologist knocked. He guided me out of the room so he could break the news to Daddy in private. I stood in the hall watching two nurses whispering to each other. They shook their white hats and scowled. Then the door opened and a hairy little hand clapped my shoulder. Yes, the doctor said: Cancer. Of the esophagus. Metastasizing rapidly. No known treatment. Too far gone. Eight months tops.

I watched his doctor's teal pants disappear up the hall. I swallowed the boulder down and turned back into the room, wondering what to say. "Sorry, Daddy"? "We'll fight this thing"? "Make the most of the time you've got"? "Why in God's name wouldn't you go to a doctor?"

What I said was this: "Geez, this really is the pits." Something led my hand to his shoulder. It was all knob and bone under the wispy fabric of the hospital gown.

"Yep," he said, staring steadily at the screen. "The pits."

Sergeant Carter's moon-pie face was spitting mad. What silly thing had Gomer gone and done now? I wondered if I should unmute the set.

"It'll be all right," Daddy mumbled.

"Huh?" I asked, even though I'd heard him perfectly well.

"Nothing." He looked up at me, then his eyes darted back to the set. The boulder churned in my gut. No, I thought. You can't cry in front of him.

"Be back in a minute," I said. I fled and didn't stop till I was in the parking lot, where I crumpled against the side of my car, trying to light a Marlboro while my insides burst open, dislodging a terrible question: He wants to die, doesn't he? And then one more: Do you?

IT TOOK THE cancer six months to rot his insides out. Between stretches of silence in various cinder-block rooms, he told me more about himself than I had ever known. How he almost died from malaria in Africa in World War II. How he loved to go skinny-dipping in the river as a boy. How on the boat back from the war, he won enough money playing poker and pool to finance his wedding and put a down payment on the house.

He had nothing to say about what happened after that.

Mostly we sat and watched sports and sitcoms in silence. I wanted to tell him what was happening inside me, but I didn't know how. How exactly do you tell a man with a feeding tube in his gut, wasting away on cans of formula in stinky beige rooms, that you have finally decided to admit you're gay, finally decided to get a life, finally decided to stop being his ghost?

I never figured it out.

Two days after he died, I was back in his old brown room, kneeling on the mud-colored rug, rooting one more time through his ancient trunk. Once again, I was desperate—this time, because I had volunteered to deliver his eulogy. There seemed so little to say. Daddy had married wrong, lived the sad gray life of a martyr, and figured out a way to die. Somehow, I didn't think that would make for an uplifting eulogy, even if I sprinkled in a few anecdotes from the hospital in Africa.

I pulled out the yearbook, thinking that I might quote the heartsick girl's bad adaptation of "Trees." There was no other good eulogy material in the trunk. I shut it and headed toward the door, happy to be leaving the depressing little room, maybe for good. But as I went to click off the ship's-wheel lamp, I noticed the blue-covered Giant Print Bible, lying now on top of the walnut chest.

Every Sunday, rain or shine, with or without us, Daddy had gone to Sunday-school and church. Maybe there was some eulogy fodder in his Bible—a favorite passage marked, a page turned down, something.

A faded yellow legal pad had been stuck into the Book of Acts. I pulled it out, seeing Daddy's familiar, cramped handwriting on the top of the first page. "Rev. Strawbridge," it said. He had been one of the retired ministers who taught Daddy's Sunday-school class. I ran my finger down the faded lines of penciled notes:

"Love thy neighbor (Paul, Romans).

"Walk humbly with thy God (Micah).

"Homosextuality an abomination (Lev?)."

My finger stopped. I tried to breathe. I tried a joke. "Jesus, Daddy, at least you could've spelled it right." I read it again, just to make sure. Then I walked out into the cramped upstairs hallway, crumpled into a ball of misery against my daddy's door, and cried and hugged my ribs for what seemed like hours.

DADDY WAS LAID to rest in a treeless slope behind his family's Methodist church, across a busy street from the farmhouse where he was born. The house is long gone; it burned to the ground when he was three or four. That was his first memory.

On a still, scorching August afternoon, a year after his funeral, I've come back for a chat. I'm not sure why. But here I sit, cross-legged, wiping shriveled grass clippings off the brass plate that commemorates his service to the U.S. Army.

"Um, Daddy?" My voice sounds loud, like the fairy-tale giant's. I glance around to make sure nobody's listening. My fingers pluck a dead brown dandelion and grind its pom-pom to dust. I stick the bottom of the stalk in my mouth and try to suck out some moisture.

Breathe.

"Okay. This is all stuff you probably know already. And now that you're dead or whatever you probably know all kinds of things even if you didn't know them while you were still alive and, anyway, what I mean is I had to come and tell you finally because I never could tell you when you were around because I could never admit it to myself, you know, and then you were dying, right? And then it didn't seem exactly appropriate to haul off and inform you that I was gay while you were lying there in those ugly beige rooms wasting away, so anyway, that's why I'm here. In addition to wanting to say hi. So, hi."

Hush, now. It's all right. I close my eyes and hug my ribs like I'm bracing for something. But there is nothing but the rumble of traffic, the sweat dripping into my eyes. I pluck another dandelion and rock back, suddenly struck with how goofy this is. I've driven all the way out to Bumfuck, so I can come out to a dead person with anti-gay propaganda scribbled in his Giant Print Bible?

I look up at Daddy's gravestone, thinking how embarrassed he would have been by its size. And its fussiness: Across the top, an engraver has tried to suggest a rainbow by carving out a series of parallel, half-moon lines. On either side, a cross coming out of broken ground intersects the rainbow, Easter style. Mother must have ordered it. Which made a certain amount of sense: Minutes after Daddy died, a rainbow had stretched from horizon to horizon with fat stripes. We all took it as a sign. Of course, we chose different signs.

I gaze at the rainbow in the bleached blue sky. No signs today.

Come on. Cough it up. What did you come to say?

"I love you anyway." It's as simple and impossible as that. I sit for a while crushing dandelions, rocking back and forth and sobbing and sobbing, until I remember that my partner is cooking dinner tonight. I don't want to keep him waiting forever. I stand up, wipe away my snot, and say so long to the ghost of my daddy.

RAKESH SATYAL

The Kitchen Incident.

For a week, just a week, I thought my father was gay.

Picture this:

It is a Sunday. I am twelve years old. I am in seventh grade. My family and I are eating lunch at our kitchen table. During meals, we have the habit of watching large-screen TV in the family room nearby. News. Never anything else, simply a choice among CNN, local broadcasts, or, at dinnertime, *World News Tonight With Peter Jennings*.

The seats at our kitchen table are part of a hierarchy, and the determining force behind this hierarchy is the TV, a sort of blue-glow deity that controls our actions all the way from its corner in the family room.

There are five people in my family—my father, my mother, my older brother, my fraternal twin brother, and I. However, only four seats are ever occupied, since my mother never sits down. Rather, she glides from the stove to the table, setting before us dishes of food: buttered stacks of oily, breadlike *parathas;* casseroles full of curried peas and potatoes, with chunks of soft, cheesy *paneer;* steaming piles of basmati rice, dyed yellow with turmeric, cumin seeds hiding amid them like flies in cotton; small bowls of smooth, plain yogurt, salt and pepper swimming on top. My twin brother and I, being the youngest in the family, have to settle for the seats whose backs are to the TV. My older brother takes one of the two seats that face the TV, although whichever twin occupies the seat directly across from him often blocks the screen with his head. Only my father's seat affords its occupant the luxury of no obstruction, and therefore it is—even more so than his well-worn recliner in the family room—the throne in our house.

I plan to eat quickly this afternoon. I have a lot of math homework to do—we have just started to learn algebra this year—and I know that if I stay too long at the table, I will have to endure hearing more about the World Cup of Cricket, which my father follows avidly. His hands are steady but hard at work as he tears off pieces of *paratha*, scoops up some potatoes, and pops the food into his mouth, talking all the while. I stare at his thumbs, which are double-jointed, the top section of each bending far backward, a thin layer of oil from the food coating them in a glossy sheen.

My father chews his food with a vengeance. His teeth chomp down, his jaws pronounced through his cheeks. At home, unabashed and comfortable, he does not mind freeing food from his gums with one swift sweep of his tongue, a mush of *paratha* and potatoes flung down his throat. Juicy clicking accompanies each of his bites, a sound that drives me crazy—and so I tell him—but it persists nevertheless. After all, this lazy Sunday lunch is only a family affair; there is no need for decorum.

Everyone always says I look just like my dad. My twin brother looks like my mom, they say, or even like my older brother, but I am my dad's one and only counterpart, so when people comment on our resemblance, my father proudly places one arm around me, giving one firm squeeze of my shoulder. There is a portrait of all five of us over the mantle in the family room, and though it is three years old, neither my father's nor my looks have changed much since then. I glance back and forth at our faces: same nose, very thin bridge blooming into a bulging tip; same eyes, brown circles, not ovals, lashes long and full; same lips, the upper perhaps too tiny and the lower thicker and fuller, jutting out just a couple of millimeters more.

At times like this, while I watch my father eat, I scorn this resemblance.

It is when I have reached the end of my patience with his *click click click gulp*, when I am on the brink of swiping my plate off the table and into the sink, washing my hands, and running upstairs to begin my math, that I hear my father say to my mother, "He's a good-looking guy, this guy, right?"

My mother responds nonchalantly, setting more potatoes on the table: "Yeah, he is." She glides back to the stove.

I instantly look at my father, who is staring at the TV behind me. I turn quickly to see the screen, but the broadcast has already cut back to the anchorwoman, a pale-faced brunette with two dark lines of rouge at her cheeks and a gaudy silver chain around her neck. I turn back around, tense without yet knowing why. Everyone carries on as usual, my father putting another bite into his mouth, my older brother reading his own section of the paper, my twin brother quietly sipping water, my mother flipping a *paratha* and sending flour dust into the air.

I will never know which man my father was talking about. I certainly can't ask him during this odd moment; I can't show him why I find such a comment so extraordinary, why finding another man attractive matters so much in my young, wistful, gay mind. Already, during this lunch, half a dozen boys and their pretty faces have swept through my head, and now, for the rest of the time at the table, I steal glances at my father and try to imagine some pretty face locked under his veined temples.

But before I can see that face, my father gets up and moves to his recliner. I go upstairs and do my homework, trying over and over, just as I have at lunch, to find the missing part of an equation.

MY FATHER WAS reborn right before my eyes. To think that I had always thought of our physical resemblance as a coincidence, merely attributing it to heredity and nothing else. What had happened in the kitchen—The Kitchen Incident, I automatically labeled it in my head, as if it were some Sherlock Holmes mystery I had recently read—told me that this physical resemblance was merely a skin that covered the blood and marrow of our relationship, that it was only one part of a complex similarity. Now, when I looked at myself in the mirror, I saw *meaning* behind the bulging nose, the round eyes, the full lower lip. I saw them all as testaments. Not testaments to my father, but to my father's sexuality. Not just to that, either; no, to homosexuality itself, to that remarkable tingling I felt when a boy I liked walked into a room, to the fantasy I entertained of kissing that boy, of linking our hands, of embracing and affirming and allowing.

We were prophets-in-crime, my father and I: We bore our sexuality on our faces; we carried it wherever we went, more twins than my twin brother and I.

LIKE FATHER, LIKE son, people have always said, and now, here, this Sunday night, that phrase starts to take on a more pressing, cataclysmic meaning. How frivolously, almost comically, people say it, but if they only knew the beauty that really lies behind it, if they only understood how my heart pumps joyfully to know that my father shares my view of love, they would say those words with the utmost reverence, as respectfully as the pope conducts vespers or a dying husband whispers last words to his widow-to-be.

I begin to spy on my father. The Kitchen Incident, I am certain, is not just an isolated event but an experience, an ongoing drama, and it is my duty, as the head detective in this case, to gather substantial evidence.

Monday night, as my twin brother and I sit doing homework in the family room, my eyes land on a sculpture perched high upon one of the bookshelves that border our stone fireplace. My father brought it from India more than a decade and a half ago, this porcelain rendering of a beautiful Indian woman. Thin, feline eyes and a long, hooked nose, key elements of the "sharp features," which, my mother says, pretty Indian women possess, and which she insists my future wife *will* have. Hands covered in intricate henna designs—*mehndhi*, a word I love to say over and over, partly because the sound of it is so beautiful, partly because I want its crimson swirls all over my own palms. Hair pulled back in a bun, surrounded by a garland of white carnations, which then cascades along her spine, a chiseled groove down the middle of her thick back. Were the garland able to break its porcelain freeze, it would swish joyfully along the woman's lower back, which is bare due to the gap in her sari, a tight, short, blue blouse and puffy, red petticoats; one sheet of gold-trimmed cloth leaps up from her skirts and jumps over her shoulder until it settles alongside the carnation garland. Her arms are parallel to the ground, elbows raised, wrists bent so that her reddened palms face each other, ready to receive a tray of glowing candles at the *mandhir,* a box of marzipan sweets, or a man's muscled waist.

Her body consists of sections stacked on top of each other. The bastions are her legs, which connect to a black, circular pedestal by way of two feet, heels together, tiny toes ringed in gold. Above this pillar is the red dome of her skirts. Then her torso, waist cinched, a dot of black paint for a belly-button, bulging breasts that the artist has emphasized by curving two lines of paint out of her cleavage. Along with this piece come her well-poised arms, which meet just under the thin column of her throat. And then her pretty head, carnation garland curling off it in one solid chunk.

This fragmentary composition conspires to make her one jiggling masterwork: One little touch makes her hips gyrate, her arms undulate, her head saucily nod a silent, assured *Yes*.

My father treats this delicate figure—the Porcelain Courtesan, I will deem her a few years later—with the utmost care, always dusting her himself, telling us that she is irreplaceable. A statue, he calls it, but come Tuesday, I, having been witness to The Kitchen Incident, see it for what it really is: a doll! Not a "statue," not a "piece," not a "sculpture." A good old-fashioned doll. And now I see a striking resemblance between this Indian woman and the Barbies I used to buy on the sly at the local Biggs store, the hot-pink boxes I took off the shelves and placed on the bumpy conveyor belt of the checkout line, saying cryptically to my twin brother, whose face turned as red as an Indian's can get, "I think she'll really like this, don't you?" This Indian doll's chest bulges just like Barbie's; her half-moon of a smile *is* Barbie's grin. Even Barbie's arms bend in the same manner, her palms facing each other, too.

Conclusion: My father plays with Barbies. Indian Barbies, but Barbies, nevertheless.

And on Wednesday, I pity him. I pity him feverishly, lamenting that he should share such a tortured existence. I writhe just thinking of my father, this man I thought to be so strong and self-assured, struggling to assimilate just as I do; I think of how inevitably sad it is that he can understand the ruses that define my day at school this Wednesday, such as changing with downcast eyes in the locker room, knowing that looking up once, however brief I intend for it to be, will steer my gaze from a boy's eyes to his budding chest, to the spare fuzz of his happy trail, and then to the bounty at the end of this path, a treasure that, once found, brings with it instant degradation and irrevocable disgust. How horrifying, to think that my father might shudder while he plays cards with other Indian men. *Thash*, they call it, during which they sit on the floor in some-one's living room—in the position deemed "Indian style," as if it were named after them—a big, white sheet their only mat, a mess of red, white, and blue chips and crinkled green bills in the middle of it, like some Dalí representation of the American capitalism they, businessmen and doctors and engineers, so thoroughly enjoy now.

Thursday night, as we all go to another impromptu get-together, I watch my father from the doorway of the living room, examining his every move. He laughs with his buddies, throws chip after chip into the center, pulls out his thick burgundy wallet and takes out another twenty dollars. And now I see, behind the façade of amusement, the slight terror in his eyes, a tiny twitch from time to time, when he, so much like me— or perhaps I have been just like him all along—thinks, "They'll find me out. They'll find me out and then . . ." But who really knows what happens *then* before *then* happens? To think that my father has cause to fear *then* just as I do!

And then, on Friday, as strongly as I have pitied him, I celebrate him, changing my mind as I do all the time, liking my sexuality in spurts. He is better off this way, I think. He is better off daydreaming, better off understanding the true beauty of the female form because he is not sexually attracted to it, better off understanding the true beauty of the male form because he *is* sexually attracted to it. Even at twelve, I know I possess a sensibility that my straight friends lack and that, in my eyes, they should want; I am fiercely proud as I curl up with my copy of *Emma* or paint lilacs in watercolors of varying purple, defiantly pleased that I am not cracking home runs in the cul-de-sac or shooting hoops. I feel elated that my father can appreciate such things, that even if he can't do them, his childhood having passed him by, he at least *wishes* he could. He is better off.

And this elation carries into Saturday, too, when I opt to help my dad mow the lawn for the first time in my life, a chore usually done by my twin brother, who, though deceptively called my mother's son, shows the strongest potential for fatherly duties like this. I plow through the backyard in straight, buzzing lines, and my movements are free and happy because I picture my father relishing the way the grass wafts into the air and floats down to the ground, as if dancing a descending ballet.

After I finish my leg of the mowing, my father gives me a short, tough hug, the sweat from our bodies sharp-smelling. "You smell like your dad," my mother once told me when I came home from a tap-dance lesson. She wrinkled her nose, laughed, tousled my hair, and told me to go take a shower. I do just that right now, going inside, stripping off my grass-strewn clothing, throwing it into the washer, and running naked to the shower.

I take a long time in the shower, loving how each green shoot that falls from my hair or my limbs represents another step closer to cleanliness. I finish, dry off, go to my room, change into a clean T-shirt and shorts, and I'm just about to go downstairs for lunch when my eyes pass over a tiny strand of blond hair that sticks out from under my bed. My stomach catches, and as I get down on my hands and knees and pull out one of my old Barbies, my stomach begins to contract, and I'm laughing, stroking the doll's hair, moving her arms and legs, making her skip across my comforter as she sings—by way of my high, light, unchanged soprano—a made-up song about girls loving boys and boys loving boys and boys boys boys . . .

When I notice my father standing in the doorway, my first reaction is to smile and pat the bed beside me, asking him to sing with me, too. My first instinct is to beam with anticipation, finally uniting these two minds that have thought the same thoughts and loved in the same way for years but have never done so together.

But his body does not want it. His body has a face whose brows furrow, whose eyes suddenly lose their usual roundness and become thin slivers, whose nose flares its nostrils, whose mouth frowns, full bottom lip tucked under tiny top lip, then opens to say, softly but sternly, "Lunch is ready," before my father walks away. And in that moment, which is really just a few choice seconds, I realize that I have created a mystery that does not exist. The Kitchen Incident is an incident and nothing more, and I don't need my mother to tell me, though she will some months later, in passing, that the sculpture in the family room belonged to one of my father's favorite aunts, that he keeps it immaculate to honor her memory. It is a sculpture and nothing more, as eventually unimportant as the white noise of the TV that glows behind me during Sunday lunch the next day.

And from then on, whenever my father gushes about one of my recitals, whenever his opinion and mine concur about the same symphony or artsy film, I will wonder what it is that makes me realize again that I love him. Maybe it is just plain old family love. Maybe it is just the fact that he is my old man, he who once tied my shoelaces and drove me to the bus stop and made me fried eggs sunny side up. But maybe, just maybe, it is the unforgettable and undeniable memory of that week, that one week when I looked at him and saw myself.

PATRICK ROSE

The End
of the
Beginning.

In 1965, when he was twenty-four years old, my father, Paul, was living in Philadelphia and was engaged to a girl named Jennifer. But close
to their wedding date he got cold feet and he left her, driving off in his
convertible in the middle of the night and ending up in Washington,
D.C. It was this impulsive act that led to my existence. He took a job as a
hotel desk clerk and met a young woman named Katherine who worked
in the gift shop. Katherine was twenty-five, divorced, and had two children. Paul asked her out, Katherine accepted; and almost immediately she
became pregnant—with me.

They eloped. Six months later I was born. Two months after that, Paul
wrote Katherine a note explaining that he was still in love with Jennifer
and that he was going back to her. He taped the note to the refrigerator,
and while Katherine, my half brother, half sister, and I were in the playground beside the hotel, he got back into his convertible and drove away.

Paul stayed in Philadelphia with Jennifer for nearly a year. We remained in Washington. In 1966, not long after my first birthday, Katherine was proposed to by a man she didn't love (but a man who was willing to marry a woman with three kids), and in an effort to facilitate an amicable divorce she tracked down Paul the only way she could: by writing to his parents in Trenton, New Jersey. Paul, as it turned out, had never told his parents he'd gotten married and never told them he had a son. Katherine's letter mentioned both and included a picture of me. Paul's mother—my grandmother—read the letter in horror, and quickly dialed up Paul in Philadelphia. It was an ugly, late-night call. My grandmother had met Jennifer, she liked Jennifer and was already envisioning her as a future daughter-in-law. My grandmother was bewildered by the sudden presence of this *other* woman and her gaggle of children, and she was convinced that Katherine had trapped Paul into marriage by getting herself pregnant. Though no one in my immediate family has ever spoken this aloud, it seems clear that the advice my grandmother gave to Paul was to forget this other woman, forget the child, and get on with his life.

It might have happened—only Paul got cold feet again. Perhaps impulsively, perhaps after a great deal of anguished talk, he turned down his mother's advice, gave up Jennifer again, got back into his convertible, drove straight down to Washington and begged Katherine to take him back.

She did.

SUCH WAS OUR beginning—mine as his son, his as my father. For the first twelve years of my life, Paul didn't seem very interested in me. We'd traced a path down the east coast, living in this or that city for six months at a time, and had ended up on Merritt Island, Florida, where NASA was hiring supply-room clerks and secretaries. When those jobs folded with the end of the Apollo project, Paul became an auto mechanic and my mother started nursing school. I turned thirteen the same year both my half brother and half sister left home for broader horizons, and Paul's lack of interest in me turned into a kind of blatant, passive dislike. I, who at that time knew nothing of our family's beginnings, didn't understand his attitude toward me, couldn't see any cause for it, and had no idea how to ask about it. In turn, I decided that I didn't like *him*. I made an appointment with a counselor at school and said, "I don't like my father." When the counselor asked why, I said, "Because he doesn't like me." The coun-

THE END OF THE BEGINNING

selor grinned and sat back in his chair and said, "You just relax." I relaxed, and privately I gave up trying to be close to Paul. If Paul noticed this, he didn't seem to mind.

The relationship Paul had with my mother was better than the one he had with me, I thought—though not by much. They slept in the same bed every night and they rarely argued, but they hardly spoke and almost never kissed (at least, not that I saw). I don't think I ever once heard Paul say my mother's first name. Around him, my mother mirrored his personality: She turned sullen, if not dour. When he wasn't around, she became lively, fun, impulsive; she would break into a laugh I began to think she reserved only for me. Once, out of the blue, she asked me how I felt about my father. I considered lying, but decided to tell her the truth. "I don't think he likes me." "He likes you," she said, with a sudden, worried look on her face, "he loves you; he just doesn't know how to show it. You love *him*, don't you?" "I love him because he's my father," I said, "but I don't like him." The worried look on her face collapsed into a kind of defeated frown. She said nothing else.

There was one advantage that emerged from my having virtually no intimate relationship with Paul: While he never talked to me about my school performance, about drinking, or drugs, or career options, or the importance of choosing good friends, he also never once talked to me about sex. Not a word about girls, dating, protection. As a result, I never once had to pretend that I was a heterosexual adolescent around him. I was allowed to be sexually invisible.

I worried, of course, about my "horrible truth" leaking out to the rest of them: my mother (who seemed obsessed with the idea of what a good father I was going to make some day), my sister (who was more than curious about why I didn't have a steady girlfriend), and my brother (who, while I was risking blow jobs with boys in a Pinto on Merritt Island, was busy turning himself into a brick-solid, foulmouthed, tattooed Navy sailor). But I never worried about what Paul would think if he found out. There didn't seem to be any relationship there to damage.

WHEN I MOVED away to college, my parents, who had started their marriage with two pre-existing children and another one on the way, were left alone with only each other for the first time in their lives. They lasted as such for another four years. The week after I graduated from FSU (and the week after my parents' twenty-third wedding anniversary) my phone rang in Tallahassee one morning before dawn. It was my mother. In a whispering, sniffling voice, she said, "Your father and I are having some problems. I'm not sure what's going to happen."

We didn't talk long (she wanted to hang up before Paul got out of the shower), but I understood that she wanted to leave him, and it made sense to me, just as it would have made sense if he had announced that he wanted to leave her. For as long as I'd known them, they had seemed to be only tolerating each other.

What followed was a strange and difficult time for my family. My sister, now twenty-seven, had just gotten divorced from her first husband and was living alone with her infant daughter in a four-bedroom house in the little town of Hamilton, Virginia. The week before I received that whispered phone call from my mother, I'd phoned my sister and asked her if she would take me in for six months or so while I worked and saved up a little money, decided on graduate schools and got my submission materials together. She gladly said yes. A week after my mother's announcement, she called my sister and asked if she, too, could move in for a while, once the house in Florida was sold, and, perhaps not quite as gladly, my sister agreed.

The house in Florida sold quickly. Within two months, my mother, my sister, my sister's child and I were all living under one roof in Virginia. Paul, as it turns out, was devastated by my mother's leaving him. Convinced that she would "come to her senses," he, too, moved up to Hamilton and took an apartment not a stone's throw from my sister's house. The proximity was an awkward one. Paul wanted nothing to do with me or my sister or his step-grandchild; he wanted only to get his wife back. He would invite my mother to dinner, she would hesitantly accept, and the evening would usually end with one or both of them crying, with Paul's trying to follow my mother into my sister's house and my mother's closing the door in his face. He would ring the bell; the baby would start crying; my sister, as newly established matriarch of a system gone haywire, would start screaming.

Amid this drama (probably because of it), my sister and I fell into a lot of intimate talks about our childhood, about why we'd become the people we were, and it was during one of these talks that I came out to her. She shook her head yes. She said she'd figured as much. Then she burst into tears. I finally got it out of her that she was crying because of the regular worries: that I would have a hard life, that I would get beaten up, that

I would get AIDS. Then a new worry surfaced on her face. "You haven't told anyone else, have you?"

"In the family? No. Just you."

"Good. Don't."

She may have simply thought the timing wasn't right. But I felt the timing was perfect. The family had been capsized and we were already in the act of getting our new bearings; why not get *all* of the waves behind us? I came out to my mother. She burst into tears and expressed the same concerns my sister had. I called my cousin and aunt in Atlanta and came out to them. I called my brother, who was out of the Navy by now, living in Missouri and heading toward his own divorce. "Yeah, that makes sense," the gruff, smoky voice said calmly over the phone line, "because you never watched *Star Trek*." When I asked him what he meant, he said guys who didn't date girls were usually either *Star Trek* freaks, or gay.

Finally, I drove over to Paul's apartment, with the intention of coming out to him.

He'd been living there for six months, still waiting for my mother to take him back, but it looked as if he'd just moved in the day before. There wasn't a single picture on the walls, there was no furniture other than a bed, a dresser, a television and a pair of aluminum lawn chairs. I'd brought a pizza and a six-pack of beer with me, and when I opened the refriger- ator, it was empty save for another six-pack and a pizza box. Paul and I were not used to being alone together. I was nervous but resolved to do what I'd come to do. We each opened a beer and sat down in the lawn chairs. There was a football game on the television and the sound was turned down. I said, "Dad, we have to talk about something."

"I know," he said, looking down at his beer. "I know what you're going to say. But you don't have to apologize, it's just the way things are."

I let this ride for a moment, then said, "Apologize for what?"

"You and your sister have sided with your mother in all this. You had to make a decision, and you made it. There's no use apologizing for it now."

"That's crazy," I said. "We didn't 'side' with Mom."

"You're all over there, and I'm *here*!" he said loudly.

I wanted to tell him it wasn't as if a custody battle had taken place and he'd lost; when would he ever have fought for me, anyway? But I could see it in his expression and hear it in his voice: It was *just* like a custody battle in his mind. He was determined to take this as hard as he could, to be as much the victim as possible, and I got so bent out of shape, I decided on the spot that he didn't deserve my coming out to him, that he'd done nothing to warrant such an intimate exchange of information between us. I left without telling him.

THE DUST SETTLED, somewhat. I got accepted into graduate school and moved to Ohio for two years. My sister remarried and had two more children. My mother moved out, bought a town house, and settled into grandmotherhood. When I finished my master's degree, I moved down to Richmond and got a job teaching at an urban college campus. I was living just two hours away from my family (with the exception of my brother, who was still out in Missouri) and I saw them every few months. I was, by this time, "out" to all of my friends, to my employers, even to some of my students. But I had yet to come out to Paul. Four years after the divorce, he was still wearing his wedding band, still living in a nearly empty apartment, still watching television at night from an aluminum chair. On the one hand, I'd stopped caring that I wasn't out to him; he never called me, had little to say when I called him, and seemed just as uninterested in my adult life as he had been in my childhood. On the other hand, he was fifty-six years old, and his own father and grandfather had dropped dead at sixty-one; I hated the idea of his suddenly dying with a gulf of unsaid things between us.

I was working up the nerve to come out to him—I was actually taking notes on what I would say—when the phone rang. "It's your dad," he said in a flat voice.

"Hi," I said, surprised that he'd dialed my number. "I was just getting ready to call you. I—I have something to tell you."

"I have something to tell you, too. I'm getting married."

He could have announced that *he* was gay and my shock probably wouldn't have been greater. "What are you talking about?"

"It's been a long time, you know. I've waited a long time, and I've accepted the fact that your mother and I will never reconcile our differences. I'm getting married."

"Okay," I said. "I'm gay."

I heard a little huff of expelled breath like an aborted laugh against the receiver, and he said, "I've known that since you were in high school."

HE HAD SAT there in that aluminum chair every night for more than four years, staring at the television with his life on hold. Then, on impulse—the same kind of impulse that seems to have dictated much of his life when he was in his early twenties—he had picked up the phone, called directory assistance in Philadelphia, and looked up Jennifer's old number. Instead of reaching her, he'd reached her father, who was ninety-seven years old and had no memory of Paul, but who told him Jennifer was living in Boston now. He gave Paul the phone number. Paul dialed Boston.

In the interim between 1965 and 1996, Jennifer had gotten married, had had two daughters, and had become a widow; her husband had died of cancer. I don't know what that initial conversation was like—it was the first time she and Paul had spoken in more than thirty years—but clearly the same spark that had been there three decades earlier was still there now, for Paul soon after flew up to Boston for a visit. Then Jennifer flew down to Virginia for a visit. Now Paul and Jennifer were getting married and had plans to settle down together—in Hamilton.

As for the rest of us: My sister had just gotten divorced from her second husband; my brother's divorce had finally come through, and he was swearing he would never marry again; my mother was going through a string of miserable, short-term boyfriends, each one reducing her to an emotional wreck; and I had become a serial monogamist, latching myself onto one man after another, craving their approval as much as I craved romance and finding that while the latter always petered out, the former was never enough for me.

But Paul was getting married. To Jennifer.

IT'S ONE THING to accept the fact that your parents were never really in love. It's another thing entirely to embrace the idea that your father might have spent the bulk of his adult life married to the wrong woman (your mother) only because he was trying to make good on a mistake (you). I met Jennifer for the first time a few weeks after their private wedding ceremony, and while I was nervous and hesitant and preoccupied with history, I couldn't help but like her. She was calm, and exceedingly polite. And Paul, around her, was a changed man: lively, engaged, *mirthful*. He was the kind of man I would have liked to have had as a father when I was growing up.

They moved into a small house in Hamilton and decorated it to the nines. Jennifer's younger daughter was still in high school, and so she lived with them, and Paul, in turn, became much more involved in her life than he ever had been in mine. I was both jealous and glad to see it.

When Jennifer suffered a stroke two years into their marriage, Paul called and talked to me for over an hour (longer than we had ever talked on the phone). He was scared, of course, and he went into every detail of what had happened, what the doctors had explained, what the prognosis was. The slight paralysis and most of the other side effects turned out to be temporary, thankfully, but there was a stretch of six months or so when they weren't really sure what was going to happen. Listening to Paul talk about his wife with such involvement and intensity during that period made me feel farther away from him than ever. He was sharing information, he was making the choice to call *me* and tell *me* what was going on, but he was talking like someone I'd never known—someone who cared about his family more than anything else in the world. He wanted me, suddenly, to be part of it, and I didn't feel up to the role.

A year later, after Jennifer seemed to be out of the woods, I wrote Paul a letter for the first time in my life. It was such an anomaly that I spent the first paragraph explaining why I was writing as opposed to calling, how I was never able to get around to saying what I wanted to say to him over the phone, or in person, and how I was going to try to say it here, on paper. Then I proceeded, over six pages, to describe how I saw the shape of our relationship, how I'd felt he disliked me as a child, how I'd eventually started disliking him and how our having never acknowledged any of this was preventing our becoming truly close. I'd come out to everyone else in the family but had waited four more *years* before coming out to him; didn't he see that as an indicator that something was wrong?

I had the sickening feeling, dropping the letter into the mailbox, that I would never hear from him again. But within days I received a reply. "What you can't realize," his letter read in the first paragraph, "is how hard it was for me when your mother ended our marriage." I was stunned. The bulk of my letter had been about events pre-1980, but here he was, hyperfocused on *the divorce*—as if my mother's leaving him was a nuclear explosion on the time line, a mushroom cloud emanating rings that wiped away all deeds past and future. I wrote back that I wanted to talk to him about my childhood; he wrote back just as swiftly that he could not "revisit those days," that it was too painful, that we had to move forward. I didn't answer that second letter. And we didn't speak again for nearly a year. When I finally broke the silence, calling him on Father's Day of 1997, he sounded glad to hear from me, and we managed an entire conversation—and have managed every conversation since—without once mentioning the letters, the year of silence that had passed, the possibility that anything was less than perfect between us.

I HAVE NO doubt that I would understand Paul differently, had I become a father myself. Straight sons who grow up to become fathers are usually provided with a template for the job, which they can choose either to ignore or modify or follow to the letter; those of us who don't have kids—still the majority of gay men—have no use for the template. What I have in place of a straight son's understanding of his father is a gay son's somewhat humbling recognition that his own adult life and his father's (so far) are not without their similarities. That is to say, I, too, have done some desperate moving around, have jumped at a few impulses; I've bailed out of a couple of relationships and been kicked out of a couple more—and I haven't always landed on my feet.

I live in Manhattan now, where I met my lover, Fred, and we've been together for three years. Fred is forty-one and has been HIV-positive nearly half his life. He's one of those remarkable comeback kids: In 1995 he had a single T-cell and a viral load so high, it forced the doctors to recalibrate the scale. He was one of the first people to receive a protease inhibitor, and by experimenting with combinations of Western and Eastern medicine he's brought himself back from the abyss more than once. Since much of this ongoing battle took place before we ever met, I'm still learning how to cope with it—how to be supportive, always, and how to step out of the way, sometimes, when Fred tells me there's no reason to panic.

Five months ago, there was reason to panic. He lost all his energy and slept for nearly three days straight. He wouldn't eat and began running a fever. At noon on the third day I came home from work to find him delirious, dehydrated, and burning up with a temperature above 104. He had chest pains, and there was blood in his urine. The next forty-eight hours are something of a blur: taxis and doctors' offices and the emergency room at St. Vincent's; blood tests and urine tests and sonograms and chest X rays. T-cell and viral load counts. His temperature dropped down to normal and rose again, then plummeted to 93. According to the doctors, he had some of the symptoms of flu, but no flu. He had all the symptoms of a kidney stone, but no kidney stone in evidence. The chest pains came and went, but like everything else: without explanation.

Eventually, he began to feel better. In the ensuing weeks, I had casual phone conversations with my mother, my sister, even one with my brother (whom I called out of the blue), but with none of them could I discuss this most recent mini-crisis, because I hadn't told anyone in my family about Fred's HIV status. The circumstance, in fact, had become a kind of second closet. I was afraid of how they might react. I didn't want to deal with their being unsupportive and couldn't face having to heap their anxieties on top of my own. And of course, this had made for a lot of conversations wherein I wasn't honest about what was going on in my life.

When Paul called in November—the first time we'd spoken in months—I asked him how things were going and he went into a happy litany of porch-building, dog-washing, steak-grilling. He told me in detail about the cruise he and Jennifer were purchasing a year in advance. Then he asked how I was. A second before the words came out of my mouth, I didn't know they were coming. Maybe some part of me—the part that was always angry with him—wanted to throw a challenge into his face (*react badly, why don't you, so that we finally have something tangible to fight about*); maybe I'd just reached a breaking point in my silence.

I told him everything. He listened to it all as calmly as if I were talking about my job. Then he started talking about Jennifer.

He talked about her stroke, her recovery, his involvement. "If you're asking my advice . . ." he said, and then hesitated.

I wasn't. But it occurred to me that I'd never before heard him say anything even close to that. "Yeah," I said—and suddenly I meant it. "I want your advice."

"Be there for him, whatever happens, whatever it takes. And make sure he knows it."

The fact that this was already my game plan didn't matter. I was thirty-six years old, Paul was sixty-one, and he was giving me advice for the first time. I would never know who the great love of his life was—he'd been so devastated by my mother's leaving him and seemed so much happier with Jennifer—but it didn't matter. He was passing on to me something he'd learned: something that may be self-evident to most people and may be even inherent, but something he'd had to *learn,* and thought I should know.

It made me feel close to him, for a while. I went to his house at Christmas and spent the day with him and Jennifer and Jennifer's two daughters who had flown in from their respective homes in different parts of the country. Paul had wallpapered a few rooms over the past year and wanted to show me the upstairs, and in taking that tour, I realized that while there were dozens of framed photographs and snapshots hanging on the walls

THE END OF THE BEGINNING ▪

and clustered on tables and dressers, there wasn't a single picture of me in the entire house. When I got back to New York, I wrote them a thank-you note for their hospitality, and I included in the envelope a snapshot of me.

A month later, Paul called and told me they'd received the note.

"Then you got the picture?"

"Yes," he said. There was a long pause—as if a radio dial had been turned to dead air. Then he said, "Jennifer liked it."

GARY REED

Mites

I dropped out of college after my freshman year and was looking for a job, still living at home. My parents didn't think I was looking hard enough, so my dad took the initiative of getting me hired at Oklahoma Steel Castings Company as an inspectors' helper, where by that time he was an inspector.

At six feet and 125 pounds with shoulder-length hair, bell-bottom jeans and platform shoes, I wasn't exactly a prime candidate for manual labor, but my dad had seemed extremely pleased at the prospect of my working with him every day, earning a union wage of nearly $9 an hour. At nineteen, my independence was as repressed as my sexuality, and while I lived beneath his roof, I lived pretty much within his control.

It was hell's Oklahoma outpost on a twenty-four-hour schedule: an incessant roar; raging pits of fire; massive crane-hung urns of molten scrap lowering, rising, swinging overhead; electric horns blasting heads-up warnings over the thunderous din; men caked in filthy sweatshirts, coveralls, helmets, gloves, leather aprons, simmering in their own sweat; everything dimmed by a grimy light; my snot and spit black with steel dust.

An inspectors' helper was an extraneous body filling a job with no actual definition. My dad was one of four inspectors who ensured that all the contracted castings leaving the plant were of sound quality, so I worked for him as well as three others. I was always in somebody's way, a clumsy obstruction in any inch of space I occupied, constantly yelled at to watch out, duck, or move. I spent the greatest part of my days looking for the most out-of-the-way place to just stand and make myself as inconspicuous as possible, blanking out as many of the torturous hours as I could before being spotted and barked into some other place.

Most often, I went to the sheet yard in a forklift looking for the chalk-marked grade and tonnage I'd been sent to retrieve for the foundry. I'd climb up on the rails to center the jaws of the crane on the top lip of steel sheets the size of double garage doors. Back on the ground, I'd slide it out of its storage slot with the mere pressure of my thumb on a compass of electric buttons and levitate the solid ton piece into the air. I'd angle it around by hand with the strain of my whole back pushing it into the most lumbering of spins, positioning it just so as it lowered onto the specially rigged fork of the lift.

On the best of days I could hope for, I'd be pointed toward dozens of barrels of raw castings in some remote shed in the yard, where I'd pass the hours with a hand grinder, shaving off the burrs and dingleberries of the molded castings, without a clue as to what the alien articles were. In the scale of the foundry's massive fireworks, the stray sparks of the grinders seemed as harmless as a swarm of gnats buzzing against my lap until the thighs of my jeans suddenly burst into flames, ignited by the misaimed shower of embers. In a panic, I hurled the grinder from my hands. It banged off the pavement with its blade still spinning and jumped and skidded across the yard until the leash of its electrical cord choked it to death. Adrenaline drove my feet backward as the fire leapt at the front of my shirt. Once I'd witlessly swatted out the blaze with my gloved hands, I critically studied the grinder and judged it most likely permanently damaged. My thoughts actually paused over the inanimate machine with more regret for its scrapes and dents than I gave to my own blistering legs.

Confessing the mishap, I showed the grinder to my dad, expecting a shameful end to my career as a foundryman and a humiliating ruination of his own reputation. He simply shrugged and showed me where the tool room was. There was neither high regard for nor short supply of grinders in hell. It did take him a day and a half to find me a leather apron.

Regardless of the potential for self-immolation, I was grateful for the solitude of the yard. Being assigned anywhere within the foundry meant bearing witness to the ritualized homophobia of the all-male crew. There were a couple of other apprentices and helpers around my age, even one other longhair who smoked joints out behind the sheet bins, but most of the foundrymen were my father's age or older and, like him, were "lifers." They'd started with the company as men my age, knew no other kind of work, and intended to retire from the same place. They were all married, even the hippie, most with children. Statistics prove otherwise, but they were all presumably straight men, as redneck and macho as Oklahomans can be. Yet, with rare exceptions, they could not do their work without the threat or invitation to fuck one another in the ass, suck one another's dicks, or the exchange of lewd tongue wags or mimed jerk-offs. They called each other Pansy and Doll and Pussy and Sweetheart as well as faggot, cocksucker, and queerbait. Once, a welder was bent over a workbench and a dye cutter grabbed him from behind and started pumping his ass doggie style. When the welder broke free of the grip, he chased the cutter away with his lit blowtorch while most of the rest of the crew guffawed. It was serious fun and it was relentless.

My youth, my build, and my hair made me the prime butt for such fun. My very first morning, when my dad introduced me to the other inspectors, Lou, a forty-year-old, bearish Cherokee with deep acne scars, turned straight to my father and deadpanned, "She's sweet, Paul. I love that ponytail, honey," he said to me with a hot whistle. "Can I feel it? Oh, I better not, I'm all sticky." He crinkled his cratered nose and lifted his pinkie delicately from the doughnut he had pushed into his mouth. I didn't know how to respond and so laughed good-naturedly but uneasily until my dad said matter-of-factly, "First rule around here is ignore anything Lou has to say—the rest of us do." What was most obvious to me was how my father was one of the exceptional outsiders to this foundry-wide code of conduct.

Not that he wasn't one of the guys in every other respect. He held no superior rank and little seniority. No one bothered to curb their inclinations on my account as Paul's son, so I couldn't believe that he was offended by what he saw and heard on an hourly basis for longer than I'd been alive. He displayed no reaction at all, really, and I certainly looked to him for reaction, because I was mortified by the vulgarity and terrified by the implications.

My fear of being a queer had rendered me an asexual virgin as well as a heterosexual poser at nineteen. Even the gay men I'd met in the theater department during my year at the state college were in the closet in 1972. To have such a nightmarish distortion of my most private inclinations played out over and over all around me by normal, average men acting out normal average contempt and disgust and with such hilarity made me unspeakably secretive. But didn't my father have any doubt about me at all? Was I so up to standard in his eyes that he risked his own reputation by bringing me into the foundry as a worker and another Doll for all the queer-baiting? Maybe he was testing me for my mettle, for my own good in the real world as he knew it to be. In his quiet way, he might actually have been proud of me, and this job, to him, was a means of showing it. "College boy" was my nickname around the plant. Even as a dropout, I was the foundry's first worker with any higher education—my dad was the first to send any of his kids to college. With his eighth-grade education in a one-room school, I guess that warranted him some pride and respect.

When I was younger, my father had been a crane operator on the night shift at the foundry. Until I started working there, the clearest image I had of his occupation was a gilt-framed, amateurish drawing on a sheet of typing paper that hung in the bedroom hallway amid all the family portraits. Other than the revolving display of my own grade-school paintings on the refrigerator door, it was the only semblance of original art in our house. The fact that my father had drawn it as an adult was a wonder to me. The picture was of a man in full figure from bulbous-toed boots to flattop haircut, a crude caricature of my father himself. The expressionless fellow had his feet balanced in the bend of a giant hook at the lower end of a thick vertical cable from which he swung out to the side Tarzan style from a carefree single-handed grip. The block print across the top of the picture read "THE FOUNDRY IS NO CIRCUS" and along the bottom warned, "SO DON'T BE A CLOWN." My mother had told me—for in spite of my intrigue about my father's singular artistic endeavor, I'd never mentioned the picture to him for fear of his embarrassment—that the drawing was from a safety-poster contest at the foundry and was the second-place winner at that.

My dad's picture betrayed none of the foundry's filth or swelter, its hivelike pace or its pervasive dangers. It certainly didn't illustrate the man-on-man fucking obsession. But maybe my dad's safety slogan explained his nonparticipation in all the sexual monkey business at the foundry. Whether he agreed with the attitude behind such clowning or not, the foundry was no circus to my dad. I saw his point just a few years later when I came home from school and found him drugged on the couch instead of asleep in bed as usual. His left hand was buried in a bandage big as a melon. A sheet of steel had slipped from the crane's grip and sliced off his index finger at the bottom knuckle. He'd carried his finger to the emergency room in his lunch bucket.

Throughout my childhood, my father worked while everyone else slept. In the kitchen with the lights off, he dressed himself: patched-up blue jeans, soot-stained sweatshirt, Frankensteinish boots. He had the key in his pickup's ignition no more than five minutes after getting up from his and my mother's bed without so much as a splash of water to his soon-to-be black-caked face.

The graveyard shift ended shortly after my school day began, which meant my dad spent the broadest stretch of daylight asleep. He'd be awakened for supper, after which he remained stooped over the cleared table with the morning's paper. He read in a thorough, methodical order, rephrasing aloud any bit of news he found interesting, maddening or amusing, supposedly for my mother's benefit, as she washed the dishes a room away. Sometimes he even described the comic strips frame by frame.

He'd watch television for a short while before returning to bed for a couple more hours and then start all over again. He worked overtime whenever he could; that was most Saturdays, occasional double shifts, and some Sundays as well.

In the way of a child, I intuited the strain of my parents' opposite work schedules in my mother's unpredictable moodiness and my father's sense of resignation. He earned a higher wage working nights and that allowed us as a family to "get ahead" or "out from under" instead of just "making do." I understood early on that my going to college figured into those overheard vague phrases between them. But in my heart, I sided with my mother's unhappiness with my dad's hours. Her unhappiness meant something to me because I was sure I loved her. Although she worked as well, she was home when I was, she made and maintained the home we had. I knew what made her proud, what disappointed her, what angered her, and what made her laugh. I knew I was her son. Whereas my dad was barely more than a tolerated stranger at the dinner table. The fact that his chronic absence was attributed to my own future benefit carried no emotional value to me as a boy. I felt no gratitude for his personal sacrifice because I had no sense of his person.

By the time I was in high school and my father was finally working day shifts as an inspector, I'd deduced that he and I had very little in common as people, even less as men. Aside from our basic human decency we had more to despise than to respect between us—temperament, intellect, politics, religion, moral and social consciousness—but time and circumstances had taught us both by then the profound advantages of silence, not only to our cohabitation but also as a means of habitation in general. As a child, I'd not even had the opportunity of his presence to make any such judgment or to have any level of relationship beyond the rather dull wariness toward his absence and the subconscious sense of something maybe amiss.

I might have been five or six years old the first and only time I ever saw my father naked. He and I were the sole occupants of a men's shower room on the shore of a lake. We'd stripped out of our swim trunks to wash the mud off our feet and change into dry clothes for the drive home. Without sexual knowledge or even curiosity, I didn't know how to account for the exotic factuality of his genitals. I was dumbstruck by the vision of his body—could not rest my eyes on the full sight. My eyes felt too small or his body seemed too great, or my modesty was too great and my reaction was too overwhelming. The furtive view of his naked body made him more man to me but no less an enigma. In the spray of the shower beside him, my own sense of physicality washed away down the drain. My own connectedness to him did not occur to me. I felt no gene within me whispering evolutionary aspirations for his masculine model. I couldn't conceive myself ever becoming such a creature.

Another time, when I was around the same age, I was sprawled on my bedroom floor one night involved in some puzzle or board game and looked up to find my dad, just home from a party, standing in the open doorframe watching me. I sensed something different about him, something in his eyes and the way he regarded me. Louder than necessary, he almost shouted, "Hello Gary," and he added my middle name, which only my mother ever used, and only when she was mad. He said it with affection and a rare smile. He swayed slightly stepping into the room and asked what I was up to. Nothing, I told him, suddenly fascinated by his loose manner and even more so by the goodwill of his interest. "You want to wrestle?" he asked. I laughed as if at the absurdity of the invitation but at the nervous thrill it stirred in me as well. "Why not?"

he said, falling on all fours on the floor beside me. "I want to grapple with my boy."

"Get off the floor, silly. You've had one too many," my mother chided, loosening her earrings as she stopped by the door.

"We're only talking," he said over one shoulder. "And I only had a couple."

"Well get up. I need help with this stuck latch."

My dad returned his attention to me. "Anything stuck in your ear?" He put his face so near mine, I felt the heat radiating from his flushed cheeks. His warmth was a new experience. In that instant, I felt completely in love with my father. It bubbled out of me in unbridled laughter as he pounced on top of me and took my ear between his lips. The tune he started humming filled my whole body with vibrations. The shaved stubble of his face and neck against my own was a sensual pleasure I squirmed closer to.

"Stop it now, Paul, before you hurt him," my mother warned, but she wasn't part of the equation of the moment. I loved the feel of my father against me as we tousled and rolled across the carpet. I loved his solid weight and strength and the incongruous tenderness of those aspects in his rowdy embraces. More than my delight in the roughhousing was my intoxication with his presence, the immediacy of his being there on the floor over, under, and around me. "You're drunk," I teased him, but I wanted my dad and me both to be so drunk always.

The elation sobered as unexpectedly as it had begun when I twisted a shoulder against the floor and cried out with the sharp pain. The playful shine of my father's eyes went cloudy with bewilderment. His hands flew off me and hung defensively at his sides as he froze, kneeling rigidly above me.

"I told you you were going to hurt him," my mother said angrily, pushing my dad out of her way as she came to my aid.

"We were only playing," my dad insisted.

"Too rough," she answered and accused him again of having too much to drink, which he again denied. It was the first time I ever wanted to defend my father against any of my mother's critical remarks, but before I could admit that I really wasn't hurt—the pain had been momentary and was more an accident of my own exuberance than my dad's—my father had gotten to his feet and left the room, proclaiming he didn't know I was so delicate I couldn't take a little jostling but he knew it now

157

and it sure as shit wouldn't happen again. His words pinched a nerve deeper than any in my shoulder. Although he came to my bed later that night and said he was sorry if he had hurt me—"You didn't, Dad, I'm fine"—he nevertheless kept his vow.

It's tempting to think my father and I both withdrew a little farther from one another after that night, but in fact, we simply returned to the emotional distance we'd always known. The reason for that gnawing estrangement is what remains unknown. In some infantile core of consciousness, I resent his early absence, having experienced it as rejection. A shrink once suggested that my dropping out of college was a vengeful ploy against all his years of night shifts and daylight hours in bed. I think I was immature and directionless, tired of school and eager for my own life to begin. What I've always felt is that my father disapproves of me, so in defense I've done my best to hide my truest self from him, including my sexuality—less fodder for the fire. Yet, I cannot illustrate any evidence of his disappointment or shame except for the equal lack of any opposite evidence. It's not that my father was particularly unwelcoming or critical or gruff. He was never mean. I've always thought him a kind man, gentle if physically ungraceful and usually soft-spoken in his highly opinionated way. Having never heard him say "I love you" or "I'm proud of you," I'm left only with his early absence and his present silence. But, I'm also left with one memory of near-perfect communion with the man.

We were on some boondock, backwoods road in Arkansas, the station wagon spitting dust, rocks banging the floorboards and June bugs splattering the windshield. My father was at the wheel, my mother next to him telling him to slow down. My grandmother, Mur, leaned forward from the backseat with a mournful groan, dabbed the snuff juice from the corners of her pursed lips with a folded hankie and asked creakily, "Oh, Lordy, Paul, idn't that it?" I was too slumped in the seat next to her to catch sight of the turnoff she indicated: just a rutted trail through wild wooded pastures that slapped at the car doors and clawed at the windows with big leafy paws.

If Mur hadn't stirred my head from her shoulder and the air-conditioner hadn't shut off with the killed motor, I might have remained where I lay in dozy lethargy induced by the springy drive and the way the August light glazed over my senses.

Outside the car, we were knee-deep in the country, the place my father was born. The gray wood remains of a house stood off in the distance, no more than a collapsed roof and a few partial walls, not enough rubble for more than four or five rooms for a family of eleven.

My mother held Mur's pocketbook while my grandmother fussed with her sun hat. My father, already a few yards ahead, surveying the field with his back to the rest of us, stood solemn and still, his forearm a visor for his eyes. Through a ditch of cattails and fountain grass, I waded up behind him, responding to his unguarded stance and deeper-than-normal silence. There was a mythic charge to the dazzling heat and the stunning aural texture of the unstirred air. The moment sizzled with light as I approached my father. It was strange how he appealed to me, how dimensional his presence on the edge of that abandoned Arkansas field. He'd rarely before been so present to me. The women with whom I'd normally have lingered and aligned my pace receded to a distant murmur somewhere behind me as I made my way to his side.

"What are you doing?" he asked. The question came out thin and aspirated. I don't think he expected to find me there with him, wasn't planning on having to speak. I couldn't even explain my own presence. Why were we here? What did he want in that overgrown field of ragweed and gopher holes?

"I want to come with you," I answered, compelled by the rare opportunity to choose my father's company even though the choice was wrought with the potential to disappoint him.

My dad straddled the gully between the road and the pasture and, without so much as a grunt of warning, latched his hands beneath my arms and lifted me over the ditch. I lost a shoe as my legs swept through the tall weeds. Telling me to stand still, he lowered me to the ground, then squatted and slapped through the grasses until he retrieved the missing dime-store thong.

"Good lands, son, you can't go traipsing through here in a pair of flip-flops!"

Not a full minute had passed between us and I already felt defeated by the effort of his company. "Yeah, I can," I assured him, hurriedly refitting the sandal to my foot, clinching my toes for traction against the flimsy rubber. As he took in the sight of me, the scrutiny felt drier than the daylight on the land. With the sun blazing overhead, I couldn't meet his eyes without squinting. The harder I squinted, the less of him I could see, which only threw me back into my own feelings of daintiness and flip-floppiness.

"All right," he finally said, "just watch where you're going—a piece of barbed wire could . . ." He put his hand on the back of my neck, drawing me alongside his reckless stride. His touch was unexpected. I felt the coarse breadth of his palm from ear to ear as we tramped toward the ruins of the old house in the most distant corner of the field. The sensation distracted me. I fought off an urge to turn my face into it—the perfect dock for the prow of my face, it seemed as if the press of my father's hand just then over my features could've changed the cast of my mother's mold.

I did my best to keep up with him, to maintain the casual back-and-forthness of his hand on my head and the guided forwardness of his assurance in the unwelcoming environment, until my ears and nose started tickling with the hum of gnats and I felt my ankles and knees nicked by the ricochet of grasshoppers leaping up from the underbrush. "Daddy, wait!" I said, coming to a spastic standstill. As if on command, the insects immediately settled so that I twitched and swatted at nothing but the blank and quiet air around my face. My father had withdrawn his hand, almost reflexively, at my whiney outburst.

"So many bugs," I explained feebly, rubbing my arms.

"Worse than bugs," he said, digging at the dirt with his foot. I looked down to see the toe of his boot pry the sheath of a snake skin from its camouflage with the earth and grass. He kicked the dried hull aside and sauntered on toward the ramshackle remains of the old farm.

There it was again, the burden of that shift between us. I felt the challenge of his masculinity—great slabs and pylons of manliness falling down between us like a catastrophe of my own misstep.

He walked away toward the house as if proceeding deeper into himself, his thumb hooked in his hip pocket. I stood right where I'd come to rest—dead center, I realized, looking around—in the hickish nowhere. The car and road were completely out of sight. A quick look back and my father's head was no longer visible; just the singed stovepipe and the few vertical beams of the house the termites hadn't yet downed could be seen through the slats of weeds that encased me.

I felt like I'd come to a painful emotional place with my father—one of overwhelming confusion—where I'd been many times before and yet had managed to forget again and again.

I wandered a few steps farther and found myself in the midst of a dense blackberry patch. Most of the berries had burst on the vine. Flies swarmed over the juicy mush, but a few still looked firm enough to eat. I plucked one particularly large berry among a number I delicately tested between my fingertips. I sniffed it, licked it with the tip of my tongue, and waited for ill effects while surveying the quiet surroundings: nothing but the buzz of horseflies and the bitchy squawk of a jay circling the empty sky. Thinking of Mur's cobblers and pies bubbling out of the oven and wondering why my dad would never let me turn the crank on the ice-cream maker, I popped the berry into my mouth and bit into it. I gagged, my throat closing at the rank, sour juice. I nearly unhinged my jaw letting the contents spill out and then spit all that I could before I dared swallow.

Just then I heard my name being called, first by my father, then by my mother's more distant voice. I yelled back and began trudging quickly toward the road.

On the drive back, I began to itch.

"Chiggers, probably," my father said from up front, "or poison ivy— you shouldn't have traipsed off like you did." When we got back to Mur's, he pushed me into the bathroom, where I peeled down my shorts. He kneeled down to take a look. From waist to ankles across my scratch marks were scores of parasites. He sighed, lifting me onto the countertop where the tiles were cold against my bare seat, and he began to pluck, one by one, each blood-filled mite. He picked them off whole and unbroken, his large fingernails working like tweezers, pinching, lifting, smashing, then flicking the little black smears of blood into the white basin.

After a while, I stopped squirming, finally gave up my humiliation and slumped back against the mirror, just a scrawny twig of a boy, naked under my father's blunt probing fingers. I took comfort in the intimacy of my father's patience with the operation and let go of some of my resentment from earlier in the day. As usual, because it was comfortable, we said virtually nothing the whole time alone together, beyond a few whines and "ows" on my part and my father's comment on my problematic peach fuzz "down there," which made us both grin.

I closed my eyes eventually, entranced by the attention, the dreamy, repetitive picking at my skin and the trust of his touch, its caring and tenderness. My mind drifted and sprawled like a blackberry patch behind a tidy woodframe house in the country. I thought I heard my daddy whistling, pictured him running through the fields with a silver bucket glinting in the sun.

THESE DAYS, IN his seventies, my father is receding into deafness. Though my mother angrily insists at times that "he hears what he wants to hear," she spends more time cajoling him to get a hearing test, to ask his doctor about a hearing aid, which he stubbornly refuses. He denies any loss of hearing. My brief yearly visits show me otherwise, in sometimes-comic misunderstandings. I've learned to speak louder to him and to make sure I face him when speaking; I try to keep my remarks simple, using short words and uncomplicated sentences. It makes me feel child-ish around him, probably makes him feel childish as well. Worse even, it keeps us from making the effort. We watch a lot of ball games on TV together when I'm home; that is, we sit in the same room with a football game on TV while he watches between naps and I either read or pretend to watch while my mind wanders as far from sports as it is prone to do.

The irony of his hearing loss saddens me. Even if his bullheaded insis-tence on ignoring it and letting it take its course means he's at peace with shutting out the voice of his family as well as the rest of the world, I hate to think of him consumed in silence for his remaining years. Maybe I still have hopes of a conversation someday, a true exchange of words, heard and felt, held and considered, tendered and returned with resolution and respect. Maybe my life is still choked with too much silence from the past and the personal pain is too great to wish on anybody I love so much, even the father who seems to have been the teacher of all that quiet.

I'm out to my parents now, but it was a long time coming. I wrote a gay novel and so we didn't even have to have a real conversation about it. We've lived in different states for twenty years and we correspond with letters mostly that my mother writes for both her and my dad. So even on the topic of my queerness, he's never said a word of his own. On my vis-its since, the issue hasn't been raised directly.

My mother wrote that the news came as a total shock—hard for me to believe at the age of forty. But then, my mother, while not exactly a prude, is a bit naïve. On the other hand, while my father can be an actual prude, he is not naïve. I cannot help recalling my days at the foundry and all those coarse queer jokes, all those slurpy air smooches and how frightening it was for me to smile along. I cannot help remembering how my dad ignored it all, never acknowledged it one way or another. I still wonder what that means. Does he think of his queer son in that demeaning way? Why would his thinking be any different from any of his lifelong peers and coworkers?

I don't know the answers to any of my questions about my father. He's the last man on earth I'd ever want to discuss my or his sexuality with, and he's the one man in my life I want most to discuss it all with. But the pattern of not saying things is too ingrained in us both.

After three months, Oklahoma Steel Castings laid me off and a dozen other men due to a lost contract. I'd never been so relieved. My father, showing no understanding of me at all, but having some apparent faith in my ability, immediately talked to a buddy at another foundry and had me reemployed within a week. I stuck it out there for as long as I could, trying to prove my masculinity to my dad and myself. After six months I quit to take a job with a landscape nursery, feeling that, as long as I continued to work with my hands and body and ended up dirty at the end of the day, even for half the salary, my father wouldn't think too much less of me.

ALFRED CORN

Daddy

"I hate you!" Words of paradoxical devotion, stirred up by something sarcastic Daddy had just said at the dinner table. But they were announced over my interior audio system, not out loud. I've often wondered what my sisters and stepmother, sitting stolidly at their appointed places, would have done if I'd blurted it out. I knew, or believed, or feared Daddy would kill me if he could have heard what was reverberating in the little cell block between my ears. My sole chance of survival was to keep my trap shut. That was the pattern: Pretend to enjoy your dinner, avoid talking, and hope the meal would pass without blood and mayhem. Even so, there were also times when I got the eerie, sweaty feeling Daddy had the power to read my mind. Come to think of it, he could—not through ESP, but just by looking at me. You didn't have to be Freud to size up a kid about eight years old, with Oedipal parricide written all over his face, bent over his plate as he shoveled down his mashed potatoes, green beans, and a pork chop so he could get it over with as soon as possible. My older sisters Margaret and Zoe looked the opposite of placid, and my step-mother betrayed a certain humid nervousness herself by constantly jumping up to take away or bring something to the table. We all knew that at some point during this family ritual, one of us kids (the designated sacrifice) would start sobbing, jerk to our feet, push back our chair, and run from the kitchen, leaving the half-eaten pork chop behind. It was the natural result of hearing your character and behavior put through the shredder; and we never knew in advance who was going to be sitting in the hot seat that particular day.

So how did this middle-aged man wearing a white shirt and bow tie, with dark hair combed straight back, carefully trimmed mustache, and a thin film of sweat on his forehead get to be such a caveman with his kids? Nobody knew; apparently fathers at some point undergo an operation replacing the heart with a flint surrogate. He was who he was, with the same kind of finality that iced his prefab answer to all our protesting whys: "Because I *said* so." Another favorite dictum was "As long as you live under my roof and eat off my table, you will do as I say." The house and table were his; we were his servants, although with no salary except room and board and a few coins dropped in our palms once a week as an "allowance." Those were the terms of servitude. Break one of his decrees and be punished by the belt, a disciplinary resource that probably amounts to child abuse. I don't doubt that Daddy himself qualified as a victim of abuse before inflicting it on the next generation. My grandfather was a museum-quality patriarch, ruling with an iron hand that must often have come down on my father when he was a kid. Not that anyone criticized their shared approach to parenting, but if it had been questioned, they could and would cite the Bible: "Whom the Lord loveth, the Lord chastiseth," or hoary old saws like "Spare the rod and spoil the child." Spoiling a child was the worst thing you could do; and we were so loved and so unspoiled as to be trembling, mute little robots, doing our Father's will in terrified obedience.

It was like living with what they used to call a "Saturday night special": You never knew when it might go off on you. Actually, Daddy really did pack heat—at least he owned a pistol, which he kept in a drawer in the bedroom. One day he told me he wanted to teach me how to shoot it (this was one of his excruciating and abortive efforts to Make a Man of Me). We drove to the woods outside town. He set up a tin can on a log some thirty feet away from us and then blew it off its perch with the practiced skill of the army veteran. If there'd been any doubt beforehand that he could, assuming the spirit moved him, actually kill me, I didn't doubt it now. Putting the can back in place with a fresh ventilation hole punctured right through the Campbell's tomato soup label, he nested the thirty-eight in my shaky hand. "Okay, son, shoot at it." I gave the trigger a little squeeze and, KABOOM, the cold, heavy metal thing discharged. But the can wasn't impressed and didn't move. I fired again: same result. Again: zip. That day I shot no more. Nor did Daddy ever run the experiment again. He would have to devise other ways to stop me from being such a sissy, to get me out of my room and away from my books and, for Chrissakes, *outside* into playing fields where complicated, butch things were done with pigskins and helmets and bats and mitts. But none of it ever worked, with the qualified exception, much later, of tennis lessons. I didn't have the killer mentality you need to succeed at sports.

All right. If I was a sissy, it was *his fault*. I remember reading a book about the Wild West and the technique of horse breaking. The instructor in this account told his apprentice that you have to be careful when you take a wild mustang and try to make a good mount of it. If you overdo things, if you're too harsh, you will "break the colt's spirit," and render it useless except for the dullest of farming tasks. I dropped the book and said to myself, "That's what he's done. He's *broken my spirit*." A statement proving false in the long run: but it sounded good, it provided an obliquely romantic rubric for the abjection I felt at that period. What emerged in the years since I got out from under that paternal roof and its basic condition of servitude is that, in fact, I have something like "true grit," the source of which has to be Daddy. I also inherited or acquired by example his short temper, which has been known to strike terror in the hearts of some who thought they could get away with denying me basic respect; and that includes those ready to put their homophobia into action. I also attribute to him, if only in a backhanded sense, my hair trigger alarm system against injustice. Because I was an underdog, my sympathy goes out instantly to any other person smarting under the heel of an oppressor. In addition to soldiering in the Gay Lib Army, I've always stood up for people of color, Jews, and women in their struggle to achieve parity with the dominant sector. When I see someone mistreated, I feel it in my gut and swing into action.

Yes, I was beaten, the rod wasn't spared, blah-blah. Like billions of other children, I survived and got over that. The one unforgivable instance of corporal punishment was this: One hot summer afternoon, Daddy said or did something infuriating, I've forgotten what, and my control snapped. The pent-up words staged a jailbreak, and they were in no mood to be flattering. Daddy slapped me hard. Silence came in a rush. But he looked into my eyes, read my mind, and realized that he'd gone too far. He never did it again, but it sealed his fate in my affections. He had gone over the foul line, and he would have to live there from then on with other shaggy, horned, and tusked demons and never expect any pity from me. Not that he ever asked for pity. Daddy would have assumed that showing weakness of any description could only result in the undermining of paternal authority, and *that* was as sacred and inviolate as the Ten Commandments. Which, goddammit, we children had better not take in vain, starting with, "Honor thy father and mother."

And yet, it turns out even unforgivable deeds can be forgiven. At least I've done so in his case. As time passed, I got to know more of his story, and on the foundation of added knowledge a structure of sympathy has grown up. Begin with him as a high school senior in the late twenties, the eldest scion of a rich, respected family, good-looking, captain of the football and baseball teams, irreverently charming, popular enough to be class president. After graduation, he goes off to college. And it's pretty much downhill from then on. The Depression hits, my grandfather loses most of his money, and my father barely manages to scrimp through his undergraduate education on a football scholarship. He logs in a year of law school, until the money runs out. He gets a job at a law firm, but there's no work, and he is let go. He starts selling insurance policies, the kind bought by poor rural families who scrape up ten cents a week to maintain some kind of minimal coverage. He meets my mother at a dance, it's love at first sight. They marry, and my sister is born six or seven months after the wedding, even though she's not premature. Six years pass and another daughter is born, followed two years later by a son, who is named Alfred D. Corn III. At this point, my father is called up in the Army Reserves and shipped to the South Pacific. For two years my mother lives alone and brings up three children. Then she gets appendicitis. The ensuing infection and rupture is fatal because penicillin supplies are low and reserved for military use only. She dies on V-J Day; word reaches my father in the Philippines, and he is immediately released. He comes back home after a long, hazardous journey, still in shock, and penniless. We children are put up first by my aunt and uncle, who have a seedling farm out in the country, and then by our grandparents. Eventually, Daddy finds a house for us, a small 1920s bungalow right at the city limits of a medium-sized town in South Georgia called Valdosta, named after a gorgeous alpine region in the Italian Piedmont, even though our flat, hot Floridian landscape had zero resemblance to that.

Daddy got the house ready for us, repainting, sanding the floors, and buying furniture. It was a modest establishment but was equipped with a porte cochère so you could drive your car under a sloping, protective wing of shelter and step directly onto the front porch. According to the usual American practice of mauling adopted French words, it is called the *portacaSHAY*. As cars got bigger in the '40s and '50s the portacashay got smaller, just as the house itself did when we grew to full size in it. Daddy at first tried to raise us with the help of a housekeeper, but she proved brutal and untrustworthy. He dated and probably slept with several women, eventually remarrying. The pretty bride was someone much younger whose fighter-pilot husband had been killed in action. So there we stood, arm in arm, a new little family circle. Although: I think my father hadn't really worked through his bereavement. Throughout childhood, my mother was a taboo topic, almost never mentioned, I suppose out of regard for my stepmother. But probably also because thoughts of her were too painful for my father to contemplate.

Like others in his generation he was a heavy drinker, and it got worse. More because of unresolved grief and alcoholic numbness than anything else, he decided to go to work for Big Daddy (yep, that's what we called him), whose fortunes had made a modest recovery in the postwar boom. Daddy wasn't entrepreneurial enough to form a business of his own, and at the age of thirty-six he was too proud to sign on as an entry-level employee. But he and my grandfather were locked into a sort of death embrace of codependent antagonism. All they had in common was a pugilistic psychology; they fought about every business or personal issue every day. When he got off work, Daddy just wanted a few shots of whisky to forget all his troubles. But soon drinking itself was one of the troubles he needed to get over. He would abstain for a while and then fall off the wagon and binge for a few days or a week, then go on the wagon again. Which meant he was often in withdrawal, his nerves frayed, his temper short. I now know enough about the symptoms of alcoholism to understand his behavior, but I didn't understand it then. I hated his drinking, hated the slurred speech and unsteady gait it gave him, hated hearing him get up in the middle of the night and pour himself a shot so that he could get back to sleep. I hated the days he was too sick to go in to work and lay in his bed trying to "taper off," as he said, the house reeking of bourbon and puke.

He must have felt an enormous guilt and a barely contained rage about his situation. In the fabulous '50s, almost everybody prospered, but not my father. The salary Big Daddy gave him wasn't exactly princely, especially considering how much of it was spent at the package store. People Daddy probably considered below him got rich and flaunted their cars and golf togs and big Tara-style houses while we slogged on as best we could with limited means. Trying to strike a blow for good health (and to avoid confronting his most serious health problem), Daddy gave up smoking. Within a few months he developed a paunch. His looks were gone. He had a loyal, subservient, worried wife and three obedient but resentful kids he couldn't really afford to bring up with ease. His life had been one long decline. I didn't then, but I now feel sorry for him. In a paradoxical sense, he became a valuable example to me. Because in the majority of cases alcoholism has a genetic origin, I, too, came down with it—the difference being that I put the cap on the bottle before my life was destroyed. If I hadn't watched him get so sick, I might not have had the sense to address my own problem. In many ways, he was a victim whose anguished existence set me an example of how not to live. By which I mean more than the jarhead thing. I made up my mind never to get trapped in a life I loathed, including sexual orientation, relationship, job, house, city, whatever. I used to say "I'll mop floors, I'll live on bread and water before I give up my identity." And sometimes (figuratively) I've had to do that.

Surprise: Daddy mellowed with time. He brought his drinking under control and even gave it up for a five-year period after he was diagnosed with diabetes. Once he no longer had to make cash layouts for us kids, his modest income was enough to live comfortably if not luxuriously, and my stepmother inherited a larger house when her own parents died. He was mostly pleased with how my sisters had turned out, even though one divorced and remarried. I, on the other hand, kept my distance by going to live in New York. Never once did he visit me in Babylon. He absolutely refused to come.

And I, for my part, rarely went back to Valdosta. I'd made the mistake, just after getting my B.A. and before going off to begin graduate work at

Columbia, of staying one last summer at home. I'd lived away for four years and had lost the requisite meekness. I'd begun my life as a gay man, though I hadn't at that time come out to my parents. I went to bars and stayed out late, waking Daddy when my headlights turned into the drive. He tried to impose a curfew. I told him, excuse me, I was nearly twenty-two. But there was also the issue of my new companions, some of them reputed to be "notorious homosexuals." I said he shouldn't worry about it, I could take care of myself. He said I didn't seem to be getting the point. "As long as you live under my roof and eat off my table . . ." Ah, that. So the next morning I skipped out, leaving a curt goodbye note on the kitchen table. I found a cheap boardinghouse in the downscale part of town and moved my few belongings there. The note included no for-warding address. For a couple of weeks I lived a weird, seedy, Tennessee Williams kind of life, not seeing anyone I knew and wandering around deserted downtown streets like a transient. There was the sleazy night I brought a stranger home and we rolled around on my bed-sitting room's sagging mattress in the glare of a naked lightbulb. I guess we weren't quiet enough because my landlady told me she'd reclaim my room if it hap-pened again.

One afternoon my parents appeared at my door. I was nearly out of cash. Daddy, hat in hand, apologized for his behavior and asked me to come home for the last two weeks before I was scheduled to leave. He was afraid the scandal would become known, sure, but he also regretted (maybe) having failed to realize I was now an adult, or at least an arro-gant snot who believed himself to be one. I relented, but after those two weeks, I never again stayed under his roof or ate off his table for more than three days. We got along best when we didn't see each other, and salutary avoidance was pretty much our MO for the next twenty years. Eventually (and not because I expected it would result in a loving and complete and supportive relationship with them), I did the politically correct thing and came out to my parents—with the assistance of the U.S. Post Office. I didn't want to pay airfare for a special trip down there to make the announcement. I mean, there I'd be, dragging a chair over from the dinner table and sitting in it backward as I flashed a big Colgate-toothpaste grin at two puzzled seniors on the sofa. My elbows resting on the chair back, I'd use my perkiest tone to say: "Daddy, Mama, I'm GAY! Isn't that wonderful?" It just wasn't me. So I wrote a well-phrased and cowardly letter; sat back and waited until it wasn't answered. What did

I expect, a dozen pink roses? I telephoned. Hems and haws from Daddy. "Got your letter. You're an adult, you can make your own decisions. But you Understand, now, that this Lifestyle has always been Condemned by all Civilized Societies throughout History." We were talking on my nickel; no way was I going to deliver a lecture about Athens in the good old days. So I just mumbled something about having thought it all through very carefully; and moved into the sign-off portion of the conversation. Daddy never said another word on the subject again.

WHEN HE WAS nearly eighty, he developed prostate cancer. An operation took care of the offending tissue, which included not only the prostate but also the testicles—news tailor-made to give young Oedipus an electric chill. Then it was discovered that the cancer had spread to the bone. Once that happens, you just sit back and wait because there's nothing else to do. Toward the end I went back for a visit. Daddy was thin, his face runneled with age, his paunch gone, his hair totally silver. He moved slowly, spoke hesitantly—drunk with terminality, you might say. We three kids behaved with filial deference, and this time we actually meant it. I spoke with him calmly and was treated in turn as an adult. When I left I gave him a hug and said "I love you," something I hadn't done since early childhood. Before stepping into the car, I looked back once and saw him standing unsteadily at the door, waving goodbye.

That was the last time I saw him. As his condition worsened, I wrote letters and tried to be supportive. I knew he was a believer and a believer in the afterlife. So I wrote that I could see an analogy between the current situation and the period just after my mother's death, the time when he'd found a house for us children and wanted to get it ready for us before the actual move. That (in my metaphor) was what Daddy would be doing: He would go first to knock the place into shape, and later on, when things were ready, the rest of us would follow. We had all had the Bible read to us throughout childhood, so I knew he would at least unconsciously recall the passage in the Gospels where Jesus says to his disciples, "Let not your heart be troubled. You believe in God, believe also in me. In my Father's house are many rooms. If it were not so, I would have told you. I go to prepare a place for you."

In October 1992, Daddy went ahead. Lying in bed the night after I got the news, I had the image of a roof's being peeled back from overhead, leaving me to face a black sky full of stars. It was sort of scary, but there was also the sensation of an influx of fresh air. When I finally fell asleep it was like falling upward into the darkness. The following May, my stepmother followed Daddy, which, besides being sad, added a note of finality to everything. Just us kids left to carry on the legend. The "rooms" are doubtless ready by now, but neither my sisters nor I have gone there to check them out. Assuming there's some advance notice of the transit, we may, when the day comes, want to avail ourselves of a small, harmless daydream suggesting that Daddy's thoughtful preparations have proved helpful. It's an appealing picture. I can easily imagine his waiting on the front porch right by the porte cochère as we drive up. But the eventuality is attractive only if the old homestead has been renovated from the ground up. I never want to go back to the cramped, melancholy space of 1954, shabby and not even genteel, pervaded as it was with the smell of defeat and vomit. That will all have to be alchemized into something else, a set of premises newly conceived. Once I move in, there can't be any obligation of total subservience, surely. Because this time we won't be staying in a house belonging to Daddy. He, too, will be a nonpaying guest, living under someone else's roof, eating off someone else's table. The house rules—informal, cheerful—should put us on an equal footing.

FELICE PICANO

Driving Mr. Picano

The messages on the answering machine told the story I'd missed that weekend: My aunt had been taken ill. Her condition was critical. She had died. The funeral was in a few days. My eighty-two-year-old father couldn't drive all the way. His doctor said it was too soon after he'd just spent many weeks in the hospital for a heart condition. Taking a train, even a plane, was unthinkable. I'd have to drive him.

Now, if you had at any time up until that moment asked me how I felt about a four-hour drive to Rhode Island with my father as the only other passenger, I'd probably place it midway on a scale between dining on broken glass and having bamboo slivers hammered under my fingernails. On the other hand, I couldn't fail to recall that what I'd come to consider the major conversations I'd had with my father as two adults had occurred during our infrequent car trips; and most intriguingly *all* of the very few conversations we'd had about homosexuality I'd had with my father had taken place while he and I were driving somewhere.

Could driving together have been our equivalent of finding a "neutral physical activity" (say the way other fathers and sons would play catch or watch a baseball game together?)? I'm from that generation that helped bring about Gay Liberation. I came out a few years before the Stonewall Rebellion. My father was born just before World War I. His was a generation of men who seldom, if ever, talked to each other about *anything* personal at any length, never mind about sex, never mind about homosexuality.

It also happened to be a lovely spring day when that phone call arrived and I had nothing to write under deadline, so I told my father, sure, I'd call my cousins to see when we should arrive for the funeral, then I'd call and rent a car.

"Don't rent a car," my father said. "We'll take my car."

My dad's car: a twelve-year-old Pontiac midsized sedan. "Formerly owned," because he refused to pay what a new car cost, despite the fact that during my childhood, when he was less well off, he always bought new cars directly out of the dealer's showroom and scorned anyone who didn't. A "formerly owned" car moreover that my dad had bought very inexpensively and that he'd driven only locally, in central Queens. Maybe once a month as far as Manhattan. No trip longer than that.

The last time we had been in a car together, also a long trip to Rhode Island for this same aunt's birthday, had been in my dad's '79 Ford station wagon, another formerly owned vehicle, this one not a sickly maroon but a lively deep green surrounding plastically fake wood, and only slightly less than half the size of your usual Caribbean cruise ship. The one time I had parked this vehicle for him I'd needed a compass and sextant as well as perfect recall of all of Euclid's basic laws. Only eighty years old for that trip and in considerably better health, my father had driven and I had "navigated."

Which had gone like this: Me: "Here's your turn coming up, Dad. Here it comes! This is the turn! . . . That was your turn!"

Besides that kind of insanity, often repeated, that particular driving trip had been notable for being the setting of our first-ever conversation about homosexuality. In all our four-and-a-half decade-long relationship we had exactly none until then. This one came about once we were cruising along on the New England Thruway, where I guess my father felt he could relax a little. He did so by beginning to complain about my older brother, Bob (now deceased), who had recently split up from his wife of many years, and was currently living about a block away from her and their daughter in Brooklyn Heights. Living, in fact, in an apartment with another man.

"I'll never understand your brother, Bob," was how my father opened that conversation. "Why would he want to leave Eraina and go live with that colored guy?"

"That colored guy is his boyfriend." I, of course, assumed everyone knew this.

My father almost crashed the car he became so excited. "His boyfriend!" Around us drivers blared their horns in a warning cacophony.

"Sure! Bob's as gay as I am."

"Since when?"

"Since forever. He's always had boyfriends. Remember Bobby, when they were kids? Then, when he went into the Paratroopers? That southern guy, Colin? Those two years in the Army, they were inseparable. Bob was depressed for years when Colin died in that car accident."

"Wasn't Colin married?"

"So what!" I replied. "And after Colin, there was J. K.? Remember him? The one who was killed on his motorcycle."

"I thought J. K. had a girlfriend?" My father groped for some way out. "What's the difference how many girlfriends he had? The first time J. K. visited me in my apartment on Jane Street, he tried to get me into bed." I didn't add how surprised (not to mention flattered—J. K. was "dreamy") I'd been. But as I wasn't yet out then I didn't take him up on it. Stupidly, since a few months later he was dead. I went on, "Bob probably had boyfriends I never knew about. But those three and Dean make four. That's as many as I had."

My father was silent a long time, then he'd muttered, "You kids!"

Following that car trip, I'd declared to anyone who'd listen that the next long trip my father and I took, I would do the driving myself.

And now I would be. At the time I was still a resident of Manhattan to whom driving is a profession practiced by people with incomprehensible accents, no geographical skills, and a compulsion to revenge themselves on the world for the fact that someone of a differing political persuasion had bombed the hell out of their natal picturesque village, forcing them to move to the outlying slums in the Bronx or Brooklyn.

However, very un-Manhattanite-like, I had been driving a great deal by the time this trip came up. Up and down California's Pacific Coast Highway, all around San Francisco and Los Angeles, back and forth to

Cape Cod, up to Vermont to visit friends who lived in the country. I loved to drive. Hell, I even drove down to south Jersey with a woman friend for a wedding—that's how much I enjoyed it.

It had been twenty-five years since I'd last regularly driven. And I'd only gotten my new license again because my companion developed cytomegalovirus "floaters'" in his eyes late in his HIV infection, and as a lawyer with business all over the state, he had to try cases in person at out-of-city, county courthouses. If he couldn't drive, I who had no fixed work hours could certainly drive him. However altruistic a reason, this never did work out as planned: He'd died before I got my license.

I had stopped driving years before, during the particularly horrible year of 1966, when I'd been involved in three auto accidents: one with a woman pal driving on the Autostrada del Sole in Italy, another in a taxi in Paris, and a third when I'd taken a fall on an oil slick along a Georgia highway driving my BMW 750 motorcycle. It was shortly before that last incident that I'd learned of my "suddenly interrupted lifeline" from a palm reader, and —belatedly—taken her hint.

As much as the accidents and the interrupted lifeline, there was other unfortunate history connected with my driving—history involving my father. He had taught me how to drive when I was a teenager. Or, to be precise, he had chauffeured me around the vast empty parking lots at Green Acres Shopping Center on Long Island a few winter Sunday afternoons, and, after long lectures on defensive driving—"You're a soldier parachuted behind foreign lines! Everyone's your enemy"—he had allowed me to get behind the wheel of his gorgeous ice-blue Bonneville sedan for three minutes at a time, to move his car at about six miles an hour as he shouted "No! No! No!" or "Not so fast!" or "Wrong way!" This happened until we were both too nervous to go on and I called a stop to the mutual torture.

Despite my father's lack of instruction, I did manage to pass the school's driver education class and it fell upon him to take me for my road test shortly after my sixteenth birthday. A glowering and dour Saturday morning, filled with gloomy predictions from him about how inattentive and dreamy I was—and therefore how much of a danger to every other human being not merely on that stretch of road I'd be driving, but also a quarter mile on either side.

The man giving me the road test, a nattily dressed, stout, fortyish, African American with a wonderful goatee, doubtless heard my father's final querulous instructions, and doubtless also possessed an irritating father, because he passed me with high marks. This further depressed my father, and we drove away from the DMV test area in a somber, speechless gloom.

Or rather he did. I clutched at the temporary driver's license I held in my hot little hands, the paper that spelled out "freedom," spelled out "grown-up," spelled out "you can do it!"

There's never been any question that in my life the car has become in many ways our era's modern male proving ground. And watching some current films would seem to bear out the fact that it's true for others, and still is, years after I first got my license. Remember the teenage girls' utterly hapless driving lessons in the movie *Clueless*, a movie written and directed by a woman? And, conversely, how the young men "prove themselves" in up-to-date hot-rod conversions in *The Fast and The Furious*? Both were immensely popular with young people. So, while it may be true that girls and women drive all over the world daily, some of them very well, and that some have race cars and are car mechanics and car-magazine testers, I contend that the car is still what sociologists call a "male site."

So . . . after arriving home from my first driving road test, my dad joined a visiting friend in the garage while I went to tell my mother the good news. When I returned with her invitation for coffee and cake I arrived at the garage door in time to hear my father's friend say, "Well, you were wrong! He passed." My father grunted some very grudging assent. His friend replied, "So? How does he drive?" I waited. Finally my father muttered, "Like a Newport debutante!"

Now to a sixteen-year-old boy, this statement impugned not only his driving ability, but also his seriousness, his future, his manhood itself. It was devastating. And I'd never forgotten it.

Decades later, I had to admit, my father had pinned my driving style to a tee. I drive fast, casual, playing loud music and singing along. My single finger on the steering wheel tapping the rhythm, my hair ruffling in the breeze of the open windows, I glide across four-lane freeways at eighty miles an hour. I'm alert, I'm careful, I don't get tickets, I don't have accidents. But you tell me it takes six and a half hours from L.A. to San Francisco? Sorry, I do it in five and a half with a half hour for lunch and two other stops to pee. When friends visiting my Cape Cod rental had to make a train, trust me, with me at the wheel, they might leave their stomachs somewhere near Wellfleet, but they always made their train in Hyannis!

And in all the years since, Dad never said anything otherwise about my driving. So, my father must have been desperate to let me drive him. I mean *desperate*.

The day of our trip I sat in the driver's seat of his car and noticed some obvious discrepancies: "Where's the hand brake?" My father didn't know. He'd never used it. And the speedometer! It read only up to eighty-five mph. "Fuel-injected," he explained, "saves gas. Work it up to cruising speed."

I'd driven dozens of rental cars after getting my second license, which meant that in no time I was relaxed behind the wheel of this car too. As I drove along the West Side Highway out of Manhattan, we began to talk cars. My father told me about his first car, a 1932 Pontiac, a sporty ragtop with a rumble seat and white walls, bought for $600. He'd driven with a friend on a new road to Montreal and slept overnight in Lake George. "Whenever we would come to another car," he said, "we'd stop, get out and shake hands."

"You're kidding? There were so few cars then?"

"You bet. And, people with cars then were a better type of person."

The first half of our trip to Providence my father and I made good time. I was bothered a bit by the fact that the car had no pickup for passing. Not that I zip in and out of traffic. But I'm also not crazy about being unable to escape a sixteen-wheeler with its nodding-off driver. So I decided to take the Hutchinson and Merritt parkways, where no trucks are allowed, and switched back onto Interstate 95 only when I had to.

Once in Rhode Island, my father took advantage of having a chauffeur. The funeral wreaths had to be bought from a particular florist's in Cranston. And where precisely was that bakery in Silver Lake that sold wine biscuits unobtainable in Queens, promised to his friends back in New York?

My father's directions were guided by memory and so very tight: I had to be alert for sudden turns, at a second's notice and very often into streets that looked more like alleyways.

On the third day of our visit, my father said, "You're not bad for a new driver . . . New," he explained, "compared to driving sixty years like me."

"When I was learning you thought I'd be a terrible driver! And dangerous!"

"Never," he protested. "Wasn't that your younger brother?"

"No. Me. You said I was too dreamy."

Coming home a few days later turned into something of an odyssey when the car began acting up. It slowed down no matter how much I leaned on the gas pedal. My father seemed unfazed by the assorted noises from the engine, the continuing slowdown, and even passing motorists who alarmedly pointed at our car's exhaust, where white smoke was sending up eloquent signals. But a little more than halfway back to New York, after I'd let him take over the driving, even he had to admit something was off. We heard one very loud clank, almost but not quite an explosion, and the car died. We babied it halfway up a highway ramp, and hours later, a local mechanic confirmed that the engine had seized up, an event akin to a fatal coronary. My dad wouldn't hear of abandoning the malodorous Pontiac. While I took Amtrak back to Manhattan, he remained with the car, riding along with the tow truck back to Queens, where they arrived sometime after midnight. He'd had the engine replaced at the dive where he had bought the car and continued to drive it, albeit more gingerly, for the next few months, until the frozen winter afternoon when, as he was driving along his own street, the car hit an ice patch and accelerated from twenty to seventy miles an hour, smashing into a light pole. Shaken if unhurt, my father sold the wreck for scrap and bought a pale blue 1990 Buick Regal coupe. Formerly owned, but in okay condition.

A year or so later, while I was on a book tour that took me back to New York, I went out to Queens to have lunch with my dad. He was in even more fragile physical condition. The "new" Buick looked good, and he wanted to drive out to Mineola to pick up something for a friend, then treat me to a good Italian restaurant he knew of on the North Shore of Long Island. As we were approaching the car, he tossed me the keys. "You drive."

I did. It was plush and smooth, comfy, a bit softly slung, with indistinct, even woolly handling, compared with the close-grip, fast acceleration, and tight feel of my sporty little Asian coupe back in California. But it was a pleasant summer afternoon drive and, even though my dad did manage to get lost looking for the restaurant, we eventually found it and had a great lunch.

Back in the car, after lunch turned out to be the setting for our second conversation about homosexuality. During this much shorter drive, my father brought up the subject himself. I'd just mentioned that I was planning to travel throughout Germany that spring. He had asked why I was going there and I'd explained: "My novel, *The Lure*, is the best-selling gay book ever published there. A new translation is coming out. A twelfth-anniversary edition. I'll do a seven-city book tour, by train."

"I don't get all this homosexuality business," was my father's response. "You don't look or act like a fairy," he added.

"I'm not a fairy. But I am gay."

"I mean, the fairies I knew were . . ."

I pounced: "What fairies did you know?"

"Well, one really. And this was a long time ago. Maybe you weren't even born yet. Barky—remember Barky, the jeweler?—he and Harry and I were friends since high school and we went everywhere together. We ended up at some party in Manhattan and there were these fairies there. Well, Barky went off with one of them, down to his car— remember that big old dark green Packard sedan with the three windows on each side? And at the same time, another fairy got interested in me. I must have been a little drunk and so I let Barky and these fairies persuade me. I went down to the car with one, and I let him blow me. But he was almost like a woman. You know, he kind of dressed that way and acted that way. He wore perfume and everything."

Although my father wasn't tall, he had been in great physical shape until his mid-fifties, had been a terrific and powerful swimmer, and had been a good-looking man. I could easily picture some gay guy dragging him out of a party to do him in the back of Barky's Clipper. And I was also intrigued by the idea of Barky himself—a much bigger, incredibly masculine guy who was known to cheat constantly on his wife with women—going to parties where "fairies" were not only present, but also potential sex mates.

"When did this happen?" I probed. "In the '50s? Late '40s?"

"I don't remember exactly," my father said, and I wondered if he'd immediately regretted telling me the anecdote, because he hurried on: "So when I heard you were, you know, homosexual, I wondered how that could be. Of course," he added, "I also remember when you were five or six years old and I saw you kids in the backyard and you were wearing— I don't know—some kind of costume, a sort of dress, jumping around with a toy sword, and I asked what you kids were doing and your sister said playing Pirates and that you were someone named Annie."

"Annie of the Indies," I said, remembering it well. I'd seen the movie at a children's Saturday matinee, and I had fallen instantly in love with the actress Jean Peters as well as the part she had played in the Technicolor extravaganza; winning sea battles, dominating and betraying men, all of them weaker. Years later, remembering, I figured that this had been some sort of a coded lesbian role. But I'd eaten it up at the time.

"Right," my father went on. "But when I talked to your mother about it a little later, you know, saying how if you kept that up you'd probably grow up to be a fairy, she laughed at me. She said, 'That was last week. This week he's Robbie the Robot. He's driving me crazy, wanting to eat directly out of cans because he says that how robots eat. So what are you saying now, Phil? That he'll grow up to be a refrigerator?'" My father shrugged. "So, I dropped it."

"All kids play out different roles. At least healthy ones do."

"That's what your mother said. But . . . I don't know. You were always different than the others. Right from the start. First, you'd been a baby model for Macy's. Remember all those teddy bears you had? Jesus! There must have been forty of them, until we gave them away to the poor kids' charity. You got a teddy bear every time you posed. And once you got older, you were always doing something—singing, dancing, acting in plays, drawing, painting, playing musical instruments. It didn't seem normal. Of course, later on you all but lived in those roller skates. Then on that bicycle. You wanted to sleep with that stupid bike. You treated it better than a person. Then you began racing go-carts, and getting into fights. So I figured you'd gotten over all that other stuff."

"All the fairy stuff?" I asked. He nodded yes. "Well, Dad, you were right that I was different than the other kids in the family. But it wasn't because I was a fairy. It was because I was an intellectual. An artist."

"I'll say an artist! You used to draw nude women!" my father said. "Eleven years old and you're drawing nude women with huge . . ." he gestured breasts. "I thought, this kid's going to be worse than his old man with ladies . . ." He concluded with another shrug, "In a million years I'll never understand!"

Now it was my turn to shrug.

As I was driving him home from what would be our last car trip, I reminded my dad of our previous long drive together, during which his underachieving previous car had attempted to commit suicide on the New England Thruway.

"After that crazy trip with the Pontiac," I said, "I was sure you'd never want to drive with me again."

"That stupid car!" he moaned. Then, "No. None of that was your fault. You're a fine driver," he assured me: a vote of confidence years after I no longer needed or wanted it—which didn't mean I didn't value it. "No, you're a good driver," he said. "Alert. Sure. . . . You can drive me anytime, anywhere."

TOM STEELE

Playing
The Game.

It's an autumn night in 1957, and we are a nice WASP family of two boys and two girls in an upper-middle-class suburb of Toledo, Ohio. I am five. In total darkness, my father is lying on the carpet of the bedroom I share with my older brother, with each of us wrapped in his arms, our heads against his chest. We are playing The Game. With him as our guide, we're on an imaginary voyage, riding our flying bicycles up into a magical forest. We take turns giving details of our expedition, what kinds of animals we see, whether it's autumn or spring, whether our forest is sunny or starlit. When we go on these voyages, sometimes all three of us fall asleep there on the floor, and we forget to dream.

We are The Happy Family. We adore being together. We go all-out on holidays, especially Christmas. We go on long family trips. We sing in the car everywhere we go, like the goddamned Trapp family. We have a beagle who actually laughs. Many of my friends are jealous. They hate their parents or their brothers or their sisters. They have lousy Christmases. They never sing.

I realize how smug some of this sounds, but we were never smug about anything. That would have been bad manners. We were just incredibly lucky.

At least for a few decades we were.

WE HAVE A beautiful summer home in Lakeside, on Lake Erie, 50 miles east of Toledo, where the whole family summers, except my father, who stays in the city during the week to sell insurance and real estate. We have a boat there—or rather, a succession of boats, successively larger, but always small enough to water-ski behind. The days are long, the lake shimmers endlessly, there are movies at Orchestra Hall, and the corn and tomatoes and peaches are better than they will ever be again.

MY BIRTHDAY IS May 30, Memorial Day. I am six. My father takes me downtown to see the Memorial Day Parade, a big deal in those postwar days. There are marching bands and floats and men in uniform everywhere. My father hoists me onto his shoulders so I can see. He shouts above the crowd, "These people are doing all this for you, you know, because it's your birthday."

I believe him, of course.

By the age of four, I'm taking piano lessons, and at eight, I'm studying violin as well, and then drums. I'm something of a child prodigy, and I continue to compose and play music on and off all my life, twice abandoning the idea of making a career of it.

My father is also musical, as is everyone in my family. He's a sax/clarinet/gut bucket man. But he has only five or six LPs, and an eclectic mix they are: barbershop quartets, Glenn Miller, Wagner overtures, and Benny Goodman.

I come home from college for Christmas to discover that he has fallen in love with the lugubrious song "Feelings" and that he has bought the single, which he plays over and over on the elaborate stereo console in the living room, wired with speakers set in various places in the house so that the music is everywhere. I find it extremely odd that he, a man of such determination and good cheer, would turn obsessively to such a disheartening song. When at last I take the single off the turntable, I notice that he has played it so many times the grooves on the disk are worn nearly through to the other side.

My father is a conservative Republican, or thinks he is. I know better. He's too much of a softy to adhere to the cruel tenets of conservatism, I later decide. And he cannot defend himself in any political argument because all he knows he's learned from the conservative garbage he reads. In his bathroom near the toilet—right where they belong—are books like *Mr. Conservative: Barry Goldwater* and *Teddy Bare*, a vanity press book assailing Teddy Kennedy—long before Chappaquiddick.

By the time I am 18, another book joins them: a howler called *How to Tell If Your Children Are Doing Drugs*. I borrow it from time to time, and my friends and I read it aloud to each other when we're stoned, which is a lot of the time, to helpless peals of laughter.

MY FATHER DROPPED out of college to fight in World War II. My mother graduated from Wellesley College at a time when few women went to schools of any stature.

There is tremendous emphasis in my family on the importance of education. My parents are both deeply involved with our schooling on every level. My father is president of the Board of Education. If one of us doesn't do well in math, we are tutored. Mostly, we excel all of our academic lives.

When I am 20 and a junior at Syracuse University in 1972, after years of describing myself to friends as "bisexual" (usually to get into their pants), I fall head over heels in love with a strikingly handsome 18-year-old boy. I go into a first-love tailspin. After a month, I fly to Toledo, where I proceed to frighten my parents half to death with some fairly wild behavior.

The first night I'm there, I stay up late drinking beer alone with my father. I tell him I'm in love with another man. He blinks as if I have slapped him, but says immediately and tonelessly, "I had a buddy in the Navy. I felt . . . that way about him. He was killed in the South Pacific. You get over it." He says it as if he were some jukebox and I had pressed the right buttons to play "Feelings."

It is the only time he ever talked about the war in my presence.

I later learn that "buddy" was often military parlance for "sex partner."

WHEN I AM 10, my father, whose own father forbade him to engage in contact sports, bribes me to play Peewee league football. To this day I know absolutely nothing about football, or any other sport, for that matter. He bribes me by buying me my first stereo, and allowing me to charge records at the local record store, where I practically live.

I hate the practices after school, the games—really, everything about football. I do not hide my dejection. But my father is so elated that I am even trying that I somehow continue. The vicarious thrill is palpable.

Sometimes he leaves work early, parks his shiny Chevrolet ninety yards from our little skirmishes, and stands leaning against the car, watching us from behind his black sunglasses.

Years later, I learn that he had subsidized the entire team, supplied uniforms, and hired the coach.

IT IS 1976. I am living happily in Boston with the same man I met at Syracuse. We live on Beacon Hill, then undoubtedly the gayest neighborhood in New England. While my mother is traveling with friends in Spain, my father flies to Boston, takes me out to Wellesley College, shows me where he proposed to my mother on a footbridge, and offers me money—or anything I want—if I will "leave the gay lifestyle." He tells me it's killing my mother, which it isn't, and that I can't possibly be happy. I actually laugh at him, then try to soothe him as much as I can.

We never talk about my sexuality in this way again. He well knows how stubborn I am, and he believes I have chosen to be gay in the same way that he chose not to be, and he resigns himself to it.

IN 1978, AFTER my lover and I go to Europe for two months, I tire of "little Boston," and decide to move to Manhattan, where I have already begun spending a good deal of time and money. Whether he will join me there remains to be determined. Throughout our relationship, though I am the only man he ever sleeps with, there is a steady succession of women. (He is now married, with two children, and is soon to divorce.)

The very night I move into the Manhattan apartment where I still live, my brother and his young wife are killed in a car accident near Lakeside on their way to the boathouse. Going about 70 miles an hour, my brother swerves my mother's station wagon—to avoid hitting a deer, perhaps?—and the car plunges into a ravine, where it is crushed.

My family is of course completely devastated. But my father crumples as I have never seen anyone crumple, before or since. He has no way of processing this loss, cannot bear the idea that all the insurance in the world cannot protect his family from disaster.

In turn, he dies as he lived: very quickly. Pancreatic cancer, just sixty years old, a little over two years after my brother.

IT'S 1957, AND I am five. In spectral darkness, my father is lying on the carpet of the bedroom I share with my older brother, with each of us wrapped in his arms, our heads against his chest. We are playing The Game. With him as our guide, we're on an imaginary voyage, soaring on our flying bicycles up into a magical forest where light and joy rule, and no harm can ever come to us. We have the only father I've ever heard of who plays The Game.

When we go on these voyages, sometimes all three of us fall asleep there on the floor, and we forget to dream.

Over forty years later, I still wonder where he came up with the idea of taking his sons on such a journey.

BILL HAYES

Home Movies.

It took time to use an eight-millimeter home movie camera effectively. Time and experience. Not just anyone was qualified. I think it was something of a calling.

Precursor to today's sleek camcorders, the eight-millimeter was mute, unpredictable, and slow. It's been retired for years now. Before the invention of easy-load film cartridges, you had to sit down and thread the film over, under, and through the camera's tiny spindles—consulting the instructions after so many failed attempts. And when you wanted to film indoors (Christmas mornings always called for this), you had to build a skeletal tree of blazingly hot "sun lamps," which, if nothing else, enforced the discipline of filming from one perspective—in between the hot lights and the nearly blinded children. There was no steadycam roving from room to room, no zoom shot. There really were no close-ups, come to think of it, that didn't dissolve into a filmic pudding of brown light. To keep things in focus, everything was shot from the proper distance. And, of course, there was no audio recording. Just images, just faces, just film.

My mother was called to the order sometime in the early 1950s. In the division of labor between male and female, which in our family followed the most traditional Irish-Catholic-U.S. Military lines, she was solely in charge of filmmaking, a position she embraced with patience, humor, and creativity. Mom was the cinematographer, director, editor, and projectionist of the Hayes family film archives.

To this day, long after the five daughters and one son have grown up and my parents have moved twice from our childhood home in Spokane, the family Bible still lies open atop the home-movie hutch in their living room. I peeked inside the hutch recently. As when I was a kid, I took great care cracking open the cabinet doors. Box upon box of small eight-mm movie reels were stacked within like a house of cards. I held one hand out to catch a pile as they tumbled from the shelf.

IN THE 1960s and '70s, when my sisters and I were growing up, occasional Sunday evenings throughout the year were designated movie nights, as were each of the five major holidays—Easter, the Fourth of July, Thanksgiving, Christmas, and my parents' wedding anniversary. Those evenings unfolded with time-worn ritual. My sisters cleaned up the kitchen while Mom excused herself to transform the living room into a movie theater. She removed a fresh pack of unfiltered Pall Malls from the good-silver drawer, lighted one, and set to work. A Burt Bacharach album played on the stereo console. Exempt, as a boy—the only son—from kitchen chores ("squaw's work," my father called it), I pulled the screen from behind the coats in our front closet. Dad, in his single contribution to the preparations, helped me set it up. *Shweeeeeesh:* The screen snapped into place, sparkling with what looked like a surface of crushed diamonds.

Mom fiddled with the projector, which was famously temperamental—the complex and often cruel husband to the eight-mm camera itself. She strung together extension cords, stacked books atop the coffee table to raise the projector's height, and, with the lights still on, began experimenting with a strip of blank leader film. Dad poured another drink and momentarily retreated to put on a bathrobe, while my sisters and I began sorting through reels of film. We each got to pick one.

Not every movie was properly labeled or in the right box, but somehow it didn't matter. We just knew, for example, that the film on the silver reel with the rubber band around it was the one where my eldest sister led a tour of our then new house—a concept inspired, I'm sure, by Jacqueline Kennedy's televised tour of the White House. That was a hands-down family favorite. Although Mom continually made new movies, we liked the old ones best. The younger we were in a film, the more enamored we were of it.

We pulled cushions from the sofas and the six of us—each just a couple of years apart in age—lay on the carpet right under the screen. Our life stories unfolded in disjointed, dreamlike juxtapositions. A black-and-white reel from 1953—Mom and Dad's honeymoon in Colorado Springs—might be followed by a color one from 1969, the baby blowing out her five birthday candles, then back to an overlit Christmas, in 1960, my mother hugely pregnant with her fifth child, me. As one five-minute reel rewound speedily atop the projector—the lights briefly up, a Pall Mall crushed—she pulled the next film from the waiting pile. Although we knew most of them by heart, Dad provided narration above the noisy projector. Mom was too involved with keeping the films running smoothly to do more than laugh and smoke.

More often than I'd like to remember, movie nights ended with a familiar sequence of events: My father drank too much, my mother grew tired, and the overheated projector chewed up pieces of our beloved films. The story suddenly stopped in place—a frame knocked off the sprockets—and imploded. Faces melted ghoulishly on the screen. We could smell the film burning.

Mom quickly stopped the projector as my eldest sister turned on the lights. Burt Bacharach still played on the stereo, while my little sister snored. Dad sought out more Scotch while Mom pulled her tiny editing contraption from the movie hutch. Snip-snip: She cut out the damaged film and hastily spliced it back together. Dad returned, lights out, my sister woke up, the film resumed. Again, it broke in the same spot.

"Goddammit, Diane, can't you get that thing to work right?" my father demanded. The six of us were as silent as had been the children on-screen. Dad stormed out, irreconcilable with one of his invisible furies. That was the signal: It was over.

Even though my mother finally traded up for a better camera and projector, she used them less and less as we grew older. Movies document our family only up to 1983—the year I graduated from college—which is also the year that, from my parent's perspective, my happy life story ended. Like a single film frame thrown off the sprocket, I stopped in place at the age of twenty-two: that's when I went home and told my parents that their only boy was a gay man. In their eyes, my life imploded, broke into separate pieces of film, a "before" and "after."

While I had long sensed it, I became profoundly aware of this irreparable break only when my younger sister, the final daughter, got married in Spokane recently. A few days before the wedding, my father called me in San Francisco to request that I not introduce my partner—the man to whom I consider myself married—to colleagues, friends of the family, and relatives. By implication, he also asked that we not "act gay" at the reception (which, he pointed out, he was paying for, after all), and give away his secret of nearly 20 years. "Do this, please," he added, "for your mother and me." I knew that it wasn't for my sisters. Unlike my parents, they had always been entirely accepting of me.

Infuriated, I refused, told him to mind his own business, and promised to avoid him during the event. I then asked a single question—one I had never asked him before, I suppose because I dreaded hearing his reply. "What do you tell people—friends, relatives—if they ask about me?"

"Well, I don't lie," he said—my father, the Catholic—ever-mindful of tallying his sins. "If someone asked outright, 'Is Bill gay?' I would say, 'Yes, he is.' But no one has ever asked. No one talks about gays here. It never comes up, so I don't say anything. If someone asks what you're doing now, I say you left Spokane for college at the University of Santa Clara, which is near San Francisco—so you live there now."

"Oh. So you don't mention that I've grown older since 1983, that I'm nearly forty, that I have an address, that I have a partner of ten years, that I have a job—"

"No. And they don't ask." It felt like a bash to the head. Twenty years gone, cut out of his version of my story.

Searching for a justification, my father added, "Spokane is very different from San Francisco."

"Why do you think I left it?"

I'm not a parent, I told myself once I'd hung up, and do not expect or hope to be. My relationship to fatherhood will always be as an only son. I will never fully appreciate, therefore, the value a parent places on memories of his young children, the expectations he has for them, and how hard it is to reconcile what he wanted them to be with who they turned out to be. Still, I couldn't deny feeling sad. I am so far ahead and my dad is so old, he'll never catch up.

The wedding was as romantic and old-fashioned as my little sister always dreamed it would be. My partner and I enjoyed ourselves immensely. We sat side by side in the Catholic cathedral, danced at the reception (with my sisters and cousins), introduced ourselves as a couple, and smiled in wedding photographs, all without incident. My father and I hardly spoke. He treated me as if I were a guest, a member of another man's family.

WHEN ONE OF our movie nights ended, following Dad's dramatic exit, the kids would just file out in defeat and try to go to sleep. I remember I'd get up the next morning to find the living room spotlessly cleaned, the films hidden in the movie hutch, as if the night before had been erased.

But now, after that last talk with my father, I have conjured up a revised version of this scene. At forty, I wake up one morning and find my parents still in the living room of our childhood home. The curtains are drawn, the screen's up, the projector's asthmatic fan is droning. And the films, strung in disarray, look like slashes of black paint on the light shag carpet. My parents have been sitting there for twenty years without leaving, but they have changed places. Dad, at seventy-six years, has taken over the home movies.

My mother is sitting on the couch, nursing a glass of wine, not saying a word. She is no longer smoking. And my father, who never had a feel for such things, is bent over the splicing machine trying to fix our fragile eight-mm films. He frantically snips apart and re-edits all our home movies, one by one, as the images of his six grown children burn up and break apart, year after year. He keeps cutting them up until nothing remains but a handful of single frames and strips of blank leader film. The home-movie hutch is empty.

TOM DONAGHY

The Rooftops of Philadelphia

When my father was dying the priests came and went. So did the hospice workers, one of whom became attached to him, writing him poems and baking us things. His brother Danny came, too—twice—and no one had seen Danny for twenty-plus years. Danny sat and spoke quietly, though my father might not have known. By that time Dad was reaching for glasses that weren't on his nose, and reading the financial section upside down.

His dying couldn't have been less clamorous. And this was odd, for he'd always been loud. When I was young he was forever raising his voice in public, and I was forever cringing. He didn't care what anybody thought. I cowered whenever we went outside.

But many things seemed to put us in natural opposition. He was stout; I was bony. He was ruddy; I was olive—like my mother. Through most of the '60s and '70s, when I was officially a child, my straight hair fell over my shy eyes; my father had muttonchop sideburns which seemed to grow straight out, clownishly.

Even his profession placed him in a realm utterly polar to the imaginary one I longed to inhabit: He worked in roofing. This was not insignificant in Philadelphia, a city that had, and still has, the largest amount of extant eighteenth century architecture in the country. There was no shortage of roofs that needed fixing and gables that needed replacing. Consequently, my father's hands were all over the city.

Still, he hardly spoke of his work. I had to piece together a picture of his working life from clues strewn about the house: There were the blueprints stacked in the corner of our dining room, leaning against the breakfront that held my mother's china; his galoshes were always muddy, and never got farther than just inside the kitchen door; and when I built a fort in the backyard he brought home shingles for its roof. These were the only indications of what my father did with his days. Evenings, I knew, he passed with poker and cigars, friends over for barbecues, or packing me and my brothers into the station wagon and heading to what was then called Kentucky Fried Chicken.

I remember most those vibrant early years, and then I remember his last three weeks. Lately, I have been somewhat foggy on the years in between, during which time he mellowed, became silver, less stout from his daily jogs, and more contemplative. He and my mother would visit me in New York, and brunch was no longer fraught. He'd ask questions and want to know the answers. My friends became less dismaying to him, or less exotic. He was more in his own skin, and he regarded the world around him benignly.

The shift, I think, had something to do with his success. Soon after I left for college, Philly changed its zoning, and suddenly developers were able to build skyscrapers. My father's business boomed. His company was involved in designing the roof of Liberty Place, the spired towers that became the center of Philadelphia's skyline. He was proud of this; it seemed to bring him a confidence that allowed him to feel he could be more accepting. He was a decent man, it turned out, and I realized not everyone is given this kind of father.

In my adolescence, though, we were at war. He was no idol and I was no chip off the old block. He had Jesus. He had basketball. He had *60 Minutes*. I put on plays in the backyard and insisted on buying a pair of two-toned platform shoes that discouraged him constantly. We circled each other, incredulous but more confounded and sad than any-thing else.

During my teenage years I smoked, drank, had sex—and did very lit-tle to cover up any of it. I was the eldest and intent on separating out through an escalating series of outrages, in effect saying, "I am nothing like you and this homogenous place you've chosen for us to live." I hated the suburbs and he was so proud to have made it there. I despised all the pug-nosed Irish people I was supposed to look like, and he was one of them. I refused to continue going to Catholic school, refused to attend Mass, refused to get out of bed—on and on. Everyone screamed for five solid years, it seemed.

Once he came rushing at me—I'd mouthed off, I'm sure—and we both tore through the house, eventually landing in my bedroom on the second floor. I can still see him barreling toward me. I can still feel the instinct to fend him off with a kick. He fell backward, winded, clutching himself. When he could finally stand upright, he retreated downstairs without a word. I knew he'd never come after me again. And he didn't. This made me a little sad, this winning.

When I was sixteen I went into his and my mother's bedroom and announced I was in love with a boy. They'd been asking where my school ring was, and why I'd been spending so much time with someone in col-lege. It seemed time to tell them. They put down their paperbacks, flat on top of their comforter. The lid, finally, was off.

In the weeks that followed, my father was uncharacteristically silent. Eventually, he bought me a book on ballet (I'd been taking classes), and we began speaking again. Soon after, I left for college, and communication between us became sporadic—phone calls, visits. Whenever I actually saw him he seemed smaller, less vivid than the image I held in my head.

He could still inspire a kind of social terror when we were together in public. There is a story famous in our family of my father's holding forth in a New York restaurant about something or other. He kept men-tioning a friend of his who was black. This friend kept coming up in the tale, as well as the fact that he was black, and my father's voice was, as usual, loud. My mother kept kicking him beneath the table, eager to silence the "black" business. He paid her no mind—he knew how to keep the flow of a story masterfully. Eventually, though, he could no longer ignore her kicking: "What, for God's sake?" At this point my mother jerked her head to the table next to ours, where a black family sat eating dinner. My father didn't hesitate: "What's the problem? They know they're black!"

He was happiest when my mother was happy. They were the lover and the beloved. From him I gleaned I was meant to be the former, and for a brief time after he died I hated him for this. In my grief I needed to be comforted, but the man I was grieving, through his silent tutorial, had prepared me only to comfort. He had encouraged me to become the barometer of everyone's emotions but my own, by coaching me to keep vigilant track of my mother's.

It must have seemed inevitable then to everyone that I would pick up where he'd left off, smoothing my mother's reentry into the world—and thus holding my family together with reassurances. But I couldn't. I was spent. My temperament, like so many other things we had in common, was ultimately my mother's. I was impatient and headstrong, and she and I were stuck with each other, useless without the great pacifier who'd calmed her and confounded me and spoke too loudly in restaurants.

Some people become like their fathers after they're gone; I realized I was unable to. This leveled me further. He had so many qualities I suddenly wanted for myself: he was sanguine, unperturbed. I had dreams where he admonished me for not shepherding the family to a new order. Eventually, the dreams faded. In the meantime, my mother made a few adjustments and had a dream of her own. In it my father came to her and said it was okay to leave the apartment they had moved to after selling the house I'd grown up in. Relieved, my mother moved out, leaving behind the views of the Schuylkill River and the den where we'd put his hospital bed, positioning it to face Liberty Place so that he could see the skyline he'd helped create.

We never talked about my being gay. That is, we never talked about what he thought about it. His actions expressed acceptance—after the initial shock and silence. But how did he reconcile it with his Catholicism, for instance? Did he mention it to his friends? I had by then achieved some success as a playwright, and some of my plays were autobiographical. How was he able to bear this? Was he?

There was one other period when we didn't speak. I'd written a play about a father driving his son to the train station. The dialogue in the play never took place between me and my father, but it could have. It was a worst-case scenario as drama using my father's regional Philly cadences and my recently acquired smart-aleck faux sophistication.

In the play, the son asks his father if can invite his boyfriend home for Christmas. In asking the question, the son blurts out that his boyfriend is HIV-positive—and that he himself is waiting for the results of an HIV test. Fraught, to say the least. But none of this mattered to my father when he sat in the audience and saw the play for the first time. What mattered, he'd later say, was he felt misrepresented as a character. He was not, nor had he ever been, the insensitive, working-class type he thought I'd portrayed. He'd felt people were laughing at him, and that, in turn, I was publicly mocking him. Most of this came through my mother, but my father's face confirmed the balance.

I was dumbstruck. Of course, the actor playing the father had leaned on the colloquialisms a little hard, caricaturizing the part a bit, but I thought the play conveyed a silent and mutual forgiveness. The character of the son was a bit of a snarky putz; what did it matter if the character of the father seemed rough around the edges? There was a truth to the play that I was proud of. It wasn't perhaps the exact truth of my relationship with my father, but it was a parallel truth that was every bit as valid. But, of course, these are distinctions a playwright makes, not a playwright's father.

Eventually, he spoke to me again. By that time I'd realized the separating out I'd begun at fourteen was nearing completion. I was stronger in some ways than he was. That is, I had a facility that he did not have. It was to be my freedom. But it put me in that uneasy place of knowing that one day I would have to take care of him.

When we brought him home from the hospital we took turns feeding him chipped ice, until, finally, he refused even that. The night before the morning he died, I leaned over and kissed him and told him I'd be staying at my brother's house, that I had to take a break from the pull-out couch my mother had provided. He nodded and winked and frowned the frown of understanding fathers. Things would continue, he seemed to convey, not at all as we planned.

MARK DOTY

The Business of Birds.

Twenty years after we buried my mother in that resentful, unvisited turf, my father reads a book I've written. It's a memoir about grief, the bitter wake of my lover's death, and in it I have described the urge to take my own life, in a hopeless hour when I didn't believe I could find the strength to participate in the world again, when pleasure seemed to lead only toward endings.

Of course I didn't write the book thinking I was speaking to my father. If I thought he'd be listening, I'm not at all sure what I could have said. But that's a miracle of the page; it feels private, interior, an intimate chamber, but it's an intimacy with all the doors and windows open.

I described walking the salt marshes in winter, at the end of Cape Cod, how their austerity and immensity suited my own grief. My father, at eighty-three, writes me a letter. He describes the way he'd walk the swampy edges of the Mississippi himself, sixty years ago, and how he loved the red-winged blackbirds that darted there, and the huge owl who'd turn his head to watch my father pass, and how in spring floods the farmers' fields would sometimes fill with fish. He remembered a tooth-less bulldog he used to feed boiled hominy. My father is a master of non sequitur—he once wrote me a letter which passed from his approval of my divorce to the number of watermelons ripening in his garden within a single sentence—so I wasn't surprised that his letter suddenly shifted registers. What startled me was what he said: how he understood, reading my book, how I'd felt when I wanted to jump from a hotel balcony. He told me a story, how he'd been so discouraged, in 1975, that he'd emptied his bank account, took his pistol, parked the county truck he drove in a garage and got a bus for Des Moines, where I lived then. He would give me the money, and then shoot himself, that was the plan. But outside of White Sands, New Mexico, he seemed to "come to." He told the driver he wanted to go back to Tucson, and the driver stopped a west-bound bus. My father picked up his truck, went back to work. "I still have the gun," he wrote.

And then it was back to flowers and shrubs, his laden grapefruit tree, the sparse new crop of pomegranates.

He's never in his life spoken to me this way, never told me a story in which he seemed so helpless or so open. 1975: a year before my mother died, year of the boxes of Miltown, his wife going mad in the back bedroom. Is it the first time he's ever actually said what he felt? It's the first time I've heard him. The gun—the gun he didn't sell after all—has divided all three of us—my father, myself, my mother's ghost—but now it turns in my memory, and manages to bring my old father and me nearer to each other, in closer proximity than we've ever been.

Which is not to say we are not awkward; too late to repair that, but it doesn't matter; I don't expect anything from him. Something between us seems complete.

Which is often the way, I think, with what ruins us: it comes back, to offer us at last—well, nothing we'd have wished for, exactly. Who wouldn't have wanted it all to happen differently! But the thing that harms turns out, sometimes, to be the very thing that restores, the exact thing.

IN THE AUTUMN of 1997, something happens I'd never have predicted. My father and his second wife come to visit Cape Cod, a day's stop on a bus tour of New England they've taken to see the fall foliage. They have, these years, traveled everywhere together—cruises to Hong Kong and up the Yangtze, up the Pacific Coast to Alaska—and my stepmother's even gotten my father to dancing lessons, and to join a square dance club. The day their group tours the Cape—looking at lighthouses and shopping for souvenirs—Larry and Edith spend time with Paul and me.

We've been making ourselves crazy with a ridiculous flurry of preparations; Paul's nervous about meeting them, after all he's heard, and he vacuums as though his life depended on it. We oil the furniture and dust the bookshelves and polish the kitchen till it gleams, or comes as close to gleaming as an old and well-used house, home to two men, two dogs, and two cats, is capable of. I decide the front of the place is looking inexcusably shabby, and two days before Larry and Edith are due to arrive we're up on ladders, wielding scrapers and buckets of paint. From the whirlwind emerge brilliant white clapboards, black shutters, everything redone but the front door, which there's no time for, and anyway we rather like its faded, scaling green, salt-air scoured to just the right patina.

We pick them up at their motel, at the appointed hour, and they chatter away in the backseat about the people in their tour group, the nice and not-so-great places they've stayed, and the colors of the leaves. They ask Paul questions about himself; I am startled that they seem to find him completely likable. The quality of affection it would perhaps be difficult to direct toward me, complicated as our history is, they offer him unguardedly. He's solicitous of their well-being, and he notices how Edith cares for my father, looks after him, and how he's always careful to make sure things are just as she likes them. We stop at a beachside restaurant— hot dogs and clam chowder, their choice—and when Paul gets up from the table they both say to me, "Such a nice young man."

I say, "He's not *that* young," but they just smile.

When it begins to rain a little and Paul produces a pair of umbrellas from the trunk of the car, my father says, "That Paul thinks of everything."

When we enter the garden gate, the newly painted facade looks bright even in the dim weather. Edith says, "You boys better do something about that front door." The dogs appear, all wiggle and charm—like us, on their best behavior. My father adores them, watching them with a frank, unclouded curiosity I've never seen in his face before. It's as if he's never seen a dog. And then it's as if he's never seen a house like this one. In fact, I guess he hasn't: We tour the little two-hundred-year-old rooms, with their low ceilings and exposed beams, their proudly cracked plaster and odd angles and old furniture.

Edith says, "Well, you boys have a lot of work to do." But my father, who has just been looking all around with that new, unguarded curiosity, says, "Gee, gee." Pause. "This is neat."

We are all a bit shy, a little tentative, and a little startled at how pleasant the visit is. We drive to a favorite beach of mine, Head of the Meadow, a wild strip of high dunes above the Atlantic where the waves break twice, once on a sandbar a ways out to sea, then again as they hurry in to shore. Sand and sky seem immense there, the wide curve endless. It's the last outpost of the continent, nothing but waves between us and Greenland, and the wind always blows in from the rimless expanses chill and fresh, with a tang of the wild.

Edith brings her purse and ties a scarf around her head; my father takes off his shoes and socks and carries them in one hand while we walk the path over a low dune. Paul makes sure they're comfortable walking on the sand; he looks so handsome to me, in his heavy new black sweater, in the shore light. I have the sensation of noticing, all over again, his open and generous face. We step down from the sandhill to the empty slope of shore. My father watches the slap of wave turn to a quick sheet of foam that hurries up the sand and back again, pulled under the dark advancing curve of the next wave, gulls drifting and settling, a racing troop of plovers. He looks simply amazed by it all. I don't think he has any desire to go closer, or to move on, or to do anything just now; his face is full of plain delight.

TO TELL A story is to take power over it. Now they—we—are part of a tale, a made thing—a perspective box! What begins as a trick of craft makes it possible to stand apart, to—forgive? Not exactly. The stubborn past is not to be dissolved by any act of will, and perhaps we ought at last to be glad for that. What happened defines us, always; erase the darkness in you at your own peril, since it's inextricable at last from who you are.

And who are *you,* anyway—with the shadow you also carry, because you are your parents' son—who are you to forgive? They were nearly helpless, as people are; they did what they knew how to do, under the disfiguring pressure of circumstance. They loved the children whom they brought to harm.

Surely their actions might be something we'd do ourselves; the hand raised to strike could be your hand, the face that trembles to receive the blow your face. The finger on the trigger yours, afraid; the heart held in the gun sights yours also.

And that is close enough to forgiveness, to find that any character in the dream of your life might be you. But you don't know that until you tell the story; caught in the narrative yourself, how could you see from that height?

Though the firebird can; that's the business of birds, to see from the correcting perspective of *above*. All along, the firebird watches, patient in ashes, smoldering till the hour to flame. Just one dance teaches it to believe in the brightness to come. All it ever needed was a practice run, in preparation for someday's full emblazoning.

A VISIT TO Larry and Edith, in Tucson. Historic, for me: At forty-four, I've finally brought my lover home, which ought to be momentous, and is in fact exhausting for us both. It isn't long before even Paul's good spirits flag and wither like some poor unwatered plant in the desert sun.

Larry: "Remember that restaurant you took us to in Provincetown? Well, that sure wasn't four star."

Edith: "Did you boys ever do anything about that front door?"

Larry, later: "Well, Mark, your house sure wouldn't pass the white-glove test."

And so the sniping continues; we sit at the kitchen table and talk and when that fails—after I lose my temper with my father, who has suggested I might get a job in the casino industry, if the college professor thing doesn't pan out—we look for things to do. We drive out to the Desert Museum, in the foothills outside of town, a beautiful place where the plants and wildlife of Sonora are displayed along long looping trails, in habitats artfully contrived to look like the real thing—a rocky cliff for bighorn sheep, a den for mountain lions, a huge scrubby enclosure for the javelinas, one of which, Edith informs us, once bit her on the butt. Larry and Edith walk more slowly than Paul and I, and fall behind, and when we come to a fork in the path I can't stop myself; I pull him in the rougher, less-traveled direction, heading off into the scrub where I know my parents won't go, and I take a deep childish pleasure in walking with him in the sun far out of the reach of their conversation, and I make sure we look at every single display.

And so my parents and I make it clear, over the course of a weekend, that reconciliation and resolution are things that happen in stories, and are never complete in this life.

PHILIP GAMBONE

Not Crying for Dad

Eleven years ago, on the evening after my father's funeral, my partner Bill decided to pick a fight. We were driving back home. For the three-quarters of an hour that it took us to make the trip, Bill kept up a steady harangue.

"Why didn't you cry?" he demanded. "The wake, the funeral—you were so goddam emotionless the whole time."

Calmly, quietly, I tried to explain that I had never been one to cry in public, certainly not in front of all my relatives.

"Three days!" Bill persisted. "I didn't see you shed one single tear. Not one. Jesus, he was your father." He paused. I knew he was about to deliver the coup de grâce, and here it came: "You sure better cry at my funeral."

Silently, I guessed that this was the real cause of Bill's upset: panic and anger at his own imminent demise. We both knew it was coming. The early signs were there: increased fatigue, occasional bouts of diarrhea, the first purple lesions of Kaposi's sarcoma on his arms. As it turned out, it would be another three years before Bill would pass away, quietly, in his sleep, his body wasted by cryptosporidium. But on that mild April night, as we got out of the car and walked up the steps into our house, I told myself that Bill's anger with me was just so much incomprehension at the merciless unfairness of death.

"Dad died last week," I wrote in my journal under the entry for April 15, 1991. "It seems necessary—mandatory—to record this, though I don't yet feel ready to say anything, observe anything, even feel anything about it. For now I just feel relief—that his suffering is over and that the stress and strain of anticipating his death is also over."

The truth of the matter is I did not have much of a relationship with my father. Although we were not estranged or hostile, we weren't buddies, either. There were no father-son outings, no long bull sessions, no camping trips—none of those classic "bonding" experiences that might have brought us closer together—when I was growing up. Gay friends tell me that is simply the way it is with gay sons and their dads. They tell me that a father intuitively senses his son is homosexual and distances himself, like an animal shunning the runt of a litter. Rather than directly confronting the discomfort and shame he feels about this queer presence in the family, the dad retreats.

My father must have had his suspicions about my sexuality, increasingly so as I reached young adulthood. In college I did not have girlfriends, I sang in an all-male glee club, I brought only male friends home for dinner on weekends. A year after I graduated, I moved in with my first boyfriend.

From my late twenties until I was forty, I lived with my second lover, a man I'll call Alfred. Alfred and I celebrated holidays with my parents, entertained them for dinner, and (except for kissing, which we did not do in public) pretty much behaved like a married couple in front of them.

Did my marriage to Alfred make Dad uncomfortable? Possibly. But did he withdraw, turn away from me, as a result? I'm no longer convinced he did. As time goes on, I find myself wondering more and more if my distant relationship with my father had anything at all to do with his displeasure at my being gay. What if, all along, I could have been close to him? What if it was I who drove him away?

■　■　■

As a GAY man, I feel fortunate to have grown up in a family where the men were not preoccupied with proving their masculinity. Many of my uncles, most of them born in Italy, took up decidedly "soft" professions. They were chefs, florists, carnation growers, tailors. They enjoyed beautiful things. Hardworking, quiet, and affectionate, they preferred a game of horseshoes to football, and family picnics accompanied by ukuleles to smoky nights hunched over a poker table with the fellas. I remember kisses from my uncles and my grandfather—my father's father, Pop—whenever we greeted each other or said goodbye. Most of the "macho" culture and customs of America, their adopted country, must have bewildered these kind, gentle men.

My dad was very much cut from this cloth. The youngest of three children, he grew up during the 1920s in Canton, Ohio, a working-class city so plagued by gangsterism that it earned the nickname "Little Chicago." He seldom spoke about his childhood; I never heard of his friends or playmates. Perhaps he was shy, or perhaps he was told to come right home after school, warned not to loiter, not to mix with people outside the *famiglia*. This would have been typical of so many first-generation Italian-Americans in those days. The family, even more so than the ethnic ghetto, constituted the nurturing milieu. Outside that protective confine lurked all manner of ills: prejudice, mob violence, and, most sinister and unpredictable of all, the *mal'occhio*, the evil eye.

In high school, Dad took the commercial course. His yearbook does not list any extracurricular activities: no sports, no clubs, or organizations. He once told me he had not been a particularly good student. From the day he graduated in the McKinley High School class of 1934 until the day he shipped off to the war, he worked in his uncle's dry-cleaning business, living at home and helping to support the family. Both of his siblings were also at home. His older brother, my uncle Cy, joined Dad in the dry-cleaning business. Their sister, my aunt Josephine, having earned a diploma from the New England Conservatory of Music, returned to Ohio to teach piano. But as to the texture of my father's life—his friendships, his pastimes, his interior life—I haven't a clue. He's even missing in most of the family photographs from those years: the picnic outings, the vacations, the trip to a Catholic renewal mission. If my father attended these events, he doesn't appear in the photographic record.

There is one photo, however, a small black-and-white from about 1940, in which Dad is the center of attention. He and his brother, in their mid-twenties, are leaning against the side of a Buick roadster, which is parked in a motel court. Their ankles are crossed—Uncle Cy right over left, Dad left over right—in an obviously rakish pose. Both "boys" (I'm sure that's how the family would have referred to them) have happy, impish grins, as if they've just gotten away with something—a couple of real wisenheimers. Dad is handsome, relaxed, boyishly sexy, his shirt untucked, his hand holding a cigarette. It's summer, a year or so before he enters the Army. The first shadow of a mustache that, in later years, will make him resemble the then-popular movie star Don Ameche, can already be seen. I would give anything now to be able to ask Dad about this photo. Where were he and Cy? What had they been up to? One thing I know: This is a family photo. I found it in my aunt's cache of photographs a few years ago. Whatever little mischief Dad may have been up to, it was undoubtedly wholesome, clean, and done in the full view of his mother and father. Except for his years in the Army, my father traveled through life accompanied by family.

During the war, Dad attained the rank of sergeant and was put in charge of a tank in an armored division that saw heavy fighting along the front. It was this division, he once proudly told me, that "liberated Saar," the German region southeast of Luxembourg. In the course of the battle, a bullet grazed one of his ears, inflicting a partial hearing loss. At the end of the war, he was so eager to get out of the Army and return home that he never filed a disability claim. In later years, my mother would complain about how Dad had lost out on all sorts of benefits that should have been rightly his. I heard her endlessly rehearsing stories of how acquaintances who had never seen action during the war were drawing handsome benefits and pensions. "Your father," she would declare with a mixture of exasperation and affection, "never took advantage of anything." Soon after the war, Dad's family moved to Boston. Pop had retired; Josephine was still teaching piano; and my father, along with Cy and their cousin Vinnie, opened their own small dry-cleaning business in Belmont, a few miles outside Harvard Square. Joining their three names together, they called it Cyvinart Cleaners. It was a modest business, in many ways perfectly suited to the modest man that Dad was. It strikes me as telling that in that anagram Dad's name appeared last.

Around 1946, through family friends—that wide-branching network of Italian *cummare* and *cumpare*—my father was introduced to my mother. Both were living at home, each the youngest in their respective families, and each—I have this on the testimony of my mother—still virgins. Their first date (to the Ice Capades at Boston Garden) included several relatives and friends. A year later, they were married. Dad was thirty-one; Mom was four years older.

The family joke used to be that my mother had proposed to my father. This was told as evidence of my father's shyness with women and my mother's anxiety at her advancing spinsterhood.

"Your grandmother always said I was too young," she would explain with an ironic smile. "I had a few dates with guys, but it was always under Nana's watchful eye."

It's a miracle my grandmother, Nana DeVita, allowed my mother to marry at all. The youngest of eight children, Mom was the only one to complete high school, graduating in 1930 as valedictorian of her class. Unmarried for the next seventeen years, Mom and her widowed mother lived together, just the two of them, in Wakefield, a working-class town ten miles north of Boston. My mother served variously as my grandmother's caretaker, confidante, protégée, traveling companion, bookkeeper, scullery maid, fellow hostess, portraitist (my mother is an accomplished amateur painter), and partner in her venture to become 'na signura, a lady. I think what Mom must have seen and fallen in love with in my father was an alternative to all this, a respite from my grandmother's lofty social project. Dad must somehow have let Mom know she was okay just the way she was, that he wouldn't put demands on her all the time, didn't need her to be perpetually achieving, climbing, rising.

My grandmother gave her blessing to the marriage, but with the provision that the new couple move in with her. There was probably no negotiation about this. It was a common enough practice among Italian-American families in those days, especially when the daughter was the youngest and the last to marry.

Even if it had not been the custom, my grandmother would probably have insisted that the newlyweds live with her. Matriarch, diva, control queen, virago, tyrant—she must have been terrified of losing my mother, her lady-in-waiting. A corpulent, busty woman, Nana combined an unrelenting passion for life with a stern, shrewd, and suspicious wisdom about the ways of the world.

From the beginning of Dad's joining the family, his mother-in-law made it clear that she would be in charge. In all things, from running the house to raising the kids, Nana DeVita expected to have her way. When things didn't go as she wanted, she would raise her voice, letting it crescendo into an angry screaming fit. She and my father had horrible, operatic fights, screeching arias that flared up from the smoldering recitatives of their warm-up arguments. And though there was never any physical violence to accompany these verbal lashings, the tone of their hostilities was often vicious, sometimes even berserk.

In the end, my father always complied. He must have believed that he didn't have a choice. Setting up a household without my grandmother was simply not an option—not in our family and not in our culture. Besides, living under my grandmother's roof was a financial necessity. On a dry cleaner's salary, Dad could not have raised four boys without the relief of having no mortgage to pay. Caught between loyalty to her husband and loyalty to her mother—conflicted, I imagine, in her attraction to what each stood for—my mother had to broker an uneasy truce. To everyone's relief, much of the time my father and my grandmother were civil to each other, though one never knew when my grandmother's disgruntlement would flare up once again into an Italian Götterdämmerung.

Despite his dismissal to a minor post in my grandmother's queendom, Dad managed, in his unassuming way, to make time for his boys. On family trips, more often than not, it was he who huddled us about him in the backseat of the car and told us stories while Mom drove and Nana imperiously occupied the other front seat. Our favorite story concerned Jack Frost, the hobgoblin who, early each October, works his magic, transforming the dull, worn-out leaves of late summer into a glorious New England landscape of gold, ruby, and bronze. "Jack Frost" was Dad's signature story, one we never tired of hearing. For me the delight was threefold: the chance to cuddle up with my father; the pleasure of listening to his jolly voice and seeing his ruddy cheeks puff out as he sprang the punch line; and the message the story conveyed, that the world was full of wonderful, gaudy, unearned delights.

From Dad I learned new words, too—hoosegow, vise, loam, hooch, whiffle—corny country locutions from "out West" in Ohio, Dad's territory, so different from my mother's high-class talk. When I brought home my report cards, it was Mom who scrutinized them, praising the "Excellent"s and asking why I'd gotten only a "Very Good" here or there. Dad, on the other hand, said little, praised little, criticized little—a complete reversal, it now occurs to me, of the stereotype that mothers love unconditionally, while dads demand excellence.

One Christmas—it must have been about 1959—my parents gave me and my brothers a Lionel electric train set consisting of a steam locomotive, a few freight cars and a caboose.

"Caboose!" I giggled. It was another new word for me.

I remember Dad's explaining what a caboose was, and my imagining what it would be like to set up quarters in that little red house on wheels: a potbellied stove, a few bunk beds, everything shipshape and cozy; a world of male friends, simple pleasures, and no frou-frou. With Dad's help, we built a plywood table in the cellar, laid out the track, hooked up the transformer. In the next few years, we added two more train sets, expanded the table, laid out villages. We built chicken-wire-and-papier-mâché mountains, set up trestles and bridges, painted, landscaped. The trains were exclusively our domain: mine, my brothers', and Dad's. Mom never came down to join us. It was a guy thing, maybe the only one my father and I ever had.

Our model-train period lasted only a few years, around the time I was eleven, twelve years old. Why we abandoned the trains I don't remember. Perhaps I grew out of them, got bored, went on to other things. I was entering junior high school, a larger world of friends, extracurricular activities, tentative sexual exploration. There were long afternoons of band practice, play rehearsal, doing homework with friends. Sophomore year I took a job at the local public library; that summer I went away to music camp, the next summer to a prestigious prep school summer enrichment program, where a counselor I had a crush on encouraged me to apply to Harvard. Unaware of it, I was playing out the agenda that Mom and Nana had decided for me: to become a studious, cultured young gentleman with high aspirations, a little *signore*. In short, someone better than my father.

I do not want to misrepresent or belittle my mother's and my grandmother's ambitions. They were remarkable women. My mother still is. Approaching ninety now, she still paints, teaches art, plays golf, bowls, does all her own housekeeping, reads, travels, and fires off angry letters to congressmen and her condo association when something that she doesn't like happens. She's a fabulous dresser and still throws a mean dinner party. She has clearly inherited my grandmother's energy, vitality, and longevity. The daughter of immigrant parents, she indeed transformed herself into a *signora*. But Dad's aspirations were never that grand, his comfort with hobnobbing in high-class circles never as great as hers.

I can still remember the peals of rapture from my mother and grandmother when a letter arrived one Saturday in the spring of 1966: my acceptance to Harvard. But Dad's reaction is gone from my memory. He must have been proud, though I wonder if he also suspected that a career at Harvard would end up pulling me even farther away from him. Nowadays, whenever I teach *Great Expectations* to my students, I often see my father in Joe Gargery, the mild-mannered blacksmith who silently and uncomplainingly watches Pip, his stepson, turn into a snobbish London dandy.

During my four years at Harvard, Dad and I occasionally met for lunch. Like most things, lunches with him were completely different from the lunches I had every few weeks with Mom and Nana. Those were posh affairs at upscale places in Harvard Square with names like Ferdinand's and Chez Dreyfus. Dad preferred his lunch breaks to be far more low key. With him, I always went to an informal German eatery known as the Wursthaus.

With its dark, wooden booths, and pungent aromas of beer, knockwurst, and sauerkraut, the Wursthaus must have reminded Dad of the old days back in Ohio. He and I would always sit at the bar, where we'd kick off our hour together by ordering a couple of drafts. We always had the same bartender, a man my father hailed as "Jimmy" as if he knew him personally—though he never introduced me and they never exchanged much conversation. I doubt, in fact, that Dad was buddies with this man, but I've come to see that, in those lonely years when the business was going badly and his anxieties about the future were mounting, he desperately wanted a pal. In fact, he wanted me for his pal.

Over our beers and liverwurst sandwiches, Dad and I would shoot the breeze for an hour. When I spoke about myself, it was with guarded, reticent words: mostly just safe talk about the courses I was taking. Condescendingly, I assumed my father wouldn't understand much about what I was learning, or wouldn't care. Tentatively, in his gentle, jocular way, he'd sometimes turn the conversation to women—was I dating anyone?—a question I'd brush off as quickly as possible. No, too busy, not yet—anything to get off the subject—and we'd move on to another topic. At one of our last lunches together, Dad asked me if I thought he should sell the business. Cousin Vinnie had long since left the shop, and Uncle Cy had just cashed in his share and moved to Vermont to run a general store. Dad had been sticking it out alone.

"I just don't know," he said. "If I do sell, what'll I do then? I've never worked for someone else before. I don't know anything else." It was probably the most intimate question my father ever asked me. It unsettled me. In the silence and terror of the closet I was in, I was uncomfortably aware of how much, and how fast, my own life was changing. I was on a trajectory that was taking me into new territory—my first love affair, my first sustained sexual relationship, my first time experiencing myself as valued for something other than my good grades and multiple accomplishments. But what, from this new self, could I offer Dad in his hour of need?

I responded with innocuous encouragement. Of course he'd find another job, of course he could do it. Dad nodded his assent, but I could tell he was still anxious. I felt powerless to help him.

"I guess I'll talk it over with your mother," he said as we parted.

I ALWAYS THOUGHT it took my parents quite a while to put two and two together, but an incident from my senior year in college suggests they knew I was gay a lot earlier than I'd supposed. By then I had met my first boyfriend, "Christopher," a graduate student with his own apartment and a decent-enough income to afford a car. Sometime that spring, Chris went out of town for a week, leaving his Volkswagen for me to use. I drove it home to attend—what else?—another family Sunday dinner.

"I think I'd better take his car to be washed before Chris gets back," I remarked to my father at one point during the meal. "What do you think?"

"Why ask me?" Dad snapped. "I don't know what kind of arrangements you made with Chris or what kind of a relationship you two have."

I was surprised by his sudden outburst. It seemed so unwarranted. But now I think I understand what was behind it. There I was, acknowledging the loan of Chris's VW, but not coming clean about what exactly had prompted such an intimate act of generosity. I was still asking my father to play along with a charade that by then he must have seen through. Did Dad also see, even before I did, how his son was drifting farther away from him, in fact, giving up on him? Through all the years that I remained silent about my homosexuality, he had never wavered in the willing affability with which he greeted the guys—my "roommates" and "friends"—whom I brought home. But he must have been tired of playing that game, must have seen how phony it was—phony, a word Dad reserved for his occasional criticisms of Mom's highfalutin ways.

When, a few years later, Chris and I broke up—or, in the language I was still using with my parents, when Chris and I decided not to be roommates anymore—it was Mom who expressed her concern ("But you were such good friends, Philip!"). Dad said nothing. Maybe his was the more honest reaction.

I think he liked my second lover the best. By the time Alfred and I bought a house together, in 1981, Nana was dead, finally leaving Mom and Dad, now well into their sixties, to enjoy their marriage together without interference. And though Dad was now working for a chain of dry-cleaning establishments where he had to punch a time card and endure the disrespect of his boss, he also had more free time to do the things he enjoyed—putter around the house, play golf, take trips with Mom. Soon, too, he was coming by Alfred's and my place, a two-family fixer-upper, to lend a hand. He'd show up on Saturdays to paint, build bookshelves, scrape calcimine from the ceilings. In all but name, Alfred had become my parents' son-in-law. These were happy times: Dad and I working on a project, Alfred and my mother in the kitchen preparing supper. But as always, while Dad and I worked, I kept our conversation safe, steering it away from deep talk or personal disclosures. Each of us—once again—was waiting for the other to make the first move. I did not come out to my parents until years later, when I was in my early forties and breaking up with Alfred. For months, Mom and Dad had sensed that something was the matter, but I'd managed to evade their inquiries as to why Alfred wasn't with me when I came home to visit. Still I knew that the days of circumventing the issue were nearing an end. When my gay cousin called me one night to say that Mom and Dad had been asking him what was going on, I knew I couldn't avoid it any longer.

And so, one afternoon, over coffee in a dreary little Harvard Square eatery, I muddled my way through the saddest, clumsiest conversation I've ever had with anyone—a conversation in which I not only admitted to my parents that I was gay but also informed them that I was breaking up with my lover of twelve years and that I was having an affair with another man.

They said all the right things—about still loving me and only wanting me to be happy, and when would they get to meet this new person, Bill. True to form, Mom also managed to work in some questions about Bill's pedigree. Where did he live? What was his family like? What did he do for work? They also wanted to know why I hadn't told them earlier. I mumbled something, perhaps about not wanting to disappoint them, perhaps about not being sure they were ready. Maybe I told the truth and said I didn't know why. I wanted to get the conversation over with as quickly as possible.

Dad was then in the first stages of his battle with leukemia. He looked tired and weak. But brave, too. Three years later, he died, never knowing that Bill, whom he had grown to love, had AIDS. Once again, I justified withholding information from him, this time on the basis of his being too sick to deal with it. But in retrospect I wonder if I still just wasn't ready for the kind of intimacy my father had probably always been willing to have with me.

I HAVE SCOURED my memories of our relationship, looking for clues as to why I never felt totally at ease with my father. Sometimes I go back to what my gay friends say, that many men of my father's generation unconsciously distance themselves from their gay sons. At other times, I think it can all be explained as the fallout from my mother's and grandmother's ambitious social project: They were telling me to stay away from him. At still other times, the answer seems to lie elsewhere: in my family's ethnic background, or in our socioeconomic milieu, or in my position as oldest son. But none of these explanations ever feels entirely adequate. I've come to accept that I may never put my finger on it exactly.

A few years before he died, Dad gave me an old cardboard box tied up with a worn piece of cord.

"Your old electric train set," he said. "I thought you might want it some day."

I still have the box, tucked away in a closet. Every Christmas I think about taking it down and setting up the tracks again. But I don't. I tell myself that the apartment I live in now is too small for model trains. It's an excuse I never could have used with Bill.

"What do you mean, 'too small'?" I can hear him saying. "We can move some furniture around. Come on, push back that chest. They're your trains. The ones your father gave you. Of course, we'll set them up." At this point Bill would have thrown out his arms, Auntie Mame style. "It'll be fabulous!"

Bill would have been right, too, the way he was almost always right when it came to seeing through my excuses for not being ready to live as hard, and as happily, and as riskily, as possible.

In the eleven years that my father has been gone, I have grown to miss him more and more. There are conversations I want to have with him—about his time in the Army, about his courtship of Mom, about his years under Nana's imperious scrutiny. I am not so sentimental as to suppose that we would ever be buddy-buddy, but I'd like to think that some of my gay life would finally be a topic of conversation between us as well. Of course, none of that is possible now. This is not a statement of regret (regret is an emotion I've learned not to indulge); it's just a fact. Like this one: I still haven't cried for my father. Perhaps I never will. Nevertheless, whenever my mother tells me that she has been talking to my father—in her dreams, in her moments of loneliness—I wonder what she tells him about me. Does she describe my new apartment? Does she tell him about my new boyfriend? Does she mention the books I've written, or the semester I spent teaching in China? I'd tell him those things, too, if I could, but what I'd most like to tell him is this: "Thanks, Dad," I'd say. "For everything."

KAI WRIGHT

Equanimity Under Duress.

There we were, in a rear bedroom of my grandmother's ranch-style house—blinds drawn to block out the bright midwestern afternoon. The whole scene seemed forced and inconsequential. I would be home for only a few days before returning to my life in Washington, D.C., and I resented this wasted time. I leaned on the dresser, struggling to focus on my father and what he would say about the coming-out letter I had sent him the previous fall. But my mind kept following my eyes around the room, which had been transformed from the tidy, white-linened guest room in which I once fought my brother and cousins for adequate napping space into an unkempt hovel in which my proud father was living out his self-imposed exile from the world. His lower leg prosthesis leaned against the unmade bed, where he sat attempting to steady his shaking hands. They trembled not from discomfort over the picture of my boyfriend that they held, but as a result of the strokes my father had quietly endured while hiding out in this room.

Today, I can't even remember what either of us said, just that the conversation felt like trivial detail compared with the other issues my family faced at the time. My aunt, who also lived in that house, was, as usual, quite ill. She would die from a not-so-sudden heart attack just a few months later, at the age of thirty-eight, joining the ranks of African Americans slain at absurdly young ages by heart disease. My father's second marriage—a taxing relationship that hastened his already rapid physical deterioration— had ended, and the ex was suing him for what little money he had left. Like my aunt's, his body was buckling under the weight of diabetes and heart disease, and the hands that once made him Indianapolis's premier black surgeon now failed to steady a razor enough for him to shave regularly. But worse, as a result of all this, my father— whose signature retort to pressure had always been the proclamation, "I'm a surgeon. Equanimity under duress!"—was profoundly depressed. Rather than continue facing life's challenges, he had retreated into this dark rear room where, he seemed to believe, he could inconspicuously await death, as though we lived in 1897 rather than 1997 and any family member's disability shamed the whole unit. So I felt we had much more pressing issues to deal with at the time than the gender of my sex partners.

Looking back, of course, I wish we nevertheless had taken a longer pause to explore the topic. That was the first and last substantive conversation my father and I have had about my sexuality. It's not that he gave me a hard time—his reaction had essentially been a giant shrug, followed by a pat on the back for having too much dignity to live in the closet. But we were both too eager to move on, to dismiss our potential differences as trifling.

In this respect, we mimicked the southern-rooted black community of which we are part. White gays often profess to me, in apparent sympathy for my plight, that black America is uniquely homophobic. They see the devout religion of our anointed leaders, and equate that with the raging hatred found in too many white evangelical circles. But by and large, the black community, both gay and straight, has chosen to deal with sexuality in much the same way as my father and I—acknowledging it when forced, but otherwise remaining indifferent to the matter, when what black same-gender-loving men and women need is support. The reasoning is often the same as my own: We've got too much else to deal with, as a community, to squabble over sexual orientation. That's true, and it's spared folks like me from ever having to respond to the likes of a black

Jesse Helms. But the victory is bittersweet, for it has also robbed people like me of the opportunity to insist that the community consider my unique needs and experiences as a black gay man.

Dad got us off to a good start on the gay thing. When he received my unnecessarily confrontational letter announcing myself to be capital-G gay, he didn't miss a beat in scribbling out a reply. At a time when I was still caught up in *Giovanni's Room*—James Baldwin's popular second novel, depicting a gay relationship between two white men in France— the old man directed me to check out *Just Above My Head*: one of a couple of Baldwin's overlooked later works that tell stories revolving around black gay characters in explicitly black settings. It was, he admitted in his letter of response, "the only book I have ever bothered to read which depicts gay love in the same way that heterosexual love is shown." He went on to note, poignantly, "The novel does not affirm being gay, just assumes it in the way straight life is assumed." This, we seemed to agree, would be our goal as well, to make my gayness a non-issue, an embraced assumption. However well intentioned that goal might have been, it was as absurd and futile as an attempt to render my race a non-issue as well.

I should have expected that he'd be ready, intellectually, to respond. Melvin Wright had never been caught off his intellectual guard in his life. This was the man who, after being told by a high school educator that his dreams of being a doctor were too bold for a black boy from a place like Indianapolis, responded by heading off to college at sixteen, going on to earn his medical degree from Howard and serving his residency on the front line of urban trauma care—the emergency room of Chicago's Cook County Hospital, the inspiration for the TV program *ER*. He further thumbed his nose by moving back to Indy and building a practice designed to serve the sorts of clients most other docs avoided: poor, urban blacks with chronic health problems, whose payments come through the small and cumbersome reimbursements of public insurance, if at all. It was a business strategy that he asserts ruined both of his marriages. And that may be true, at least in part, but it is equally accurate to assume his stubborn nature loosened the bonds of matrimony as well.

But that intransigence has aided as much as it has hurt him—it is, after all, also what drove him from one long workday to the next, propelled him above Jim Crow and carried him through the poverty that comes with attending school and serving out an inner-city residency while raising two young kids. And it played a large role in shaping my worldview, for there were few things that inspired as resolute a stance from the good doctor as his obsessive drive to inoculate his sons' minds against the narrow perspectives that permeate a place as conservative and vanilla as the State of Indiana.

Sundays were spent with both the *Chicago Tribune* and the *New York Times*. A seemingly endless parade of PBS specials on black history and politics—compulsory viewing for all—were interrupted only by the occasional art flick by some aspiring black director whom the old man was jazzed about. Who knew, as I sat bored to tears watching *She's Gotta Have It*, that this Spike Lee guy would become famous? No theater in Indy was showing the film, of course, but Dad found a video and made sure his boys would be able to say "I remember when . . ." And despite the fact that he never quite unlearned the knee-jerk misogyny of the Black Power movement, he marched us out to the opening of *The Color Purple*. I still smirk at the memory of catching him and my barber Mr. Cheatham surreptitiously wiping away tears when Celie finally got up the gumption to tell Mister where to stick it.

So, while I may have just really begun to consider all the ramifications of sexual identity when I fired off my coming-out missive, it turned out not to be Dad's first intellectual encounter with the topic. The man is well read, and, frankly, he was downright showing off in his letter of reply. After pointing me to Baldwin's work, he couldn't resist the requisite parental warning about health. But his wasn't just AIDS hysteria, he highlighted, rightly, things about gay men's sexual health that too many of us still haven't learned. "Education is very good about HIV," he noted, "but poor about hepatitis, condyloma, and perianal disease. So educate yourself!" He warned me to keep my new identity in perspective, to allow it to be among the things that help shape me without limiting me. And finally he reinforced a message he had sent, more through action than word, my whole life. "I have no knowledge or understanding of what being gay is about," he wrote, winding into his close with a flourish of false humility, "but I do believe the best life is the honest life. It has lost me jobs and two marriages, but I must be true to myself and wouldn't have it another way."

These weren't just good words. I've always proudly marveled at the old man's ethical stands, like his refusal to participate in the close-knit social scene of the city's black middle class, because it meant hobnobbing with ambulance-chasing lawyers eager to build illicit partnerships with black docs. He preferred to be ostracized or characterized as aloof to risking even the impression that he would be part of such shenanigans. And rather than run up patients' bills with expensive procedures and tests, or grease profitable relationships with pharmaceutical firms by pushing brand-name drugs, he prescribed generics and spent as much time counseling preventive health care as performing surgery. At home he was equally absolute about doing the Right Thing. I still cringe at the memory of my fifth-grade birthday party, in which I joined a number of black friends in taunting one of our white compatriots, calling him honky. Dad not only made me apologize to the kid, but to his whole damn family. I absorbed all this from my earliest days, and by the time I got around to facing personal decisions such as whether and how to deal with my sexual orientation, "the honest life" was the only possible choice.

Understand that coming out to myself was no small feat. Many of my current friends, such as my partner, grasped their homo proclivities from the onset—and it's an awareness that's either a blessing or a curse, depending on your perspective. But well into college I continued to thickly assert that my failure to connect with girls had little to do with my odd obsession with boys' torsos. One and one simply did not equal two, partly because there was no such number in my range of answers: I understood gay people to be white people. Mind you, I knew of plenty of black faggots and punks—such as the Wayans brothers' insultingly depicted snap queen characters, or the father of the kids who lived down the street from my maternal grandma in Alabama, the missing-in-action bum whose mention always prompted the speaker to suck his or her teeth and note how no one had heard from him since he ran off to California with that white boy. But gay people—people with a proud, self-proclaimed sexual identity—well, those were white folks and had little to do with me. Dad had meticulously prepared me to navigate the traps life puts up for a young black man; he just never considered the possibility that I might have to face those obstacles as a young black *and* gay man.

As a result, it wasn't until late in college, when I finally came into substantive contact with some openly gay people, that I began to actually consider my own sexuality beyond the normative straight model to which I had always passively aspired. And it wasn't until I arrived in Washington, D.C.—hundreds of miles away from my previous lives—that I stumbled into accepting the fact that I was gay.

But once I got there, I had little debate about how to proceed. I plunged in with no fear, for what threat could homophobia possibly offer that racism hadn't already trumped? Would sheriffs pull me over and search my car because I was gay, as they regularly did when I drove my old 1979 Buick Regal around too late at night in the wrong Indianapolis neighborhoods? Would three cop cars come screeching onto my front lawn because I was gay, as they did when they saw me leaving a drugstore that had been robbed, even though witnesses had identified someone in a car of a different make, model, and color?

Still, there are other types of threats that I hadn't imagined, those that emanate from places closer to home than the actions of bigoted cops.

I HAD DISENGAGED myself from most social dimensions of black life pretty early on. Mom could make me physically enter the church—three times a week at our peak attendance, for Tuesday Bible study, Saturday usher practice, and the marathon Sunday services—but she couldn't make me stick around mentally or emotionally. I had what I now recognize as a crush on the pastor's youngest boy, so I didn't mind hanging out with him on the balcony, using the offering envelopes to play tick-tack-toe and make "favorites" lists—your ten favorite cars, songs, supermodels, etc. It got me through the service, and helped me ignore the drivel about man and woman and their varied roles in the world that spewed from the pulpit. Somehow I knew I'd never get that part right, and didn't wish to be reminded of the fact.

Similarly, once boys became young men, I had a hard time living up to the increasingly important "hard" persona black males were supposed to affect. I looked butch enough, but when it came to chasing tail and walking the talk, I left plenty to be desired. I was the only guy on the football team who actually cried when the coach told us he was quitting. Dr. Dre and Eazy E surely never shed public tears, let alone over some white man walking off the job. I wasn't cut out for membership in the cult of masculinity that any black man worth his salt was supposed to join by his late teens. So I mentally and emotionally bowed out of that institution as well. In one area of social life after another, I found my body physically situated inside the black community, but my mind and heart floating somewhere else, alone in some undefined space.

When I finally confronted my sexuality in D.C., I first thought I had found in the gay community a place to reengage. But it didn't take long for me to realize that the most important color in that community's professed rainbow is white. Here I was, living in the city's gay ghetto, and feeling as much like an outsider as I had in church back in Indy. The same businesses that welcomed job inquiries from my white gay friends looked at me as though I had asked where to buy crack when I applied. The same neighbors who fell over themselves to greet my white lesbian housemate glanced at me sidelong, as if to ask what I was doing on this block. Gay or not, I was an unfamiliar young black man—a threat.

This wasn't a problem; I faced the gay white cold stare in the same way I faced the straight one—with the tools Dad had taught me. But where did that leave me? Still floating in some undefined space. Eventually, I would find the black gay community, and land there. And increasingly, the larger black community has welcomed us within it as well, not just tolerating our presence as silent members, but affirming our participation as valuable and our needs and concerns as relevant. With one in 50 black men and one in 300 black women estimated to be HIV-positive, sexuality in general has suddenly become a legitimate topic of discussion. And with more than a third of young black gay and bisexual men believed to be infected, homosexuality in particular seems a much less trivial subject to consider.

But in my own family, as we moved from the crises of that winter afternoon five years ago to the next and the next, my father and I have never paused to revisit my sexuality. The closest we've come is to dance around the issue of whether one is black first or gay first. For underlying his letter's seemingly innocuous warning that I not let my sexual identity define me lurked a fear that I would allow it to supersede the racial identity he had spent so many years nursing.

I remember his reaction when I brought home a copy of the gay newspaper I had begun writing for. He sat at my grandmother's old wooden kitchen table, drugstore glasses perched on his nose, the rickety chair creaking under his weight as he awkwardly shifted about while thumbing its pages. Unable to find a graceful reaction, he finally mumbled, "It's awful white." A fair criticism. Hoping to spark a conversation about my own simultaneously black and gay identity, I directed him to my front-page story about black AIDS activists who were complaining that the Centers for Disease Control organized epidemiological data only according to either race or sexuality, offering no insight into what goes on in the unique space where the two intersect. But he was trapped within the same "boundaries of blackness," as political scientist Cathy Cohen puts it, as I had been when I was unable to translate my homosexual desires into gay identity. The activists had it wrong, he grumbled, these men were first and foremost black. Whatever health disparities black gay and bisexual men faced were a function of race not sexual orientation, and should be addressed accordingly. For him, there is no gay, no straight, no female, no male—just black.

But what other perspective can be expected from an African American who lived through Jim Crow? (And on one level, he's absolutely right. As far as the world is concerned, I am simply black. That's what those white gay neighbors and business owners saw, and nothing more.) So if I want my father—my community—to understand the other dimensions of my experience, I will have to insist on it rather than apologize for it. I will have to demand that my needs be considered equally important as those we have already accepted as critical. This is where I have failed; this is where the black gay community, as a whole, has failed.

ON MY LAST trip home, during the Christmas holidays, I resolved to revisit our brief opening discussion about my sexuality. I make it to Indy only a couple of times a year nowadays, and as usual the image of my father's deteriorating body stunned me. The diabetes had by then taken most of his eyesight, and he'd given up most any pretense of connection with the world. But his spirits were up, and I figured, after Christmas, in one of those post-holiday lazy afternoons, I'd broach the subject once more. I wasn't sure then, and still don't know now, what it is I want from him—to join some PFLAG-type group, to profess greater curiosity about sexual orientation, to just have a longer conversation on the issue than we originally accepted? But I know I want more.

On Christmas night, I joined my cousin in going to visit her father, my dad's older brother, who had been sentenced to spend the season laid up in the hospital. For some undiagnosable reason, he'd suddenly begun shedding so much skin that infections set in. Everyone had a theory, and most of the holiday conversation centered on this debate. Smart money blamed the sugar pills he was taking; the more spiritually minded folks quietly suggested a link to his wife's painful diabetes-related death the previous year. The visit made me and my issues feel small, once again trivial and insignificant. How could I demand more attention, I thought, more overt support to combat the challenges I face as a gay man, when Dad's already got this to deal with? So I decided to defer, once more. Maybe next time I'll bring it up, I figured . . . next time.

DAVID MASELLO

Double Vision.

I was sitting with my father at night by the pool in his Florida rental complex. For those tenants who have lived here long enough, my father is known as that old man who goes out there every night to smoke a pipe and greets anyone, no matter what their age, with a "Hello there, son," or "How are you, young lady?"

Although it's easy for me to imagine these neighbors of his as guests on the *Jerry Springer Show,* I am surprised every time by their genuine and ready politeness. "Fine, sir, thank you, and how about you?" I hear them reply to my father.

"Just when you get to know somebody in this place, they're gone, with no word of goodbye," my father says to me. "It's all part of this transient society we live in. There was one kid I got to know. I saw him every day on the way to my car, always working on his motorcycle. A real friendly person—down here from Missouri, I think he said. Then one day, the motorcycle isn't there and I never see him again. All that's left is a grease stain on the pavement. Every time I walk over that spot, I think of him and wonder where he went."

If you didn't know what lay beyond the pool and eight-lane roadway that begin fifty yards away, you could mistake the locale as country. Much of the surrounding land is empty but it is no longer pastoral. My father's apartment, in a complex called Shadow Run, is eleven miles inland from the Gulf and occupies a parcel of an industrial park. Beyond the baby-blue, two-story apartment units and the manmade pond with its fat, Cheese Doodle–fed swans are long, low warehouses that stretch deep into their lots. In distant fields, visible from the Shadow Run parking lots, giant heaps of gravel and sand rise like perfect breasts. Tapered radio towers vault across the land, their silver cross bracings drawing an infinity of X's into the horizon. Across the road, and visible from the pool, is a barbed wire–bounded facility I have heard is a missile-parts plant. Sometimes its lot is filled with cars during workday hours, and children can be seen playing in the day-care outbuildings; other times, for entire months, the whole facility seems abandoned.

On the night we sat by the pool, there was only one swimmer, who remained silent. It was easy to forget he was there. He stood in water up to his chest, which reflected a kaleidoscope of shadows from the ripples and submerged spotlights. His body was frantic with this movement, even though he was still.

Shirtless, barefoot young men padded in and out of the adjacent laundry room, the dryers clicking with jeans rivets and zippers. The slap of feet on the smooth concrete sent vibrations beneath our chairs. During wash cycles, some of these young men would feed coins into the shuddering vending machines and we would hear the sequence of a can tumbling, a retracting of the airtight flap, the metallic pop when opened.

On my visits to Florida the ages of these young men and who they are—whether fellow roommates, children of tenants, or fathers themselves—are never clear to me. It is not uncommon here for people eighteen years old to have a couple of children they push around on plastic tricycles—children they call Tiffany or Brandy or J. P. When showing affection, the parents caress the wispy, cultivated tail of their youngster's hair as if it were a swan's feather they had found on the bank of the pond.

At about nine o'clock at night around the pool you hear these couples talking about the sixty-cent-an-hour wage increases from their chain-store employers, how many ten-minute breaks a day they're allowed, where else applications are being taken, and which shifts are available. When the young men emerge from the bright laundry room, it's as if their bodies had been charged in there, made phosphorescent. They carry into the night some of that fluorescent light for a few moments, before it fades away. In this way, the bare parts of their bodies are like amorphous segments of the moon.

"I think I'm fading," I say to my father. "I need to head back to the motel and get some sleep, but I'll see you again tomorrow—remember we've got three more full days together." He rises from the chair with a groan, disappointed that the company he's had all day is leaving and that the days are ticking down fast to my returning home.

On the walk back to my car, past the cryptorium grid of mailboxes and through spider-webbed cinder-block breezeways linking buildings, we come to an attractive woman in her late sixties. She is sweeping her doormat depicting a scene of roly-poly children in a gingerbread house. I make a point of saying hello because I instantly spot her as someone who could be right for my father.

"Hello, gentlemen," she says back. "Beautiful night." A homemade stained-glass ornament hangs on her door, and every blind in her windows is pulled to a precise three-quarter height.

"This is my father who lives over in the N building," I say, aware of how little transition there has been in our exchange for me to mention this. But there is no time for subtlety. "I'm his son, visiting from New York."

"Why, how nice for you," she says to my father.

He then asks the first question he always asks anyone in Florida. "How long have you been down here?"

"Four months. I came from Ohio."

"Why would you leave a beautiful state like Ohio," my father says as both statement and question, "for this heat? You'll see it's constant down here—every day, ninety, ninety-three, ninety-two, with equal humidity. I dream about going back north."

"Well, I have a daughter down here, a sister, and two nephews. After all, home is where the family is."

When she says this, my father grabs the lighted pipe from his mouth so quickly that the stem knocks against his teeth. The red glow of the bowl extinguishes.

"You're right about that," he says. "Absolutely right."

When we say goodbye and walk on I tell my father, "Now *she's* someone you should meet. Ask her out for lunch one day. Ask her to sit out by the pool with you some night."

"I appreciate your concern."

"I mean it. Meet her again. Get to know her. She's very attractive and, besides—and I probably shouldn't mention this—I think she looks like you know who, an uncanny resemblance, in fact." I am referring to my father's ex-girlfriend, but I've discovered on all my visits to Florida that there are many women who resemble her—neatly dressed and thin, hair in place like some champagne-colored cotton candy confection, a small gold pendant cross against a vector of tan skin, careful eye makeup.

"I have to admit, since you brought it up, I thought the exact same thing," he responds. "Isn't that something? But I'll tell you, there's *another* woman who I sometimes see in the Golden Bear," he adds, referring to a restaurant he goes to every day for breakfast, "who's the spitting image of her," her being the ex. "It's weird, is all I can say. I swear, it's either her double or I've been having double vision."

"So follow through on this," I continue, "meet this one who lives in the complex. You said it yourself, she's nearly a double. And she seems very sweet. Remember her apartment number. You can get her full name from the girl in the rental office."

"Now how am I going to ask her out?"

"Write her a note saying you met her tonight with me and that you sit out by the pool in the evenings. It's a perfectly natural invitation. And don't wait a week to do it before she forgets us and our little exchange. You could even say she reminds you a lot of your ex or however you're referring to her these days, if that makes it easier."

I pull out of the parking space quickly, punch the trumpet icon on the padded steering wheel until a beep sounds. I drive off without lowering my window and saying goodbye again because my father might suggest following me to my motel, hoping to come to the room for another smoke and more conversation. I'm tired, nearly drugged by the pool's chlorine vapors and the sweet detergent smells from the laundry room. But I also want to get back to the Howard Johnson's as early as I can because I know there is a chance I will see the young man again I first saw two days ago.

■　■　■

MY FIRST SIGHTING of him was in the middle of the afternoon, while my father and I were sitting on the balcony of my motel room. On this trip to Florida to the same motel where I always stay, I was given a first-floor room. From the balcony, a recessed slab of concrete, we looked to the grassy strip along a snaking branch of the inland waterway, with its thin parade of kayaks and sputtering motorboats.

I needed some ice and took the room's plastic bucket to the machine in the lobby. As soon as I turned the corner, I saw the young man at the pay phone. He appeared to be of college age, at least I hoped; still, I might have been twice as old. He had on a tank top, baggy swimming trunks, and sandals. His blond hair was layered like the gradations of sand near the shoreline. I could see the way the bones—small, protruding knobs—emerged atop his gleaming shoulders.

The tiny motel lobby was defined by two walls of glass, one giving out to the parking lot, the other, behind him, to the traffic on Gulf Boulevard and the open expanse of Treasure Island beach. Within this perspective, he was part of a scene where distant motorboats streaked and bounced across the Gulf, sending up white spray like the tails of comets.

Ice clattered into the bucket and overflowed. Dice-size cubes skittered like mercury pellets across the lobby floor. He looked at me bashfully, but carefully, as I kicked the cubes into a corner.

When I was back on the balcony with my father, he walked past us on the grass. He threaded his fingers through the cyclone fence that ran along the waterway and stared down into the green water, then to the houses on the other side, their jalousie louvers flush. He looked at these sights with the concentration and interest of those newly arrived at a place. At this early point in his trip, these ordinary sights were alluring.

In a landscape so undistinguished, a young man like this is going to stand out, I realized. He is a tourist on vacation with his family, probably from Europe, as was most everyone in the motel. He looked longingly at that neighborhood across the water, but I knew he would find it lifeless because I, too, am often lured there. No matter where he goes into that sprawl of boxy buildings, that ever-expansive grid of fast-food stands and chain stores, he will stand out. He is that beautiful.

"All this development, it goes on forever," I imagine his thinking when he first sees the inland Florida landscape. "How does a person find his way through it, not get confused, know where he is? Can all this ever become a person's home? Can he say, 'This is where I live'? One place looks like another, a double of it, then a triple, then so many I forget how many. This is not what I expected America to look like." But these are not the conclusions he has yet reached, because this motel and the vistas from it are all he has probably seen so far, or so I guess.

After sending up a final cloud of cherry-scented smoke, my father knocked the pipe against the chair leg to empty the bowl and went inside to take a nap. I took my camera and stood on the balcony, focusing on the young man who was only yards away. I adjusted the lens, desperate to get his image before he left. But as the shutter clicked, he turned and looked at me over his shoulder. The wind was picking up and the masts of moored boats clanged, alarmlike. Blue tarps draped over masts snapped and the tops of palm trees shook as if wind was generated from within their dense fronds. The chilly wind sent him back to his room. He walked away rubbing his bare arms.

AS SOON AS I reached the motel after leaving my father's complex, I checked the lobby and the pool for the young man. After realizing I might not see him again, I instead walked over the waterway bridge into the neighborhood called the Isle of Palms, as I did every night. And it was there I saw him—at Pelican Place, one of the finger-shaped streets on one of the hands of land. Every street, lined on both sides with one-story houses, dead-ended at the water. He was walking toward the water, and I knew he'd have to turn around.

"I don't mean to startle you, but I recognize you from the motel where we're both staying," I said when I caught up to him.

"Yes, I do know you. I saw you in the lobby, I think, the other day. Getting ice."

"I'm visiting from New York," I said. "My father lives down here."

"I'm from Sweden with my family. This is our first time to Florida. To America even. Well, for me it is. My father has come before for business. I'm on break from my college."

"It's awfully quiet here, isn't it? On the streets in Florida, sometimes all you hear is air-conditioners or the mumblings of TVs. Only tourists walk anywhere, even at night. Why are you over here, in this neighborhood, especially now when it's so hard to see anything?"

"I just wanted to take a walk and see some American houses. An American town."

"These aren't very attractive houses, I'm afraid, or a very typical town. These are just Florida beach houses. Most of the people don't even live here all the time. And it's all an invented place. This land we're on is created, not natural. It's landfill. But I suppose even seeing these houses is interesting for you because it's all new to you."

Where we were was a couple of hundred yards inland from the motel. The city of St. Petersburg, where the sky was a pink wash, began on the far shoreline of the inlet. The little scene we created was lit by a street-light lost amid the fronds of a palm. It was windy and the floppy branches cast a frantic film noir shadow on the pavement. The tarantulaed treetop shook over and over as if trying to rid itself of something.

We introduced ourselves. "Do you mind if I walk with you?" I asked. "I come over here every morning and again at night and I know what little there is to see. I can show you a block of houses, for instance, where every mailbox is a miniature of its actual house, except for one that's shaped like a porpoise. There's also a house with three antique cars parked in the driveway—really old ones from the early 1900s—and sometimes a yellow T-bird convertible from the mid-'60s, the kind with sequential tail-lights, if you know what I mean by that."

"Yes, I'd like to see those things," he answered, although I wasn't sure he understood the details I had described.

As we strolled toward the end of the street where the water thunked against pilings, a pair of headlights swung into the road, blinding us when we turned around to look. It was my father's car and someone was sitting in the passenger seat.

"I thought I'd find you out here," my father said as he cranked down the window, yellowed from pipe smoke. "You remember Lucille," he said, gesturing to the woman we had met earlier at his complex.

"Hello again," the woman called over.

"Funny thing, just as you left I got immediately restless, even a little depressed, and so I went down to the pool for another smoke," my father said.

"Lucille was there too and we got to talking and she decided to accompany me on my nightly drive. I said to her, 'How about joining me for a visit to my son down at the beach?' I figured, if we didn't find you in the room we'd find you out here, where I know you like to take a walk."

"By the way, this is Christopher," I said, "who's staying with his family in the motel. I was just showing him this neighborhood."

"Hello there, son," my father said. "So hop in and we'll go for an ice cream at that place down the road. And you, young man, you're welcome to come with us, although I wouldn't want a son of mine going out at night with strangers. You better ask your parents."

"It's okay, sir," Christopher said. "My parents are at a karaoke bar across the street until eleven o'clock. They wouldn't mind my going with you."

As we drove along Gulf Boulevard, I realized the four of us were on a kind of double date, Christopher and I in back. Soon we arrived at the ice-cream stand, its ziggurat sign of a soft-serve vanilla cone spotlighted. We sat at a round metal table on a raised deck, ice cream streaming down the backs of our hands and wrists, shards of chocolate-dipped shell sloughing off. We licked at our limbs like injured animals attending wounds.

"One thing about my three sons," my father said, as much to Lucille as to the two of us, "is that they all like blonds. Whether it's their friends or—how should I say this, their love interests—so often they're blond." He then laughed and attended to the ice cream caught in the grid at the bottom of the cone.

Although my father knew of my situation—the result of an essay published in the *New York Times* years earlier about love-life secrets I had kept from him—being gay had never been discussed, to the relief of both of us. When the essay appeared and he found out about it from his older sister, my father called and cried into the phone. Eventually, the receiver fell from his hand and bounced across an end table—blunt, dissonant notes in my ear. His girlfriend picked it up and hurriedly told me to call later in the week. My father had told me once, "I've been having nightmares about your personal life," which I interpreted as code, and now his fears had been realized.

The day after the essay's appearance, I sent my father a note by Express Mail explaining matters the piece didn't address and that I knew would make him feel better: that I was healthy, my boss knew I was gay (and had even complimented me on the piece), my best friend was a woman named Donna, and that I was not a drag queen, nor had I ever contemplated dressing as a woman. But for years, the blue cardboard envelope with its image of a bald eagle remained unopened. I saw the eagle's white wings sticking out from atop a shelf of books in my father's apartment, the envelope's pull-tab safely in place. The information in my letter would have relieved my father, but he preferred not to risk finding out additional information that would unsettle him more. For him, it was better to limit what he knew, and learn to accept that.

Maybe my father had said what he said about blonds because he had taken a risk that night, out of character for him, and asked Lucille out. My father's usual strategy would have been to obsess and assess, delaying asking her out until inertia had become the stronger force. As all sons are at some point, I had been the father that night—given him worldly dating advice and a nudge of confidence sufficient to get him to ask her out. He was giddy with the result, and it had translated to a kind of recklessness with Christopher and me.

And yet, as we four sat at the ice-cream stand, there was never an indication from Christopher that the event was anything resembling a date. I felt more like an English-as-a-second-language tutor to him than a prospective sexual partner—explaining terms like *double-dip, banana split,* and *Fudge-o-Rama bars,* avoiding complicated idioms, spelling out words on napkins. But Christopher was with strangers in a strange place, and it couldn't be easy for him to read the situation. Still, there was much about our being out together that, for me, was like a date, only one that was formal and chaperoned.

After finishing, we remained at the table and watched cars pass on Gulf Boulevard, its course emblazoned with the language of the region, neon words of motels and attractions: Algiers, Thunderbird, SeaJay, Beach Star, Pirate's Cove Golf. Cars passed, their undercarriages and license plate frames lit by purple phosphorescent tubes. Eventually, the outside lights of the ice-cream stand were extinguished and the last of the customers walked to their cars with a percussion of snapping beach sandals.

Back at the motel, my father and Lucille got out of the car as if they had agreed on this beforehand. "We'll all sit for a while on your balcony," my father announced. "And you, young man, you need to check in again with your parents. I'm sure my son will be seeing you again during his stay here."

"Thank you for the treat," Christopher said to my father, just before leaving us. "This was my first American experience—with real Americans."

I knew then that it was unlikely during my final days on this trip for Christopher to appear on my balcony, as I had been envisioning, some late morning—dripping from a swim in the pool, a towel wrapped over his shoulders that he clutched below his chin. Saying goodbye to him and knowing that nothing else would happen was not difficult, for this was where my father lived, and he was alone. Had I encouraged my father and Lucille to continue on to Shadow Run instead of returning to the motel with me, the spell of attraction and companionship between them might have broken.

The moment I had sat in the backseat of my father's car on the way to the ice-cream stand, all my sexual longing and scheming for Christopher had dissipated as quickly as my father's pipe smoke. Nothing could have been more inappropriate than desire under my father's eyes—though I had often witnessed my older brothers express overt longing for girls in front of him. My body and my mind responded accordingly to the situation. Both would reactivate—but in another place with another person— to the pitch I felt when I had caught up to Christopher on the dark Isle of Palms street with its sounds and scents of the tropical.

I dragged a chair from the room onto the motel balcony and my father, Lucille, and I took our places.

"That new friend of yours—he's a nice kid, I can tell," my father said. "Try to stay in touch with him while you're down here—especially because he's foreign. Remember, the Swedes were allies of ours during the war. Give him a good impression of America."

As he spoke I looked at Lucille, who nodded in agreement. She was a stranger who I knew something about the moment I first saw her; I had read her correctly. She was now sitting on the balcony with my father like an expert companion. She, too, had worked all her life in some now ruined northern industrial city, for years imagining a retirement in Florida with nights spent just this way. She knew how to please a man like my father, recognized his loneliness and simple need for companionship. She had become an immediate fill-in for his ex-girlfriend. And even though she remained and Christopher had left, my father and I had each met the stranger we wanted.

PAUL LISICKY

Tools

"So what kind of recorder do you need?"

My father's bent over the open hood of the sedan, loosening a nut on—is that the carburetor?—with a wrench. I'm home from Loyola for the weekend. Beyond the open garage door, rain pours down into the driveway drain, wetting the birch clumps, the veined leaves of the silver maple, the spreading junipers leeching across the licorice root.

"Daddy," I say. (How I hate to say "Daddy," but what else to call him? "Dad" sounds like someone you'd throw a football to, and "Father" sounds like it's from the last century.) "We don't have to do this today, really." And I absolutely mean it. While I leapt at his offer to buy me a four-track recorder last week, I feel differently today. Don't I already hear him in the kitchen yelling to my mother late one night about the checks written to Clover, the local supermarket? the small iced cake we had for dessert last night?

He turns his head to the left. "Hand me those pliers."

I pick out a wrench before delicately putting it back. A part of me wishes I had the aptitude for car repair (wouldn't my help mitigate this boredom, this dizziness?), but my father and I mutually gave up on my mechanical abilities when I started playing piano at six. Not that he expects me, or my brothers, for that matter, to be him. If anything, he wants us to live lives that are bright, extraordinary, that spin off and away, laughing at how simple his own is: taking back roads to bypass toll bridges, wiping doorknobs with a pink T-shirt each time he locks the house, helping to catch the burglar who never seems to arrive, but who will certainly take every last thing we have when he crashes an ax through our front window. Still, that doesn't stop my father from marshaling us to his side whether he's putting on roof shingles or digging trenches in our enormous front lawn to lay pipes for sprinklers. If we can't truly be helpers, then we can be witnesses, provide company. And a little suffering can be good for the soul, can toughen it, can't it? Too much pleasure, too much of the easy life, and, before you know it, you're losing your brain cells, slouching on the couch before the TV, eating, well—cake.

"I don't have the right tools. Ah, shit." He rubs his face vigorously with both palms then holds them there for a second, breathing into the torn up skin. "Let's go get your machine."

"I think we should reconsider."

"Listen," he says solemnly. "You need a four-track recorder to make demo tapes. That's what you told me, right?"

"Yes, but—"

"You want to be famous?" he says more quietly now.

The question stops my breath. Famous? The way he says it is absolutely sincere, with only the slightest tinge of force; he doesn't hear anything embarrassing above, beneath, or suffusing the word. He believes in my potential with such a steady, practically holy conviction that I'm moved and strengthened by it, though I'm reluctant to admit it to myself. Yes, I do want to be known and recognized for my songwriting; I'd like to sing back to Laura and Joni, to enter the conversation. But admitting to a desire for fame sounds shameful—and as moral, frankly, as bulldozing acres of Arizona saguaros to sell lots.

"You have to earn a living," he says.

"I know, but—" This doesn't seem to be the moment to talk about claiming a self, creating something that resists the problem of death. Anyway, I don't have the language for such thoughts. "If I was after money—"

A delivery truck drives by, flinging a wave of puddle water on the flooded lawn. "There are probably more efficient ways to earn a living."

He stands facing me, shoulders relaxing backward, neck lengthening until it makes a tender crack. We sigh at once, together. It still startles us both that I've turned out to be six inches taller than he. We smile tentatively, then glance away. "I'm going to change these clothes," he says.

The wind gusts: a yellow chrysanthemum flower blows across the floor of the garage, hitting one wall, catching somewhere on the undercarriage of the car, absorbing the scent of the back tire. It occurs to me that if I'd stayed back at school, I'd have been able to finish the new song I've been struggling with for weeks, I'd have gotten those French conjugations finished. But, in spite of the agitated particles in the air, the sense of constant motion, the occasional blowup, the stifling routine of things, I love it here. (Where else can I sit and read the newspaper or work on my songs in silence and not feel the burden of presenting myself in an acceptable way? Where else but in their lamplit kitchen, with my parents attending to their tasks in other rooms, can I be absolutely alone but together with people at the same time?) Is something wrong with me? At least Sister Mary Jonathan, the school therapist I see on Tuesday afternoons, thinks so. She's suggested more than once that I'm too attached to my family, that it's time to separate, that I'm not giving the luminous Loyola College, a school I've come to loathe more than simple three-chord pop songs, a chance. The problem is that she's so convinced of the school's intrinsic value that she'd never let me go. Two months into my first semester I still can't figure out whatever possessed me to choose a small Catholic school with a heavy concentration of business majors and no established traditions in the creative arts. Was it only that they made a fuss over me when they found out about my work in music? Or was I so sick and tired of hearing my parents' worries about my desire to put off college, their fears that such a decision might turn out to be "low class," cutting off the ladder of our climb, that it was easier to give in to the first school who'd said yes? (Didn't my brother Bobby do that when he signed on to four years at LSU, causing the whole lot of us to weep silently for hours after we left him, driving back north through the swamps of southern Louisiana, devastated?) Whatever it is, I've gone wrong. And time's running out: I need the nerve and audacity to get myself the hell away from school, from home, to fly out to Los Angeles, to rent a little apartment, to perform at Doug Weston's Troubadour, to pound the streets, to work myself ragged, to get my tapes into the right people's hands.

"Ready?" My father's changed his T-shirt, but he's still wearing the same pants he wore while working on the car.

"You're wearing that?"

"What's wrong?"

"There's a spot on your pants."

He looks down at the hem, squints his left eye and rubs it—protein? blood?—with the tip of his thumb. He shakes his head. "You worry too much."

Within minutes, we're inside a cramped electronics store across from the Cherry Hill mall. In one corner: a taped-up photo of the Ayatollah Khomeini with three red circles superimposed over his face. Opposite: a potted mother-in-law's tongue that hasn't been watered in weeks. There's a stale smell of baking; cherry lozenges; the slightest tinge of cigarette breath. The salespeople, all with bushy, black mustaches, stand with their backs to the register counter, trading jokes, though they're sending out signals—I swear I'm picking them up—like hammerheads that haven't smelled anything like human flesh in weeks. (How tasty we must look to them. Who's buying luxury electronics during an oil embargo and hostage crisis?) We paddle out between the displays, trying our best to look like energetic, capable swimmers, only occasionally grasping onto a raft before we swim on. How to tell the difference between one machine and another that costs a thousand dollars more? I know I should probably care more about the mechanics of popular music, but it's as comprehensible to me as the dusty wires inside the hood of my father's car. To me an amplifier is an amplifier, and I'm inwardly distrustful of those who'd give as much credence to the sound system itself as to the quality of a performance. Perhaps this has to do with my years of playing guitar in 1960s-era Catholic churches, where we had to make do with a humble microphone attached to a blond lectern embossed with an abstract fish. At such moments I feel the grave tug that I should offer myself up to the realms of church music forever—that this obsessive need to turn myself out to the world, this wanting, is simply going to do me in. Look up to God, I think, but such thoughts are almost unbearable to take on right now: a lifejacket with weights sewn inside the collar.

A salesman with brass-colored freckles moves in our direction. Suddenly my father folds his thick arms over his chest with the instinctive distrust he holds for anyone who's out to take something from him. My headache pounds. "The youngster here," he says, before the fellow has the opportunity to extend his hand, "is a singer-songwriter."

"Is that right?" The salesman's gaze goes right to the tiny spot on my father's pants, then fixes a spot on his own. "We get a lot of young singer-songwriters in here. We just talked to a composer from Juilliard."

My father's features settle into a harder, more brutal version of his usual expression. Looking at him, you'd never know that he tears up, in public, at most movies, regardless of their content.

The salesman glances up, rubs his mustache with a ringed finger. "How can I help?"

"He needs a four-track recorder."

"A four-track recorder—okay. And mikes, and stands, and head-phones, and—?"

My father nods once, firmly, with emphasis.

"The whole nine yards," the man says somberly.

He leads us down a passageway. Walking, I'm trying to hold myself together, but second by second, my edges are melting, flowing. I'm all over the floor now, a cold clear puddle of ammonia that could make your nose run, scalding the skin of your hand if you let it linger on me too long. Why should it make me so uncomfortable to receive something? Of course my father spends the better part of each weekend working himself to death, but he's choosing that, for God's sake; he's an electronic engineer; he has two graduate degrees; he's certainly not as cash-strapped as he makes himself out to be. And yet, such thoughts are not enough to lift me off the floor, to take away this smell, which can only be described as guilt, guilt, the domain of the lazy, the muddle-headed, a state of being that was sup-posed to have gone out of fashion with Vatican II. I'm a solid, coherent adult at Loyola: no "youngster." Why can't I be that here?

We're standing next to a small tower of boxes.

"A songwriter," says the man. He looks at me directly, for a second, for the first time since I've entered the store, then turns away again. (Is there something about me that scares him, and him me?) He says these words with a brisk casualness, a lifted corner of the lip, as if such declarations are familiar from the mouths of ambitious Cherry Hill parents and their misguided offspring. A part of me wants to tell him you don't know who you're talking to, but I'm keeping my mouth shut if only to move things along.

The salesman reaches for a box marked TEAC. "Who do you sound like?"

I pause. It doesn't occur to me that the question requires a complicated answer, that I should probably just say "John Cougar Mellencamp." Instead, I choose to pose the truth as a question: "Laura Nyro?"

The corner of his eyelid pulses. I'm not even sure he's ever heard of her, but whatever he thinks of my answer, it's wrong. He tears open a box and gingerly removes a bright machine with simulated walnut on the sides and two twelve-inch reels. He clicks a bar to the right, turning the reels with a satisfying sshh, like tide moving through a marsh. He holds up a mike.

"Test, test."

"Sing something," my father says.

I roll my eyes, glare.

"Come on," he says softly, with a hint of flirtation. My father turns to the man, a kinder, more relaxed expression softening the set of his nose, the length of his upper lip. He makes a slight nudging motion, even though he's a full four feet from the man. "He's bashful."

"Daddy."

"Go sing one of your church songs."

The man hits the rewind and plays our conversation back for us. Church songs? What to do: Sing Psalm 150 in a public space for someone who'd have to pretend he'd appreciate my performance? Or worse, disappoint my father? But wouldn't he love it, though, talk about it for years, just the way he talked about my brother Michael when he played "Day by Day" on the piano in that restaurant in Mexico, with the ocean out the window behind him, to the applause and cheers of everyone at the tables—one of the many things that Michael's done to lift my father's gloom.

Fortunately, the salesman must know what I'm thinking. Or maybe the thought that we might be fundamentalists or fanatics of some sort rallies his attention. (But you don't understand, I want to say: Catholic folk songs. Guitars! Liturgical dance!) He quotes us a price that's at least $150 under list, so shocking my father that he's entirely disarmed: He's stunned that there could be something like luck or good fortune in the world.

"You're sure you're not selling me something returned?" My father squats, running his hand on the surface of the machine to check for nicks, scratches, dents.

"You have my word, sir. It's in tip-top shape. It's just last year's floor model."

My father turns to me. He lifts his brows until his forehead wrinkles; he squints. "And you're sure that's what you want?"

I nod.

"You're not making this up? You want this, right?"

I put more effort into my second nod, though I'm thinking, well— too much is depending on this, no object in the world should ever carry so much meaning and possible defeat. But when I switch the knobs to the left, then to the right, imagining myself with headphones on, my lips barely touching the spongy black bulb of the mike, a soft glow warms the underside of my arm from the palms all the way up to the shoulder blades. "Man, oh man," I murmur.

"Ring it up, then," my father says in a resigned, dehydrated voice. He pats his front pants pocket, slides out a stained caramel-colored wallet, extending a credit card to the man. "BankAmericard."

In no time at all we're walking across the slick parking lot. The clouds are blowing to the ocean now, the undersides glowing pink, umber, "muscular with gods and sungold," as Joni would say. The air's cooler, drier on the tops of our heads. Tomorrow I'll be back on the train to Baltimore, but why dwell on that now? "Thank you," I say. "Very much."

JESSE GREEN

The Daddy Track

Like mother, like son.

She had studied architecture; I studied architecture. She had studied Italian; I studied Italian. Neither of us ever built a building or lived in Italy—though we each, in our own time, supervised renovations of existing homes and read Dante. Our tastes were nearly identical, mine perhaps even more painfully refined than hers, unalloyed as they were by contact with my father's. I am surely not alone among gay men in having tried on my mother's metaphorical, or sometimes literal, shoes—and if the shoe fits, wear it. The shoe need not even be sensible; in fact, the less sensible the better.

Our shared distastes were as telling. It was my mother who concocted the list of forbidden professions, too dangerous, physically or spiritually, for a son of hers; it included anything to do with sports, wars, cars, or the clergy. By the time she imparted the list, it was unnecessary.

Also on that list, at least implicitly, was banking. My father was a banker. His father was a banker. Their business had financed the imaginations that deprecated it. But it wasn't money itself that was distasteful; it was the character of some of the people who dealt in it.

My paternal grandfather had a fine Talmudic intelligence but was vacant emotionally. The proof text, as my mother would call it, was this story my father, even now, does not know I know. One morning when he was a young boy, he woke up, late, to find himself alone in the house. The day went by, and the afternoon. That night, when his parents finally returned, he was huddled beneath his bed, no longer sobbing. They had been—where was it?—to a county fair, his older brother in tow, merely forgetting the not-as-healthy, musically inclined boy who perpetually came second, if at all. Wasn't he supposed to be at a friend's house? Wasn't the cleaning lady due? In any case, he was, apparently, forgettable. Forgivable as well, I would later learn.

The patriarch treated my mother poorly, early in her marriage, and to some extent my father acquiesced in that treatment, just as he had been subject to it earlier. And so, though she had married him, and loved him, my mother did not want me to be like him. It was a strange if not atypical dynamic, but I tried to comply; in some ways it was easy. Yes, I looked like him, had the very same feet, but it was nevertheless her heart in me.

This is the way we are often given to understand gay sons. We are supposed to be like our mothers, and in many ways we are. Not just in our sissified boyhoods, when the apron strings, which tie both ways, advertise the connection. But also in our adulthoods, sissified or not. We are mama's boys. As depicted in popular culture, and in ordinary conversation entre nous, the gay son is bound in myriad ways to his mother, some of those ways deemed immature at best. At worst, an unsavory 1950s odor—the byproduct of shared delusions, with a suggestion of incest—hangs over the bachelor apartment. Talcum, magnolia, chicken fat.

But because we are also men, we are cold and predatory. That these images are contradictory does not mitigate their power. We are, somehow, both harmless and hostile, fussbudgets and outlaws. Indeed, like women, we are suspect no matter what we do; we are, after all, the sons of Eve. But we are inevitably the sons of Adam as well. Where is Adam in all this? In the approved gay midcentury story, he is "distant": sequestered—or is he trapped?—in the small space formed by the arc of newspaper in front meeting the embrace of easy chair behind, with a ceiling of pipe smoke above.

My father wasn't like that. The pipe was outlawed early on. For a man of his generation—he was born in 1926—he was reasonably involved in his children's lives. He rarely missed dinner with us; it was, in fact, my mother who ended up missing meals, when she went back to school for her graduate degree, leaving us males to defrost and serve what she had prepared and frozen on weekends. In some strange codependent ritual, my father took me to my oboe lessons each Saturday and patiently pretended to enjoy my awful playing. He came to the musicals I was in or directed, and actually did enjoy them. He was kind and lovable, my friends all said, and even I knew he was more easygoing than my mother: slow to anger, slow to judge. If there was no way to convince him about the truth of one's emotions, well, I could look elsewhere for that—and it was, in part, his very obtuseness that made him so easygoing. Still, I was shocked by how little he seemed to know about the unregulated black-market economy of the heart. Once, in second grade, I described, over dinner, something embarrassing that had happened in school. I can't remember now what it was, but I know I wound up my tale of woe by saying, grandly, that I was then at "that age" when kids were "particularly sensitive" to how other people saw them.

My father laughed and said, "Why on earth?"—not curiously or angrily but merely with incomprehension, as if a waiter had lifted a silver dome with a flourish to reveal a steaming plate of gravel.

Admittedly, my comment now seems suspiciously canned, something I must have learned to say from an adult, possibly even my mother. Still, if it was not especially true then, it was no less true than if I had said it at any other point in my life—which is to say, it was true enough. My mother nodded supportively. But my father just shook his head. "Why on earth?" he repeated, this time resigned, and yet with some deference to an inexplicable, self-evident reality, as if at a foreign film.

Why on earth? Exactly. Where one's feet met the ground, if they did, was no place for self-consciousness. For my father, this wasn't a lesson but a given; for me it would take years—and, it seems, several lives—to recognize it as my patrimony.

IF HE WAS the banker by trade, it was my mother who was the banker by instinct: the banker of feelings. She borrowed them and kept them safe, or loaned them out judiciously. But she wasn't in it for profit. She paid more interest than she charged.

Whether for profit or not, the banker has the power, as my grandfather, a Much Beloved Pillar of the Community, could have told her. Even where the currency belongs to others, the banker—as usurer or philanthropist—controls it. Just so with the banker of feelings. It was through my mother that I approached my father, and through her that he approached me. If I was angry or needful or merely had a question, I applied to her first. She took it up with management and reported the result.

That's saying too little, as she often had to finagle to get me what I wanted—sometimes, indeed, it was money, but as often not—and make it appear to be their mutual decision. Perhaps it actually was a mutual decision, but one she preferred me to think was finagled. In any case, by the time I left home for college, and thence to a quasi-adult life in New York, she answered the phone whenever I called, or if she didn't, was quickly summoned: "Let me get your mother." My father's language and mine, different to begin with, grew apart until they were only marginally intercomprehensible. That, too, was part of my mother's modus operandi; by now she had finished her graduate training and become a marriage counselor: an expert in, and perhaps an aficionado of, triangulation.

I now think gayness per se had little to do with my likeness to her and separateness from my father, little to do with her being my primary point of attachment to my family. For in essence we were all, gay or straight, mama's boys, my father and brother no less than I. Many males raised in the 1960s and earlier came from a similar family constellation—in the suburbs there was almost no other constellation to come from—and most of them, like my brother, married according to plan. What it had to do with gayness was the way this constellation led me to navigate my own ideas of family. It is one thing to understand how mothers control their households; another to feel so painfully what they give up in order to do so. Or how doing so is sometimes the best that can be made of having had to give up so much.

An incipiently straight boy has little reason to identify with the plight of a woman in a man's world, or to explore how the woman's world she makes of her unpromising suburb may be insufficiently fulfilling. The difference between me and my brother, or between me and my father, for that matter, has to do with the presumption of fitting in: People who intuit that they are different are more likely to be "particularly sensitive" to how people see them. How people see them or don't, I should say. I boiled when my father, not meaning it as a slight, introduced my mother to business associates as his no-name attachment: "This is my wife." And I saw her boil when the business associates smiled condescendingly and changed the subject to house and children.

My mother eventually did learn to fend, and by the time we children were out of the house, she let no one address her in those terms or tones. But my lesson had been learned by then: Having a family consumes you, down to your very name. To do it right, you let yourself be eaten alive, and even this is not enough; you must not regret the choice, even if it wasn't a choice, and you must know you will not regret it. My mother didn't regret anything, except perhaps this: She was such a good mother, all but dissolving for a time in the process, that she taught her younger son why he should never have children himself.

BUT THEN I did. Not on purpose, though not exactly by accident either. When I was thirty-seven I met and fell in love with a man who had adopted a baby boy. Nine months after we met, Andy would adopt another. Eventually, I would adopt them, too, making legal what by then had long been the practical truth: that we four were a family. But as much as I treasured the fact, and in some way even welcomed it, I was not prepared for it. I was prepared for its opposite: childlessness.

For the beloved son of a powerful mother, gayness may be an advantage. I was well suited by my mother's training to life as a gay man, or perhaps I should say I was well unsuited to any other kind of life. I had been taught how to not suffer fools, how to disengage from impossible situations, how to design my life and every inch of my apartment according to my eye's own passion. This would be a stance impossible to maintain if children, or even a moderately assertive lover, were about, but a largely unrequited homosexuality upheld that stance quite nicely. My very few boyfriends, whether from the ends of the earth or from midtown Manhattan, barely imposed themselves on my literal and figurative decor. They demanded no change in me, and my every decision stood, even if on occasion I wished that one of those sturdy decisions would get knocked on its ass.

This outlook might have suited me for a certain kind of parenting: the kind where father knows best and everyone else hangs on his word. The kind practiced by my grandfather, in fact, whose wife, in her tiny embroidered silk jackets, was so squashed and obeisant she was virtually Japanese. That kind of fatherhood was distasteful to me, and yet surely I was not suited to my father's kind of fatherhood, either: sweet, yes, but second fiddle, subtly or unsubtly overruled. Perhaps he understood this deeply when, one night shortly after I came out—and after the inevitable lament about the offspring never to be—I proposed that it wasn't in fact inevitable: Why couldn't I have children by myself, by adoption, or in some kind of "arrangement"?

"God forbid!" my father said. And though he meant that a child should not be raised in anything but the traditional manner, his tone also suggested the horror of seeing one's son—and by now he had come to accept me as a properly free spirit—incarcerated. Perhaps he himself had felt fatherhood to be a jail.

In any case, my children changed both of us. Most predictably, the protoplasmic reality of their flesh utterly dispersed his airy notions of what could constitute a family. In a very few years my father moved from saying he could never consider as family any children that Andy, or even I, had adopted, to asking us to have the boys stop using his first name, and switch to calling him "Grandpop," just as my brother's children did. Wills were rewritten, Hanukkah gifts started arriving, letters stuffed with paper money. He even phoned them himself, on occasion. If it was a painless progression, perhaps that was because it led him to a level of involvement with children that suited him better than had parenting itself.

My progression into fatherhood was rockier. I discovered, to my dismay, that much as I loved the boys, I was inadequately prepared to face the crashing onslaught of their ordinary, chaotic lives. Many of my natural tendencies and learned inclinations had to be reversed: If I had been taught not to suffer fools, how could I master a skill virtually defined by that phrase? Sometimes I wanted to retreat behind a newspaper and metaphorically smoke a pipe. I pushed Andy to do the "front office" work (food service, transportation), while I managed the "back office" (toy repair, bill payment). I would exile myself to the laundry room, where the air was cool and the cries were distant, to remove what stains I could. And it was there between the Tide and Final Touch I began to wonder what kind of parent I was supposed to be, what kind I was capable of being.

Certainly I'd known that becoming a parent diverts you from the natural course of your gayness, at least as that course was charted on maps of the last thirty years. I'd often referred to the way "fatherhood trumps gay-

THE DADDY TRACK ■

ness": Andy and I were now regarded by gay people as existing on the axis of posterity rather than the axis of contemporaneity, and thus barely gay; by straight people who might otherwise have been afraid (or envious) of us, as neutered nurturers instead of sexual freebooters—and thus, also, not gay. Even to ourselves we found it difficult to remember, as all parents do, that we existed in relation to one another's bodies, not just in relation to our children's.

But fatherhood trumps gayness in a way I hadn't yet imagined when, after only a few years of parenting, that phrase occurred to me. As if reasserting a genetic prerogative, my essential maleness, as embodied in my father and grandfather, burst out of its closet just as my homo-sexuality, as such, vaporized in the full light of day. When, one afternoon, the guard at my children's school stopped me as a stranger, I realized that after a life spent becoming my mother, I was, in relation to my children at least, becoming my father. And not in the good way. I wasn't becom-ing easygoing and slow to judge. (How much I began to value those traits in him, and forgive the others!) I was becoming distant. In response to their emotional development and ever more complex needs, I was becoming rigid and withdrawn, more likely to mutter under my breath—though at least not say aloud—phrases like "Why on earth?" and "God forbid!"

To the extent I was able to reverse that transformation, it was largely thanks to my mother. She encouraged the habit of working around or ahead of problems, probably the key intelligence in child-rearing. She sug-gested different ways of distributing duties, so that our interests merged with our responsibilities instead of fighting them; now Andy and I share back-office and front-office responsibilities according to taste, not cate-gory. (He still cooks and I still do the laundry, but he handles the playdates and I honcho the homework.) Most importantly, my mother reminded me that my sons were merely warm little boys, not cold little men—boys who needed a patient parent, not an angry son. As a result, I did learn (at my best) to step back without disappearing, to come forward without over-whelming: in short, to try to be the kind of father my father might say he wishes he'd had, wishes he'd been.

But if I've managed to break the Y-linked chain of recessiveness in my family, I've not become my mother, either: a fact reflected not so much in how well I nurture the boys as in how well, or poorly, I nurture Andy. And so, in answer to the question we are so frequently asked—"Don't you think the boys need a mommy in the house?"—I'm likely to say that the answer is no. They don't need a mommy; Andy and I do.

LOGIC AND FEMINISM do not condone this parceling of traits as male and female, motherly and fatherly, but experience, unfairly or not, is a bully in the schoolyard of theories. My gaucheries as a parent defiantly report themselves as male, my skills as maternal. Undoubtedly these reports are entirely mediated by the particular mother and father who gave substance to these concepts in my life: by the way my mother succeeded in almost every engagement with me, by the way my father often failed to engage at all.

Or did he? Recently, I have begun to see how much we are formed, as parents and as people, not only by our own failings but also by the overweening successes of those around us. Perhaps my mother, a genius at feeling, prohibited the development of the "feeling" trait, admittedly not a dominant one, in my father, just as my genius at folding the boys' tiny underwear prevents Andy from mastering this important skill—indeed, subverts any nascent abilities he may have in that direction. For the thing about a triangle, even the most obtuse one, is that it has not only three points but three sides. There are three sides to every child's story, and one of those sides is the one he can barely see. It's the one that explains the mysterious connection between his parents, what they were like before they were together, and what makes it impossible to guess what one of them may yet be like, unexpectedly, when the other one is gone.

I suppose I will find out in the coming years. The day after last Thanksgiving, when my boys were just shy of eight and six, my mother unexpectedly died, and our lives were spun out of their usual orbits. Strange new gravities, and terrible antigravities, pulled us all in new directions. My father has had to learn to cook for himself (when the line of casserole-bearing widows outside his door disbands from time to time), to manage his own social life, and, most difficult of all, to try to mother his mourning sons. He doesn't have the right words (nor I the right ears) for the job, but perhaps he has realized the lesson, and undone the damage, of his own abandonment, so many years ago. A father who forgets his son forgets himself.

In any case, he knew what to do when, after months of not working, I suddenly realized that no one was paying me to stare at my computer and cry. In the past I would have gone to my mother for help in applying to the banker for a loan. Now, the banker came to me. The resulting check was a new, unfamiliar one, imprinted with his name and, beneath it, a phrase I did not want to see. "The estate of Sally Green," it said. Fitting, for the check represented part of her bequest to me: not the money, but the father I never thought I needed.

BERNARD COOPER

Winner
Take Nothing.

When I received word informing me I'd won the PEN/Ernest Hemingway Award for my first book, I held the letter in trembling hands while the following thoughts, in precisely this order, shot through my head:

(1) I won the Ernest Hemingway Award!

(2) I don't deserve it.

(3) My father's heard of Ernest Hemingway!

There I stood, elated by a last-ditch chance to impress my dad.

Not that my father disapproved of my being a writer; he understood it to the extent that he could understand my gambling with my life in order to pursue a profession he found frivolous and fiscally unsound. Whenever I mentioned to him that I'd had something published in a magazine or a literary journal, the first question he'd ask was, "How much they pay you?" A retired lawyer, he probably thought of "they" as a faceless jury, twelve arbiters of taste. He'd pose this question with considerable enthusiasm, arching his white eyebrows, his face a picture of impending pride. Imagine telling a man who keeps a wad of twenties in a gold money clip shaped like a dollar sign that, after working on a piece of writing for months, you've been compensated with a complimentary copy of the publication. "You're kidding," he'd say, shaking his head as if I'd told him I'd been duped in a shell game.

Over the years, I'd cultivated a certain temperance when sharing literary news with my father: I'd come to consider it unfortunate, but not devastating, that he was unable to recognize the arc—or was it the bump?—of my career. Still, I ached to have him slap me on the back, wanted to hear his unstinting praise, and in it the honeyed pronouncement: Son.

Toward this end, I once gave him an essay of mine to read. It was a brief reminiscence about my mother who, up until her death, dreamed of writing a book into which she'd cram every anecdote she could think of, starting with her emigration from Russia to the United States at the age of two. She never so much as wrote a word, but the persistence of her wish struck me as oddly noble, and the tone of the piece was, I believed, unmistakably fond. And so, one night at The Brass Pan, the restaurant where my father and I occasionally met for dinner, I handed him the pages, neatly stapled. Before I let go of the manuscript (feeling him tug it from across the table was the closest I'd come to his tangible enthusiasm), I told him I hoped he'd enjoy reading it and assured him he was under no obligation to offer comments.

Days went by. Weeks. Months. For nearly half a year, in all the times we saw one another or spoke on the phone, he never mentioned the essay, and pride prevented me from coming right out and asking whether he'd read it. If it hadn't been for a chokingly potent vodka tonic I drank during one of our dinners, I may not have asked him to this day.

"Hey, Dad. You've never mentioned the essay I wrote about Mom."

"Well," sighed my father, shrugging his shoulders. "What can I tell you? You wrote down your opinion."

In the dim light of the restaurant he looked anything but adversarial, his brown eyes peering at me over the rim of his bifocals. I took another swig of vodka. My father, I had to admit, had managed perfectly well without literature, and I had no illusions that writing, especially mine, could enrich his life. At the age of eighty-six, his reading material consisted chiefly of *TV Guide,* a map by which he navigated nights in front of the Sony console, its huge screen the only source of light. He also subscribed to *Consumer Reports,* but largely, I think, to sustain through retirement the image he had of himself as a citizen with buying power. The issues were stacked on a shelf next to his law books—and a yellowing paperback copy of *The Snows of Kilimanjaro.*

My father wasn't the first person I called with news of the award, but when I dialed his number and invoked the name of Hemingway, his "Oh" was as round and buoyant as a bubble. For a moment, I thought the elusive approval I'd wanted might be close at hand, compensation for years of his lack of interest in my work. In much of that work, I'd tried to capture the moodiness with which he presided over my childhood: A C on my report card, say, could meet with his indifference or detonating rage. One never knew what familial infraction or offhand remark might cause him to suddenly leave the room and brood for hours. He was also capable of lavish generosity, bursts of goofy humor, and, whenever these traits prevailed, I finally felt at peace with a man whose livelihood was, as he liked to put it, suing the pants off people.

"Listen," he said, "we'll fly to New York for the award ceremony, share a room, and take in some Broadway shows." I was stunned by his offer, and more than a little touched. Since he had no compunction about expressing bemusement at my small successes, it never occurred to me that he might need to take an active part in my large ones.

I told my father that nothing could make me happier than knowing he was proud of me, and as terrific as a trip with him sounded, I wouldn't have time to go to Broadway shows or give him the attention he deserved. Besides, I'd already made plans to go with Brian, the man I'd lived with for many years, our hotel and flight already booked. I offered to take my father to The Brass Pan so we could celebrate properly, and suggested the three of us take a vacation together another time, when I could relax and we could really enjoy ourselves. "I hope you understand," I said finally.

After I stopped talking, I gave my little speech high marks; it had been, I thought, a good mixture of respect and autonomy. But the longer he remained silent, the more aware I became of the telephone's static, a sound growing vast, oceanic. "Dad?"

"Fine," he said. "If that's what you want."

▪   ▪   ▪

THE PLANE FLIGHT, as always, made me claustrophobic. But when panic finally gave way to the Valium I'd taken twenty minutes before takeoff, my hands and feet grew rubbery, the view of earth, abstract.

Once inside the terminal at JFK, the firm ground acted as a conduit, diffusing fear. At the baggage claim, watching as luggage spilled onto the carousel, it finally dawned on me that I had survived the flight to receive an award. Sunlight burned through a bank of windows. People swarmed toward a fleet of cabs and were whisked away to meetings and reunions. Possibility charged the air, dense, electric. In my happiness I turned to Brian and faced my father.

At first I thought I might be drugged or dreaming, though by then, only the mildest trace of Valium remained in my system. I looked at him and couldn't speak, the entire busy terminal contracting to a point the size of his face. Was he omnipresent like Santa Claus or God? Dad looked back and blithely smiled.

"Surprise," he said.

"How? . . ." I sputtered.

"Your plane. I went first class."

Suddenly I understood that all the questions he'd asked about the details of my trip—time of departure, name of the airline—questions I'd interpreted as paternal concern were part of a perfectly executed plan.

Brian, who at first had been as incredulous as I, rushed in to fill the conspicuous silence. He shook my father's hand. "Are you staying at our hotel?" he asked.

I recalled with a start that we'd booked rooms at a gay hotel. "I'm at the Warwick," said my father. "Quite a fancy place, according to the Automobile Club." Two familiar carry-alls were making aimless circles in the periphery of my vision, and before I knew what I was doing, I yanked them off the carousel. Vacillating between guilt and fury, I felt like a small, unstable electron. "We're leaving," I announced. I fled toward the taxi stand, leaving Brian no choice but to dash after me.

"Share a ride?" my father shouted.

I didn't look back.

ONCE WE SETTLED into our hotel room, I began to worry that I'd acted rashly. Had I been a different person, I might have poked my father in the ribs and teased him for being a stubborn coot. But in order to be a different person I'd have to have been raised by a different dad. The one

I had was an old Jewish genie who materialized wherever he willed and granted any wish—as long as it was his.

When I called the Warwick, my father answered on the second ring. "We'd better have a talk," I said.

"It's your dime."

"I thought you understood that I wanted to do this on my own."

"Fine. I'll pack my goddamn bags and go home."

"No. I want you to stay now that you're here. I'm just trying to explain why I reacted the way I did at the airport."

"So now you explained it. Is that what you wanted to talk about?"

There had to be more. During the cab ride, I'd rehearsed ways to tell him that his surprise was an intrusion disguised as kindness, a success usurped. But now, I couldn't recall what I'd wanted to say, or why we found it so important to win the other's capitulation.

"We'll have lunch tomorrow," he said.

THE DINING ROOM at the Warwick, with its ambient chimes of silverware and ice, offered a quiet retreat from the city. My father looked small and harmless as he sat waiting for us at a table. He peered around the spacious room, bifocals flashing, hands folded before him in a boyish pose, almost contrite. As Brian and I walked toward the table, it struck me that he was not at all the giant of the nursery I was prone to imagine; when I didn't have the actual man before me, he ballooned into myth.

There arose a somewhat leery conviviality as we seated ourselves at the table.

"So, Mister Cooper," asked Brian, "what have you been doing?"

My father toyed with the silverware. "Nothing much. I watched a little TV."

"What did you watch, Dad?"

My father cocked his head. "How about that. I can't remember."

Brian and I looked at each other.

"Is there anybody you know in New York who you could go to dinner with tonight?" Please, I prayed.

"I got relatives in Jersey. Or used to twenty years ago. I should look them up next time I'm here." His hearing aid squealed with feedback and he fiddled with its tiny dial.

"The thing is, Dad, we can't go to dinner with you tonight."

"I know," he said curtly. "You're *very* busy."

The mâitre d' brought us huge, glossy menus, the covers printed to look like marble. I opened mine, expecting an engraving of the Ten Commandments: *Thou shalt honor thy father, who gazeth at the entrees.* Without lifting his eyes from the menu, he waved his hand in a gesture of largesse. "Get whatever you want. Sky's the limit."

The next day, I decided to add a paragraph to my acceptance speech. In it, I thanked my father for reading me stories as a child. His rapt voice had transported me, I wrote, and his enthusiasm for telling tales had introduced me to the power of language. I wasn't certain whether my father had, in fact, read me stories as a child, but neither he nor I would object to the sentimental prospect. Collusion, after all, would be a kind of bond.

At the ceremony that evening, half-a-dozen awards were handed out. Almost every author who received one had written a speech identical to mine, a sort of apologia in which they expressed surprise at having won and either implied, or insisted, they were undeserving. The motif of modesty had been exhausted by the time I walked up to the podium, but I'd already revised my speech that morning and was too nervous to change it again. When I came to the part about my father, I looked up from the wrinkled sheet of paper, eager to find him and make eye contact, but I had to look back quickly for fear of losing my place. The paragraph I'd added struck me as a little schmaltzy, and I worried that my apparent sentimentality would discourage people in the audience from buying my book. In the end it didn't really matter; my homage was meant for Dad's ears alone, and reading it aloud righted the night.

Or so I thought. Immediately after the ceremony I found my father milling in the crowd and raced up to ask him how he'd liked my speech. "Couldn't hear a damn thing," he said, chuckling at his rotten luck. His hearing aid, unable to distinguish between foreground and background noises, had amplified both. From the rear of the auditorium, my dad could see me reading in the distance, but he heard ubiquitous coughs and whispers, a battle of crackling leather coats, the rubbery acoustics of someone chewing gum.

IN THE YEAR that followed, I began to publish essays and memoirs in a few well-paying magazines. My income was still meager by any standard except my own, but at last I could speak my father's language, a lexicon of hard cold cash.

By that time, however, it had become difficult for him to react to news of my solvency with anything but the foggiest acknowledgment. At the mention of money he'd look at me wistfully, nod his head, then look away. My father was going broke from the lawsuits he'd recently filed against neighbors and in-laws and strangers. Vines and retaining walls trespassed his property. A relative missed a payment on a loan. An uninsured idiot dented his fender. Someone blundered, someone would pay, someone would rue the day he was born. He represented himself in court (such a sadly incriminating phrase) and lost each case. The judges were corrupt, he'd claim, his witnesses inarticulate. Defeat never seemed to give him pause or lessen his zeal for prosecution.

Dad remained fairly amiable during our dinners, and I found it flattering to be one of the few people in his life exempt from litigation. We both preferred not to talk about his lawsuits when we were together; to do so only soured his mood and caused us both considerable confusion: The facts were vague, the court dates ever-changing, the numerous parties hard to keep straight. He was in the throes of a lawyerly tantrum; if the world refused to yield to his will, he'd force it to yield to the letter of the law.

Some nights, when the waitress at The Brass Pan asked for his order, my father stiffened and eyed her with suspicion, tense as a man being cross-examined. She'd hover above him, pencil poised, while he blinked and slowly returned to his senses, finally lifting his tremulous hand and pointing to an entree on the menu. The decline was apparent in visit after visit. Time took a belated toll, as though weariness had waited till now to irrevocably claim his face; his eyes were puzzled, hair unkempt, chin bristling with patches of stubble the razor had missed.

Eventually, he grew too distracted by his legal battles to return my phone calls. On the rare occasions when we spoke, he said he was too busy to meet me for dinner. More often than not, the answering machine picked up after several rings and played its halting, unassailable refrain: *I am not at home at this present time.*

AFTER MONTHS OF an elusiveness he couldn't be coaxed out of, I drove over to my father's house one afternoon to ask why he'd been unwilling to see me, why he hadn't returned my calls. Dad answered the door of his Spanish house, blinking, beleaguered, but glad to see me. At my insistence, we sat in the dining room in order to talk. Briefs and appeals and depositions were scattered across the mahogany table, his makeshift desk.

Pencils and paper napkins saved his place in the law books he hadn't opened for years, piled now in precarious stacks. The windows were shut though the afternoon was sunny, dust motes whirling in shafts of light. The odor of mothballs wafted from his clothes, their cut and color long out of style.

"Are you sure you're not angry at me about something?" I asked. "Because, if you are? . . ."

My father laughed, fiddled with his hearing aid. "What makes you think I'm angry?"

"You're so . . . unavailable these days."

"How many times do I have to tell you? I'm busy. Swamped. Do you need me to spell it out for you?" He rose to his feet, and I thought he might start to sound out the letters. "You have no idea. No goddamn concept."

I stood, too, trying to rise above the childlike vantage point that came with being seated. "All I'm saying is that you have to eat dinner anyway, and we might as well . . ."

"Who says?"

"What?"

"Who says I have to eat dinner? Where is it written? Is it written here?" He hefted a law book and let it slam back onto the table. Stray papers jumped and fluttered. I made a move to calm him down, but he began to prowl around the table, stirring up the sunlit dust. "Don't you ever tell me what to do!"

"Having dinner is not something to do! I mean, it *is* something to do, but I'm not *telling* you to do it." At a loss for logic, I was barking back.

"Don't you raise your voice at me!" He rushed up and grabbed the back of my shirt, a hank of fabric twisted in his grip. "I'm eighty-six years old," he shouted. "I'm an old man and I can do whatever the hell I want whenever the hell I want to do it." He pushed me toward the door, breathing hard, his face red and alien with effort.

"Dad?"

"That's right," he said. When he opened the door, daylight was blinding. "Don't ever forget that I'm your father. Now get the hell out and don't come back."

Since high school, I've been both taller and stronger than my father, but just as we reached the threshold of the door it occurred to me that I might flatter him into relenting if I let my body be heaved outside as though from an admirable, manly force. Instead of resisting or fighting back, I yielded to his elderly arms.

Acquiescence didn't help. Before the door slammed shut behind me, I turned and glimpsed his indignant figure sinking inside my childhood house. The door hit the jamb with a deafening bang, the birds falling silent for half a second before they went back to their usual racket.

ON A DAILY basis I relived the particulars: the shirt taut across my chest, the heat of his breath on the back of my neck, the flood of light as the door swung wide. The sheer abruptness and implausibility of what had happened made me worry that perhaps I'd said something inadvertently thoughtless or cruel—a spark to his incendiary temper.

In lieu of an explanation, I started making hypothetical changes in the story. Suppose I hadn't mentioned dinner? Suppose I hadn't raised my voice? Suppose we'd stood instead of sitting? Say the day had been cooler, the hour later, the dust motes churning in another direction? Would the outcome of my visit have been any different?

Several nights a week, I had to drive past my boyhood house on the way home from teaching, and the closer I came, the greater its magnetic pull. More than once, I turned the steering wheel at the last minute, aiming my car through a tunnel of trees and parking across the street from his house. The urge to spy on my father was nameless, as deep and murky as the darkness it required.

There was little to learn from my nights of surveillance. Light would suddenly burn in a window, but I couldn't see anyone move through the rooms. Even if I had, what would a glimpse of his silhouette tell me? A walkway led toward the large front door, the stepping stones flat and blank in the moonlight. His Cadillac took up half the driveway, gleaming, impassive, white as an iceberg. Despite my watchfulness, nothing happened, except that every now and then I'd glance at my phosphorescent watch, its ghostly hands advancing.

Throughout the first year of our estrangement, my entreaties and apologies and furious demands for contact were recited into his answering machine. On a few occasions he picked up the phone, then slammed it down at the sound of my voice.

By the second year, resignation took hold. I'd lost the desire to drive by his house or reach him by phone. I recalled that afternoon less often, and when I did, I refused to probe the memory for meaning.

By the third year, his absence settled inside me like a stone, impervious to hope or hurt.

"I REALIZE THIS phone call must come as an unpleasant surprise," the social worker told me. "But I believe your father's deterioration is significant enough to make legal guardianship a necessary step."

Mr. Gomez assured me that I didn't have to make up my mind right away; it would be several months before the case came before a judge. An anonymous caller had phoned Adult Protective Services to say my father needed help. If I assumed responsibility, my father's Social Security checks would be placed in a trust, and he'd need my permission for every expenditure: medicine, groceries, clothes.

"Careful monetary management is especially crucial in your father's case," said Mr. Gomez. "As you may know, the bank has begun foreclosure on his house."

"I had no idea."

Mr. Gomez cleared his throat. "On a positive note, I should also tell you that your father spoke with great pride about your many accomplishments. What's the name of the book you wrote? He couldn't remember."

I mumbled the title to Mr. Gomez, promised to give our discussion some thought, and said goodbye. I'd become so guarded against any emotion having to do with my father that the prospect of seeing him again roused only a dull ambivalence. After three years, I'd finally decided it was *I* who didn't want contact with him, a decision that redefined circumstance and made my exile bearable. And now, out of the blue, the county urged a reunion, reminding me (as if I needed to be reminded) that the man was my inescapable relation.

I'D BEEN WRITING when the phone rang.

"Bernard?"

"Dad?" Saying the word made my mouth go dry.

"I sold the house and the people who bought it want to move in pretty soon, so I've been cleaning out closets, and I came across all sorts of drawings and photos of yours. You wanna come get them? Is 4:30 good?"

"Four-thirty's good." My assent was automatic, though I wasn't sure I was ready to see him.

"Okay. See you later."

"Wait," I blurted. "How have you been?"

"Fine. And you?"

Three years. "I'm fine, too."

"Good," he said, "as long as you're fine." His harried voice softened. "Well," he said, "I'm really swamped."

Only after I hung up the phone did I realize he hadn't said hello.

I APPROACHED THE house with apprehension; who knew in what condition I'd find him? His Cadillac sat in the driveway, dented and missing strips of chrome. Since I'd last spied on the house two years ago, the first-floor windows had been covered with bars. The front door stood behind a wrought-iron grate, and no matter how decorative its design, it made the house look forbidding, aloof.

No sooner had I rung the doorbell than my father appeared behind the bars, jangling keys like a castle keep. All the while he burbled greetings in the high-pitched voice of his jovial persona. Arms folded across my chest, I couldn't act as if things had been normal, not without damaging a sense of reality that, especially in my father's presence, could flounder and bend like a little boy's. "Come on in," he said, unlocking the grate. I found his hospitality suspicious, and as much as I wanted to make amends, I also wanted to run the other way. I'd come to think of my boyhood house as a place I'd never visit again, and now that I stood on the verge of return, I practically had to astral project and give myself a push from behind.

The house was even more crammed with memorabilia than I remembered. He must have strewn souvenirs about the rooms as he cleaned out the closets, a last-minute effort to make his mark on the home he had to forfeit. A velvet painting of JFK hung above the fireplace. A birdcage he'd won on a cruise contained a wind-up canary whose jerky movements and monotonous song he insisted on demonstrating as soon as I walked in the door. Showing either a sign of delight or dementia, he watched it warble with childlike glee.

Piled on the coffee table, old boxes contained the egg-tempera paintings I'd done in elementary school, the colors still vibrant though the paint had turned as powdery as talcum. Crude landscapes and blotchy figures called back the distant triumph of my being able to shape the world and contain it on a piece of paper. Pictures from photo booths showed a mugging ten-year-old who bore as much resemblance to me now as I to my father; I wanted to warn that oblivious boy of what was to come. I couldn't look at the stuff for long, and I gathered up the boxes, ready to go.

"Sit," said my father.

I did as he asked.

"What's new?"

"Lots."

"Written any more books of yours?"

"Yes."

"Have they won those Hemingway awards?"

"That's only for a first book."

"I see," he said. "Tell me what else has been going on." He leaned forward in the chair, cocked his good ear in my direction.

"Look, I appreciate your willingness to have a reunion, but I think I deserve to know why you haven't spoken to me in three years."

His brows furrowed in puzzlement. "You live, things happen, you go on. That's the way it works."

"That's not the way it works for me."

"Well, the truth of the matter is that you were getting irritated with me about my hearing aid. You were always screaming, 'What? What? I can't hear you! Turn up your damn ear!'"

"First of all, Dad, you're the one who shouts 'What? I can't hear you.' Second, I'd never scold you because you're hard of hearing."

"I'm telling you, that's what happened."

"It didn't."

"Did."

"Okay. Suppose it had. Is that any reason not to speak to me for three years?"

My father sat back, stared into space, gave the question due consideration. "Yes," he said, lurching forward. "Yes, it is." He looked at his feet, then back at me. "I've lived in this house for fifty years. Do you remember when we moved in?"

"I wasn't born yet."

"Do you remember what day it was?"

It seemed pointless to repeat myself. "Tuesday?" I guessed.

"No," he said. "It was your mother's birthday. Boy, that was a long time ago. I sold the place to two very nice guys. By the way, how's that friend of yours, what's his name?"

"Brian's fine, he . . .

"What do I need all these rooms for, anyway? It was either sell the house or get kicked out on the street."

I shook my head in commiseration, pretending to know nothing about the foreclosure.

"Some crazy social worker said I shouldn't handle the sale myself. But I showed him. Closed escrow on my own, then told Hernandez to take a hike."

I stopped myself from blurting *Gomez*.

"The kicker," he continued, "is that I paid someone to report me to the guy in the first place."

"What!"

"See," said my father. "You *do* shout 'What.'" He bristled a moment, shifted in his seat. "It was the only way to save myself. If they said I was, you know, soft in the head, the bank couldn't foreclose."

"Did you know that Gomez called me?"

"I figured he might." My father sighed. "I got a pretty penny for the place, but I owe a lot too. There are liens and things. A second mortgage. I'm looking at a mobile home in Oxnard. Not the best, but it's what I can afford. And it almost looks like a regular house. You'll come up and visit." He stared at me a moment. "You sure have grown since the last time I saw you."

"Dad, I've been this tall since high school."

"Taller than me?"

"For years," I said.

He shrugged his shoulders. "Then I guess I'm shrinking."

AFTER LOADING THE boxes in my car, I came back inside the house to say goodbye. When my father saw me walk through the door, he slapped his palm against his forehead. "Almost forgot your present," he said. I followed him into the kitchen, where he stationed himself in front of the counter, then beamed at me and stepped aside.

A pink bakery box yawned open to reveal a cake, its circumference studded with glazed strawberries. Beneath the kitchen's fluorescent lights, they looked succulent, aggressively tempting. Slivered almonds, toasted gold, had been evenly pressed into a mortar of thick white frosting, every spare surface dotted with florets. In the center was written, in goopy blue script, *Papa Loves Bernard*. For a second I thought there'd been some mistake. I'd never called my father Papa. Dad, yes. Pop, perhaps. The nickname belonged to another parent, didn't mesh with the life I knew.

My father had begun yanking open drawers and kitchen cabinets, offering me anything that might not fit into his new trailer, which was just about most of what he owned: a punch-bowl set, napkin rings—artifacts from his life with my mother, a life of friends and fancy repasts. His barrage of offers was frenzied, desperate. All the while I politely declined; "This is more than enough," I said, gazing at the cake. I knew a slice would be sickening, dense with sugar, a spongy glut. Yet it looked so delectable sitting in his kitchen, Betty Crocker's Sunday bonnet. If the years of silence between us had an inverse, that clamorous cake was it. While my father jettisoned old possessions, I swiped my finger across the frosting, and debated whether to taste it.

Permissions

About the Contributors

Kevin Bentley is the author of *Wild Animals I Have Known: Polk Street Diaries and After,* and *Sailor: Vintage Photos of a Masculine Icon;* and the editor of *Afterwords: Real Sex from Gay Men's Diaries* and *Boyfriends from Hell: True Tales of Tainted Lovers, Disastrous Dates, and Love Gone Wrong.* His writing has also appeared in the anthologies *Flesh & the Word 4* and *5, His 2,* and *Bar Stories.*

Alexander Chee is the author of the novel *Edinburgh* (Picador, 2002). He lives in Brooklyn, New York.

Bernard Cooper is the author of four books, most recently *Guess Again,* a collection of short stories from Simon & Schuster. He is the recipient of a Guggenheim Fellowship, an O. Henry Prize, and a PEN/USA Ernest Hemingway Award. His essays and memoirs have appeared in four volumes of *The Best American Essays.* Mr. Cooper is currently the art critic for *Los Angeles Magazine.*

Alfred Corn is the author of eight books of poems, including *Stake: Selected Poems, 1972–1992,* published by Counterpoint in 1999. Copper Canyon Press will bring out a new collection, *Contradictions,* in 2002. He has published a collection of critical essays, titled *The Metamorphoses of Metaphor,* and a novel, *Part of His Story.* Fellowships and prizes awarded for his poetry include the Guggenheim, the NEA, an Award in Literature from the Academy and Institute of Arts and Letters, and one from the Academy of American Poets. He has taught for many years in the Graduate Writing Program at Columbia.

Jorge Ignacio Cortiñas's awards include first prize in the 1998 *Bay Guardian* Fiction Contest; "playwright of the year" in *El Nuevo Herald*'s 1999 year-end list; the 1999 James Assatly Memorial Prize; the 2000 Beth Lisa Feldman Prize; first prize in the 2001 Southwest Festival of New Latino Plays; and an NEA/ TCG supported residency with New World Theatre in Amherst. His plays have been workshopped at INTAR, South Coast Repertory, the Magic, and the Arena, and produced in Miami, San Francisco, and Atlanta. His first play, *Maleta Mulata*, led the *San Francisco Chronicle* to herald "the debut of an impressive new voice." *Sleepwalkers* has been awarded a Carbonell Award for Best New Work by the South Florida Critics Circle.

Tom Donaghy, a Guggenheim fellow, is the author of the plays *The Beginning of August*, *Minutes from the Blue Route*, and *Northeast Local*, among others. The plays have been published in a collection by Grove Press, and are archived on video at Lincoln Center Library for the Performing Arts. His new play, *Boys and Girls,* had its off-Broadway première at Playwrights Horizons in May, 2002. Donaghy's work can also be seen in the short film *The Dadshuttle*, which appears regularly on The Sundance Channel.

Mark Doty is the author of six books of poetry, most recently *Source* (HarperCollins, 2001); and three books of nonfiction prose, including *Firebird* (HarperCollins, 1998). His work has been honored by the National Book Critics Circle Award, two Lambda Literary Awards, the *Los Angeles Times* Book Prize, and Britain's T. S. Eliot Prize. He lives in Provincetown, Massachusetts, and New York City.

Jeffrey Escoffier writes on sexuality, gay history and politics, and dance. His most recent book, *Mark Morris' L'Allegro, il Penseroso ed il Moderato: A Celebration* (Marlowe & Co., 2001), was coedited with Matthew Lore. He is the author of *American Homo: Community and Perversity* (University of California Press, 1998) and of a biography of John Maynard Keynes in the Chelsea House series on the Lives of Notable Gay Men and Lesbians.

Philip Gambone's collection of short stories, *The Language We Use Up Here* (Dutton, 1991), was nominated for a Lambda Literary Award. In addition, his essays have appeared in a number of anthologies, including *Hometowns* (Dutton, 1992), *Sister & Brother* (HarperSanFrancisco, 1995), *Wrestling with the Angel* (Riverhead Books, 1995), and *Boys Like Us* (Avon, 1997). Phil's collection of interviews, *Something Inside: Conversations with Gay Fiction Writers* (University of Wisconsin Press, 1999), was named one of the best books of 1999 by *Pride* magazine. He has taught writing at the University of Massachusetts, Boston College, and in the freshman expository writing program at Harvard. Currently, he teaches at The Park School in Brookline, Massachusetts, and in the creative and expository writing program at Harvard Extension School. Phil's novel, *Beijing*, will be published next year by University of Wisconsin Press.

Jesse Green, a much-anthologized, award-winning journalist, is a regular contributor to the *New York Times Magazine*; his articles over the years have appeared in such other publications as *The New Yorker, The Washington Post, Talk, New York, Premiere, The Yale Review, GQ, Philadelphia, Out, Mirabella, Elle, O, Rosie*, and the late, lamented *7 Days*. He is the author, most recently, of *The Velveteen Father: An Unexpected Journey to Parenthood* (Villard/Random House, 1999), which was named one of the best nonfiction books of the year by *The Los Angeles Times Book Review*, one of the ten best memoirs or biographies of the year by amazon.com, and one of the best parenting books of the year by *Child* magazine. It was also the recipient of the 1999 Lambda Literary Foundation prize in the biography/autobiography category. His first novel, *O Beautiful*, which *Entertainment Weekly* called "one of the best first novels of the year," was published by the Available Press imprint of Ballantine Books in 1992 and was reissued by Ballantine in June 2000, along with the paperback of *The Velveteen Father*. He has lived in New York City since 1980, and is currently working on a second novel.

Eric Gutierrez spent the better part of a decade scuba diving, skydiving, white-water rafting and collecting stamps in his passport as an adventure travel writer. He is the coeditor of *Suave: the Latin Male,* and writer of the Imagen Award-nominated theater work *By the Hand of the Father* that is scheduled to air on PBS in September 2002. He wrote the gay episodes of the award-winning Telemundo sitcom *Los Beltran,* resulting in the first, and to-date only, GLAAD Award nomination for a Spanish language program as Best Television Series. His entertainment journalism, cultural commentary and celebrity profiles have appeared in the *Los Angeles Times, Newsday, Ocean Drive, US* and elsewhere. He is currently making amends by studying at Harvard Divinity School.

Joseph Hansen has published some thirty novels and six collections of short stories, and has received an NEA grant, two Lambda awards, and the Lifetime Achievement Award of the Private Eye Writers of America. His latest books are the novel *The Cutbank Path* (Xlibris, 2002), and a story collection, *Bohannon's Women* (Five Star, 2002). He lives in Laguna Beach, California.

Bill Hayes is the author of *Sleep Demons: An Insomniac's Memoir* (Washington Square Press, 2001) and is currently working on a book about the history of blood, which will be published by Ballantine. His essays have appeared in the *New York Times Magazine, Salon, Details,* and *Out,* among other publications. He lives in San Francisco with his partner, Steve.

Andrew Holleran is a novelist and essayist who lives in Florida. His latest book is a collection of stories, *In September, the Light Changes* (Plume, 2000).

Peter M. Krask is the librettist of the prize-winning opera *With Blood, With Ink* (with music by Daniel Crozier) and the opera *Henry and Clara* (with music by Jorge Martín), both of which were featured on the New York City Opera Showcase of New American Opera. In addition, he has written the text of *Rendezvous of Light*, which was premièred in Baltimore in a production he also directed and designed. He has written features and criticism for *The Baltimore Sun, The City Paper, The Boston Phoenix,* and *The New York Blade*. His essay-memoir, "The Way the Stars Come Home," was published in the anthology *Wrestling with the Angel* (Riverhead Books, 1995). He holds a master's degree in music criticism from the Peabody Institute of the Johns Hopkins University. Also a noted flower designer, his work is seen daily nationwide on NBC's *Today Show*. He lives in New York City.

Paul Lisicky is the author of the novel *Lawnboy* (Turtle Point Press, 2002), and the memoir *Famous Builder* (Graywolf Press, 2002). His work has appeared in *Ploughshares, Boulevard, Best American Gay Fiction 2,* and in other magazines and anthologies. A recipient of awards from the National Endowment for the Arts, the Michener/Copernicus Society, and the Fine Arts Work Center in Provincetown, Massachusetts, he teaches fiction and creative nonfiction at Sarah Lawrence College. He lives in New York and Provincetown.

Brian Malloy's debut novel is *The Year of Ice* (St. Martin's Press, 2002). His writing has appeared in *A View from the Loft* and *Minnesota Monthly* magazines. He lives in Minneapolis, where he is at work on a second novel.

David Masello is New York editor of *Art & Antiques* magazine and publishes essays, feature articles, poetry, and book reviews in many periodicals, including the *New York Times, San Francisco Chronicle, Art News,* and *Massachusetts Review*. He is a former editor at *Travel & Leisure* and worked for several years as an editor of hardcover nonfiction at Simon & Schuster. He is the author of *Architecture Without Rules: The Houses of Marcel Breuer* (Norton, 1996) and *New York's 50 Best Works of Art in Public Places* (City & Co., 1999).

Daniel Mendelsohn is a contributing writer for the *New York Review of Books* and a Lecturer in Classics at Princeton University. Mr. Mendelsohn's 1999 memoir of sexual identity and family history, *The Elusive Embrace: Desire and the Riddle of Identity* (Knopf, 1999; Vintage, 2000) was named a *New York Times* Notable Book of the Year and a *Los Angeles Times* Best Book of the Year. He is currently at work on a book about Archimedes for the "Science Lives" series (Norton/Lipper), and on a new translation of the complete works of C. P. Cavafy, to be published by Knopf in 2003. He lives in New York City and outside Princeton, New Jersey.

Bob Moser was born and reared in Winston-Salem, North Carolina. After earning degrees from Elon University and the University of North Carolina-Chapel Hill, he fled academia for journalism and served as arts editor and editor-in-chief of *The Independent Weekly*, an investigative newsmagazine in Raleigh/Durham, North Carolina, from 1990 to 2000. He was a John S. Knight Fellow at Stanford University for the 2000–2001 academic year. He now lives and writes in Montgomery, Alabama, where he is the senior writer for *Intelligence Report,* a magazine that investigates and exposes the activities of hate groups across the United States.

Felice Picano's first book was a finalist for the PEN/Hemingway Award. Since then he has published twenty volumes of fiction, poetry, nonfiction, and memoirs. Considered a founder of modern gay literature along with the other members of the Violet Quill Club, Picano also founded two publishing companies: the SeaHorse Press and Gay Presses of New York. Among his many award-winning books are the novels *Like People in History* (Penguin, 1996) and *The Book of Lies* (Alyson Publications, 2000). His most recent novel, *Onyx* (Alyson Publications), was published to acclaim in 2001. Picano's exhibit, "Early Gay Presses of New York," debuted at the ONE Institute in L.A. and will tour the country. San Francisco's New Conservatory Theatre will première Picano's new comedy-thriller, *The Bombay Trunk*, during the fall 2002 season.

Gary Reed is the author of the novel *Pryor Rendering* (Plume, 1997). Originally from Oklahoma, he has lived in New York City since 1980.

Patrick Rose has a story in the forthcoming *Penguin Book of Gay Short Stories*. His fiction has appeared in *Ontario Review, The Nebraska Review, Denver Quarterly, The Chattahoochee Review*, and other journals. He lives in New York City.

Douglas Sadownick has been writing about gay-centered inner work as the next stage of gay liberation for the last ten years. He has contributed essays on the process of "coming out inside" for various periodicals (including the *Gay and Lesbian Review*) and has written two books, *Sacred Lips of the Bronx* (St. Martin's Press, 1994) and *Sex Between Men: A History of the Sex Lives of Gay Men Postwar to Present* (Harper San Francisco, 1996). His work advances a vision of gay people's taking up the burden of facing their unfinished family business to open up the infinite treasures of homosexuality hidden inside the Gay Mind, and in this way effecting a truly revolutionary grass-roots gay activism. Currently pursuing a Ph.D. in clinical psychology, he works as a gay-centered psychotherapist in Hollywood, California, teaches clinical psychology at Antioch University, and provides "gay soul making" workshops and talks with colleague Chris Kilbourne at the L.A. Gay and Lesbian Center.

James M. Saslow is professor of art history and theater at Queens College and the Graduate Center, City University of New York, where he was one of the cofounders of the Center for Lesbian and Gay Studies. His books include *Ganymede in the Renaissance: Homosexuality in Art and Society* (Yale University Press, 1986) and *Pictures and Passions: A History of Homosexuality in the Visual Arts* (Viking, 1999), a winner of two Lambda Literary Awards. He served as New York editor of *The Advo-*

cate for many years, and is currently cochair of the Queer Caucus of the College Art Association.

Rakesh Satyal is a native of Cincinnati, Ohio, and a recent graduate of Princeton University, where he studied comparative literature and creative writing. He lives in New York City and works for the Doubleday/Broadway Group, a division of Random House.

For nineteen long years, **Tom Steele** was editor of *Christopher Street* magazine and founding editor and associate publisher of the *New York Native, Theaterweek, Opera Monthly*, and other publications. He has ghost-written nineteen books in the last four years, and is writing a cookbook for people with small kitchens. He contributes regularly to *Out* magazine, and reviews restaurants for a variety of other publications, including Fodor's *Cityguide/New York*. He lives in Manhattan with his equally overachieving partner, novelist-poet-playwright-filmmaker Raymond Luczak, and Elsa, a lesbian basset hound.

"James A. Webb"'s alter ego graduated *magna cum laude* from Yale University with a B.A. in English, and was in the M.F.A. program in filmmaking at the University of Southern California School of Cinema-Television. He has written articles on film, stories for a bestselling interactive CD-ROM, the librettos for operas and musicals (two of which were performed at Yale), and eight screenplays. Currently he is working on a series of GLBT adventure novels.

Kai Wright is a Washington, D.C.-based freelance journalist. His work focuses on health and sexuality in minority communities, particularly among people of African descent globally. He writes for publications ranging from *The Village Voice* to *Venus*, a magazine focusing on the lives of black LGBT people, and he is a former reporter for the *Washington Blade* newspaper. You can learn more about Kai, and read some of his work, at www.kaiwright.com.

▪ ▪ ▪

Bruce Shenitz is executive editor of *Out* magazine, where he oversees social, cultural, and political coverage. He was a reporter at *Newsweek* for fourteen years, as well as a freelance writer and editor for other national publications. He lives with his partner in New York City.